VISUAL QUICKSTART GUIDE

ITUNES 6
AND IPOD

FOR WINDOWS AND MACINTOSH

Judith Stern and Robert Lettieri

 **Peachpit Press**

Visual QuickStart Guide
iTunes 6 and iPod for Windows and Macintosh
Judith Stern and Robert Lettieri

Peachpit Press

1249 Eighth Street
Berkeley, CA 94710
510/524-2178
800/283-9444
510/524-2221 (fax)

Find us on the World Wide Web at: www.peachpit.com
To report errors, please send a note to errata@peachpit.com
Peachpit Press is a division of Pearson Education

Editors: Clifford Colby and Karen Reichstein
Production editor: Becky Winter
Proofreader: Alison Kelley
Compositor: Danielle Foster
Indexer: Julie Bess
Cover design: Peachpit Press

Notice of Rights

Notice of Liability

Trademarks

ISBN 0-321-32045-X

9 8 7 6 5 4 3 2 1

Printed and bound in the United States of America

Dedication

In loving memory of Marvin Stern, a wonderful father and father-in-law, a great thinker, and a man of quiet strength and humor.

About the Authors

Judith Stern is a digital media specialist and instructional technologist. Her background includes corporate training, expert systems development, educational research, and multimedia development. She holds degrees in psychology and education from Cornell University and the University of California at Berkeley. She currently works for Educational Technology Services at the University of California at Berkeley, where she's a product manager responsible for bringing new Web video and audio tools to Berkeley's learning community.

Robert Lettieri has been experimenting and working with digital and analog video for more than 15 years. He has taught many people how to use graphics and desktop publishing software, both individually and in training workshops. He holds degrees from Rutgers University and California State University, Hayward, and currently works at the Space Sciences Lab at UC Berkeley.

Together, Stern and Lettieri are the authors of many books and articles on digital media, including all of Peachpit's QuickTime and iTunes Visual QuickStart Guides.

They can be reached at itunes@judyandrobert.com and will post updates and corrections to this book at www.judyandrobert.com/itunes.

Special Thanks

Many, many, thanks to Cliff Colby, executive editor at Peachpit (and the nicest taskmaster one could ask for), whom we were lucky enough to work with. We also deeply appreciate Karen Reichstein's additions and Alison Kelley's keen eye. Thanks to the rest of the Peachpit folks responsible for the production of this book: Becky Winter, Danielle Foster, and Julie Bess.

There would be far more errors in this book had it not been for testing and proofreading by Samantha Lettieri (with a little help from Paula and Eva) and Lois Stern. (Any errors remaining are our fault, not theirs.)

Other folks who helped along the way include David Schwartz and Beatrice Stonebanks; Greg Paschall; Jason McPhate; Pamela Roccabruna at Altec Lansing; and Betsy, Lucy, and Garrett.

Linda Lettieri kept us going with her positive attitude in the face of great adversity (and the use of her PowerBook at the last minute).

Last but definitely not least, we couldn't have done this without the cooperation and patience of our wonderful children, Sam and Jake. Nor could we have done it without the assistance of those who helped care for them (and us) during the process: Grandma Lois, Lara and Michael, Sandy and Michael, Karen and Phil, Nancy Balassi, and others in the NOCCS community.

If we missed anyone, it's because of the hour at which we're writing this. Our apologies and sincere thanks.

TABLE OF CONTENTS

TABLE OF CONTENTS

INTRODUCTION

If you've never used iTunes or an iPod, you're in for a pleasant surprise. Listening to music will never be the same again!

iTunes—Apple's free, wildly popular, and revolutionary digital jukebox software—lets you listen to music from a variety of sources, burn CDs, purchase music and videos online, and share music with friends and coworkers over a network. All that on top of being the best software to use for synchronizing your media collection with a portable music player, such as an iPod!

The iPod is an amazing portable music player and the perfect complement to iTunes. This device is, admittedly, more expensive than other MP3 players, but when you compare it to any of those other devices, it blows them away. It's small, light, sleek, and very easy to use; it just feels *good* in your hand. It can store songs and audiobooks in a variety of formats (not just MP3). The internal hard disk on the beefiest iPods makes it easy to carry around many thousands of songs or hundreds of audiobooks in your pocket. Some versions can also store and show photos, and the new video iPod can even be used to play video. You can store other stuff on most iPods, too, such as contact info, calendars, and notes. And because the iPod doubles as a portable hard drive, you can use it to transfer or back up files.

What You'll Find in This Book

This book is divided into 2 parts.

In Part I (Chapters 1 through 6), we cover what you need to know to get started with iTunes and your iPod: setting everything up, getting some music into iTunes and onto the iPod, playing it, creating playlists, and burning CDs with music. Nothing fancy is in Part I, but all of the tools' primary functions are covered.

If you're new to iTunes or the iPod, you'll probably want to use Part I as a primer: Go through it from beginning to end, working through all the step-by-step instructions. As in all Visual QuickStart Guides, we've used lots of screen shots to illustrate instructions and speed learning. We also provide lots of tips and sometimes may refer you to later chapters; don't be afraid to jump out to Part II if we refer to something there that hugely interests you.

On the other hand, if you've already been using either iTunes or an iPod or both, you may want to skim through Part I to see if there's anything new to you and begin reading in earnest in Part II.

In Part II (Chapters 7 through 11), we return to many of the topics we introduced in Part I but go into more depth and provide more details, as well as cover some topics that aren't audio-related. We assume you're now comfortable with iTunes and your iPod and desire to become a power-user of sorts. We cover many tasks that you don't necessarily need to do when you're getting started but that will make your experience more efficient, more pleasurable, more fruitful, or more *you*.

Why a Book About Both iTunes and the iPod?

The basic relationship between these two Apple products is incredibly simple: You put music in iTunes and then transfer it to the iPod.

The iPod is a hardware device. The only way, currently, to get music onto the iPod is to synchronize it with a music library on your computer. While other software applications can serve as that music library, iTunes does it best.

iTunes is free music software from Apple. While it has many other uses besides getting music to iPods (and can even be used with other portable music players) it's the iPod that Apple has designed iTunes around these past few years. We might even venture to say that, without the iPod, Apple wouldn't have had a reason to continue to develop iTunes.

Even if you're already quite familiar with iTunes and the iPod, you should still find this book to be a useful reference. You can look up specific tasks in the table of contents or index. And in some cases, the screen shots may be all you need to accomplish what you set out to do.

As you use this book, we hope that you'll come to enjoy iTunes and your iPod as much as we do. There's a lot to learn, so let's get going.

Music Not Your Thing?

Yes, you can store media that's not music on your iPod. For years, audiobooks have been available. Now podcasts (another form of spoken-word audio) are making the scene in a big way. We know that spoken-word audio (and *not* music) may be all or part of the reason *you* bought an iPod. Or maybe you bought a new iPod because you want to watch video on it. We've made sure to cover nonmusical forms of media in this book.

iTunes and the iPod, however, often treat all media items in the same way. Thus, we'll sometimes use the term *song* to refer to a discrete media item that may have no melody whatsoever. We may also use the term *music* to refer to audio in general, or even video. Please don't be offended or feel excluded if your pleasure is listening to a novel on a long trip, getting a daily fix of Jim Lehrer during your commute, or even catching up on a TV series. Our usage of these terms is simply a convention and a friendlier way to communicate.

Part 1:
Getting Started: Basics

SETTING UP iTUNES AND YOUR iPOD

1

iTunes and the iPod are very closely related. There has to be music in iTunes before you can have it on your iPod.

This chapter helps you install the latest version of iTunes and gives you a quick intro to the windows you'll see most often in the software. Then we do the same for the iPod: make sure you have the current version of the software needed to use the iPod, help you set up your iPod, and introduce you to the iPod's main menu.

Neither installation nor updating is particularly tricky, but sometimes it helps to get a bit more explanation of what you're doing and why.

Clearly, this is not the most exciting chapter in the book. If you've already got the current version of iTunes and the iPod software installed and have a basic sense of how iTunes and your iPod operate, please skip right ahead to Chapter 2.

Hardware and Software Requirements

To run iTunes on a Macintosh, you need:

◆ Mac OS X version 10.2.8 or later

◆ 500-MHz PowerPC G3 processor or better

◆ QuickTime 6.5.2

◆ 256 MB RAM

To run iTunes in Windows, you need:

◆ Windows XP or 2000

◆ 500-MHz Pentium-class processor or better

◆ QuickTime 7.0.2 or later (included when you install iTunes)

◆ 256 MB RAM minimum

Recommended enhancements

◆ **512 MB RAM**

For faster performance and fewer problems with other applications open, you'll want at least 512 MB of RAM.

◆ **Internet connection**

If you want to use the iTunes Music Store, download or stream music from any online source, subscribe to podcasts, or have information automatically added about songs you copy from an audio CD, you'll need an Internet connection; you'll want this to be a DSL, cable modem, or other high-speed Internet connection if you don't want to go nuts waiting for screens to update and music to download.

What's Different Between the Mac and Windows Versions?

As you read this chapter, you'll find blocks of text devoted to a single platform, which may lead you to believe that the Mac and Windows versions of iTunes are quite different. Not so. While installing iTunes may differ on the two platforms, you'll find that when it comes to *using* iTunes, the two versions are remarkably similar.

Any differences are largely due to operating system interface standards. For example, on the Mac you'll find the Preferences menu choice under the iTunes menu, and in Windows it's under the Edit menu. Modifier keys (Ctrl key on Windows and Command key on Mac, for example) and window control buttons are also platform-appropriate. On occasion, one platform or the other will have an extra option, an extra setting, or an extra feature.

In this book, we use screen shots from both platforms interchangeably, since the majority of menus and windows contain the same content on both platforms.

When keys, names of screen elements, or procedures differ between the two platforms, we note both options—for example, "Press the Option key (Mac) or the Alt and Ctrl keys (Windows)."

In the very few cases in which a feature is available on only one platform, or when the sequence of steps to follow is significantly different, we'll label the section accordingly (for example, "Mac only").

HARDWARE AND SOFTWARE REQUIREMENTS

◆ **CD or DVD burner**

If you want to burn CDs, you'll want a CD or DVD writer. All Macintosh internal writers, such as the built-in SuperDrive or combo drive, will work. Most external writers will also work on both platforms, as will most internal writers for Windows computers.

◆ **Latest system updates**

So that iTunes functions at its best, make sure you have the latest Windows *service pack* (visit the Microsoft Update Web site at http://windowsupdate.microsoft.com) or have the latest system updates on your Macintosh (run Software Update in your System Preferences pane).

◆ **Faster processor and additional video RAM**

If you want to play video from the iTunes Music Store, you'll need a 1.5 GHz Pentium-class processor or better and 32 megabytes of video ram for Windows, and 500 MHz G4 processor or better and 16 megabytes of video RAM for Mac OS X.

◆ **QuickTime 7.0.3 (Mac only)**

You'll also need this for playing video from the iTunes Music Store; get it through Software Update. (iTunes 6 for Windows installs QuickTime 7.0.3 automatically.)

◆ **Mac OS X 10.3.9 (Mac only)**

Mac users need also need this for playing video.

HARDWARE AND SOFTWARE REQUIREMENTS

Getting the Current Version of iTunes

You'll want to have the current version of iTunes (iTunes 6.0 or later). Some of you may need to download iTunes anew; others already have a version. (If you're a Mac OS X user, odds are very good that you have some version of iTunes already preinstalled on your computer; iTunes has come installed with every version of Mac OS X since Mac OS X 10.1.) Either way, it's easy to make sure you're current.

Ways to determine which version of iTunes you have:

◆ (Windows) Find the iTunes.exe icon (most likely in the Programs Files folder in a folder called iTunes), and then right-click and choose Properties. Click the Version tab; you'll see the version number listed at the top of the tab (**Figure 1.1**).

　If you don't see a Version tab, you may be looking at properties for an iTunes shortcut. You'll need to click the Find Target button on the Shortcut tab to see the true iTunes icon.

◆ (Mac) Locate iTunes in your Applications folder. Select the iTunes icon while in column view, and you'll see the version number (**Figure 1.2**).

Version number

Figure 1.1 In Windows, you'll find the iTunes version number in the Version tab of the Properties window for the iTunes.exe file.

Figure 1.2 In Mac OS X, you can determine which version of iTunes you have by selecting the iTunes icon in the Finder's column view.

Figure 1.3 (Windows) Choose About iTunes from the Help menu to open the About iTunes window.

Figure 1.4 (Mac) Choose About iTunes from the iTunes menu to open the About iTunes window.

Version number

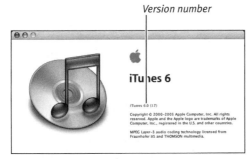

Figure 1.5 When you open the About iTunes window, the version number is the first line of text that scrolls off the screen.

◆ Once you launch iTunes, select About iTunes from the Help menu (Windows; **Figure 1.3**) or from the iTunes application menu (Mac; **Figure 1.4**); you'll see a window with scrolling text, starting with the version number (**Figure 1.5**).

✔ Tip

■ In the About iTunes window, text scrolls out of view pretty quickly! On either platform, however, you can reverse the direction of the scrolling text: Hold down the Alt key (Windows) or Option key (Mac).

GETTING THE CURRENT VERSION OF iTunes

Ways to get the installer for the current version of iTunes:

◆ Download the current version from the iTunes download page (www.apple.com/iTunes/download) and install it (see next pages); the new version will overwrite any older version. (Be reassured, however, that your existing iTunes library won't be touched.)

◆ (Mac) If you already have iTunes, in System Preferences, click the Software Update icon to open the Software Update pane, then click Check Now (**Figure 1.6**). In the window that appears, make sure the check box next to iTunes is checked, and click the Install button (**Figure 1.7**).

◆ (Windows) If you already have iTunes, from iTunes' Help menu, choose Check for iTunes Updates (refer to Figure 1.3). If a new version is available, iTunes tells you so and asks if you want to download it. Click Yes.

◆ Recent versions of iTunes are set to look for new versions automatically. If iTunes tells you there's a new version and asks if you want it, click Yes.

✔ Tips

■ Hate typing URLs? In the address field of most Web browsers you can simply type itunes.com (just iTunes in virtually all Mac browsers) and get whisked off to Apple's iTunes Web page at www.apple.com/itunes. On this page you'll see a "Download iTunes—Free" button; click it, and you'll be taken to the iTunes download page. Or, if you're a Windows user with an older version of iTunes, choose Check for iTunes Updates in the iTunes Help menu, and you'll be taken to the iTunes download page.

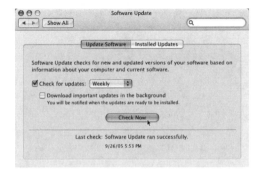

Figure 1.6 In the Mac OS X Software Update pane (which you'll find in System Preferences), click Check Now to find the latest Mac OS X software updates.

Figure 1.7 Make sure the iTunes check box is checked, and then click Install. The iTunes installer downloads and automatically runs.

■ New Macs come with iTunes, and iPods ship with a CD that includes iTunes, but that version of iTunes is likely to not be as current as what's on the Web download page.

■ iTunes' default preference is to look for new versions automatically. You can turn this off if you want. See "About iTunes Preferences" later in this chapter for instructions on opening the iTunes Preferences window.

Installing iTunes (Windows)

For the most part, installing iTunes is pretty straightforward. It's merely a matter of launching the installer and clicking through several screens.

To install iTunes:

1. Download the iTunes installer, as described earlier in this chapter.

2. If the installer isn't already open, locate the file iTunesSetup, and double-click to open it.

3. When prompted, choose a language and click OK.

   A series of progress indicators are displayed, and then eventually a window appears welcoming you to the installer.

4. Follow the prompts.

   Most of the screens you see will be similar to those you've seen in other software installations. When you see the Setup Type screen (**Figure 1.8**), choose from the following options:

continues on next page

What's QuickTime Got to Do With It?

Wondering why QuickTime comes up in iTunes installation? QuickTime is Apple's media architecture, and it provides various audio and video services to iTunes. The most obvious example is iTunes' ability to play video, but QuickTime is also responsible for iTunes' ability to encode and play AAC audio, a highly touted audio format used extensively by iTunes and the iPod.

Thus, on Windows computers, QuickTime is installed with iTunes. (On the Mac, users already have QuickTime preinstalled.)

Since QuickTime is being installed, the iTunes Installer may ask you a QuickTime configuration question: Do you want QuickTime Player (an application that gets installed as part of QuickTime) to become the default player for media files? You don't have to worry that agreeing to this will allow QuickTime to take over all media types; for the most part, it's just the ones that are Apple-bred, such as QuickTime movies and PICT files, plus a few others, such as MPEG-4 and DV. To see or change the list of file types that QuickTime can play, go to the QuickTime control panel (Start > Control Panel > QuickTime Control; you may have to click Other Control Panel Options if using Category view), and click the File Types tab.

▲ **Install desktop shortcuts**. This installs an iTunes icon on your desktop and in your Quick Launch toolbar.

▲ **Use iTunes as the default player for audio files.** This sets iTunes as the player to open audio files that you double-click or encounter on the Internet. Think of it as a temporary setting, however, since other applications may take over as the default player.

▲ **Use QuickTime as the default player for media files**. (You won't see this choice if you already had QuickTime installed before starting the iTunes installation.) This sets the QuickTime Player application to open any video, audio, and animation files that QuickTime is capable of handling and that iTunes doesn't handle. (That is, most audio files and some video files will be handled by iTunes.)

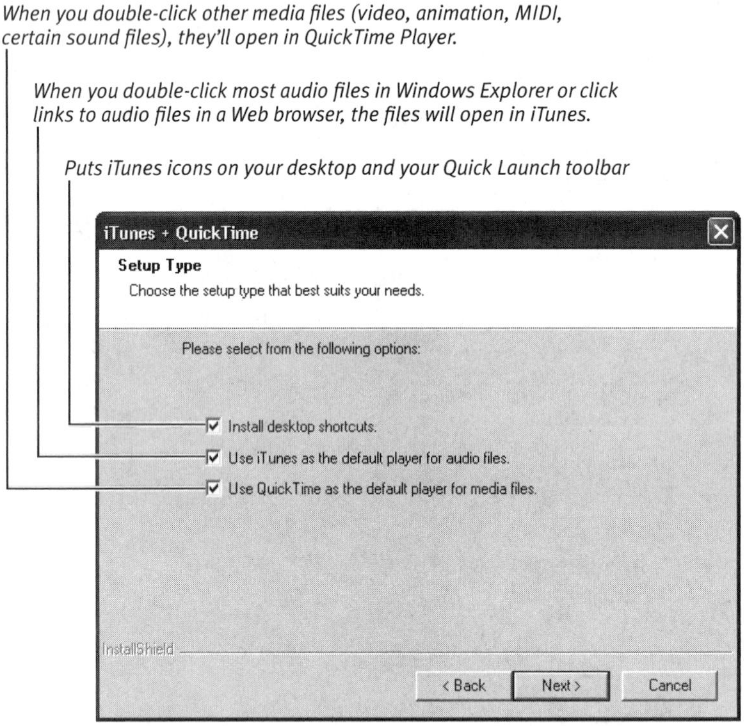

When you double-click other media files (video, animation, MIDI, certain sound files), they'll open in QuickTime Player.

When you double-click most audio files in Windows Explorer or click links to audio files in a Web browser, the files will open in iTunes.

Puts iTunes icons on your desktop and your Quick Launch toolbar

Figure 1.8 Use the Setup Type screen in the Install Wizard to choose where you place iTunes icons and to set up a default player for your audio files.

Figure 1.9
When Safari users download iTunes from Apple's Web site, they'll see what appears to be an iTunes "disk."

Figure 1.10 Users of other browsers will see a .dmg file that they should double-click to mount the "disk."

Figure 1.11 When you double-click the disk icon, this iTunes.mpkg file appears. Click it to run the installer.

Figure 1.12 During installation, you'll need to enter your user name and password. (This assumes you have administrative privileges on the computer on which you are installing.)

Installing iTunes (Mac)

If you've downloaded iTunes from the iTunes download Web page, you'll need to manually run the installer, as we describe on this page. But if you run Software Update, skip this page; iTunes is installed automatically.

To install iTunes:

1. If you're running Safari as your Web browser on Mac OS X 10.4 or 10.3, the iTunes disk image, once downloaded, automatically mounts on the desktop as a disk (**Figure 1.9**); click to select it.

   If you are using a different browser or Mac OS X 10.2, locate and double-click the file called iTunes6.dmg (**Figure 1.10**) or whatever the current version number is (for example, iTunes6.1.3.dmg) to mount the disk.

   A window containing a file called iTunes.mpkg appears.

2. Double-click the iTunes.mpkg file (**Figure 1.11**).

   The Installer opens.

3. Follow the prompts, clicking Continue on most screens (and clicking Agree to agree to the license agreement). At the last screen, click Upgrade; you'll be prompted to enter your Mac OS X user name and password (**Figure 1.12**); this needs to be the name and password for a Mac OS X user account with administrative privileges.

   iTunes is installed in your Applications folder.

INSTALLING iTUNES (MAC)

Launching iTunes

You have a variety of ways to launch iTunes; use whichever method you find most convenient.

Ways to launch iTunes (Windows):

◆ Use the Start menu. In Windows XP, choose Start > All Programs > iTunes > iTunes (**Figure 1.13**). In Windows 2000; choose Start > Programs > iTunes> iTunes.

◆ If you selected "Install desktop shortcuts" during installation, you'll find an iTunes icon on your computer's desktop and in your Quick Launch toolbar; you can double-click the former or single-click the latter. (If you're using Windows XP, your Quick Launch toolbar may not be visible; you can show it by right-clicking on the task bar and choosing Toolbars > Quick Launch.)

◆ Connect an iPod that's been properly formatted for a Windows computer. This will only work once you have installed iPod software. See "Getting the Latest iPod Software" later in this chapter.

Ways to launch iTunes (Mac):

◆ An iTunes icon should be in your Dock, unless you've removed it; click it to open iTunes (**Figure 1.14**).

◆ Find iTunes in your Applications folder, and double-click to open it.

◆ Connect an iPod that has been properly formatted for Mac OS X. This will only work once you have installed iPod software. See "Getting the Latest iPod Software" later in this chapter.

✔ Tips

■ On a Mac, you'll find that double-clicking many audio files in the Finder launches iTunes; this method isn't failproof, however, as sometimes other applications open.

Figure 1.13 To open iTunes in Windows, navigate from the Start menu.

iTunes icon in the Dock

Figure 1.14 On the Mac, click the iTunes icon in your Dock to launch it. (You'll also find iTunes in your Applications folder.)

■ On Windows, if you selected "Use iTunes as the default player for audio files" during installation, double-clicking some audio files will open iTunes.

LAUNCHING ITUNES

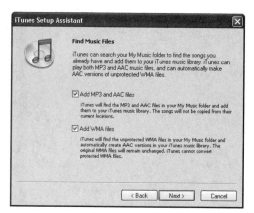

Figure 1.15 If you select Yes, audio files in your My Music folder will be listed in iTunes. Nothing changes on your hard drive.

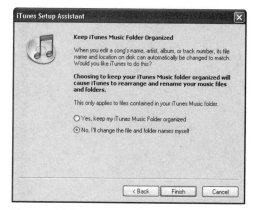

Figure 1.16 Selecting No is safer. You can change this preference later.

✔ Tip

■ You'll understand more about MP3 and AAC files when you read Chapter 8.

Setting Up iTunes

The first time you launch iTunes, you'll see a screen on which you'll need to agree to a software license agreement. If you've never had a version of iTunes installed, you'll next see a Welcome screen, directing you to click Next so you can answer some questions. While the process is mostly self-explanatory, and agreeing to the defaults (by simply clicking Next) is OK in most cases, a few screens require some explanation.

Setup screens on Windows:

◆ **Find Music Files**

You are asked if you want iTunes to search your My Music folder for MP3 and AAC files as well as WMA (Windows Media Audio) files (**Figure 1.15**). Selecting these ensures that these music files will be available to you from within iTunes. The screen lets you know that the MP3 and AAC files will not be copied to a new location; this means that there will be a listing for each of them in iTunes but the files containing the audio will reside exactly where they were on your hard disk before iTunes installation. For the WMA files, a new file will be created leaving the originals untouched.

◆ **Keep iTunes Music Folder Organized**

You are asked if you want iTunes to keep your Music Folder organized (**Figure 1.16**). The default is No. We recommend leaving this option set to No for complete safety, although the risks are actually minimal and there are advantages to having iTunes keep your music folder organized. You can always change this setting later. You'll find out much more about what keeping your Music Folder organized means in Chapter 9.

Setup screens on Mac OS X:

◆ **Internet Audio**

You are asked whether you want iTunes to handle Internet audio (**Figure 1.17**). Choosing Yes is generally better for most users. The only reason to choose No would be if you have a different preferred application for handling the audio (typically MP3 files) that you come across when browsing the Web.

◆ **Find Music Files**

You are asked if you want iTunes to search your Home folder for MP3 and AAC files (**Figure 1.18**). Answering Yes ensures that these music files will be available to you from within iTunes. You are told that the files will be copied; this means that each file will be duplicated (with the copy being put in the iTunes Music folder) and that changes made via iTunes will affect only the copies in the iTunes Music folder.

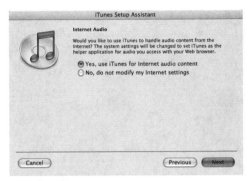

Figure 1.17 Select Yes for using iTunes to play Internet audio content unless you have a different preferred application for handling audio. Select Yes for connecting to the Internet if you want iTunes to be able to get information about the audio CDs you insert.

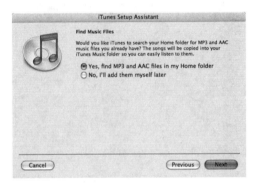

Figure 1.18 Select Yes to have audio files in your Home directory listed in iTunes. Copies of all files will be placed in your iTunes Music folder.

iTunes Quick Overview

When you open iTunes, you're presented with the main iTunes window (**Figure 1.19**). You'll find the interface quite easy to use. Let's take a quick look at the various controls and panes. (The majority of these are covered in detail in Chapter 3, "Playing Music and More in iTunes," but many of them come up in other chapters as well.)

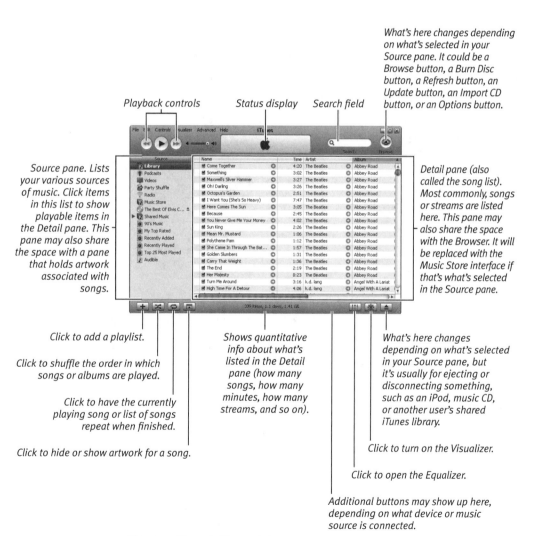

What's here changes depending on what's selected in your Source pane. It could be a Browse button, a Burn Disc button, a Refresh button, an Update button, an Import CD button, or an Options button.

Playback controls   *Status display*   *Search field*

Source pane. Lists your various sources of music. Click items in this list to show playable items in the Detail pane. This pane may also share the space with a pane that holds artwork associated with songs.

Detail pane (also called the song list). Most commonly, songs or streams are listed here. This pane may also share the space with the Browser. It will be replaced with the Music Store interface if that's what's selected in the Source pane.

Click to add a playlist.

Click to shuffle the order in which songs or albums are played.

Click to have the currently playing song or list of songs repeat when finished.

Click to hide or show artwork for a song.

Shows quantitative info about what's listed in the Detail pane (how many songs, how many minutes, how many streams, and so on).

What's here changes depending on what's selected in your Source pane, but it's usually for ejecting or disconnecting something, such as an iPod, music CD, or another user's shared iTunes library.

Click to turn on the Visualizer.

Click to open the Equalizer.

Additional buttons may show up here, depending on what device or music source is connected.

Figure 1.19 The main iTunes window.

iTunes Quick Overview

About iTunes Preferences

You'll be coming across the iTunes Preferences window throughout this book, so we figure it's time for a formal introduction.

The Preferences window is probably the window you'll see most frequently after the main iTunes window (shown in Figure 1.19). It has more than 50 options you can set; we'll be covering almost all of them in this book. For now, though, we'll just explain how you open this window and briefly describe what you'll find on each tab.

To open the iTunes Preferences window:

◆ (Windows) From the Edit menu, select Preferences (**Figure 1.20**) or use the keyboard shortcut: Ctrl-, (comma).

◆ (Mac) From the iTunes menu, select Preferences (**Figure 1.21**) or use the keyboard shortcut, Command-, (comma).

The iTunes Preferences window opens, showing the General tab (**Figure 1.22**), unless you previously had it open to another tab.

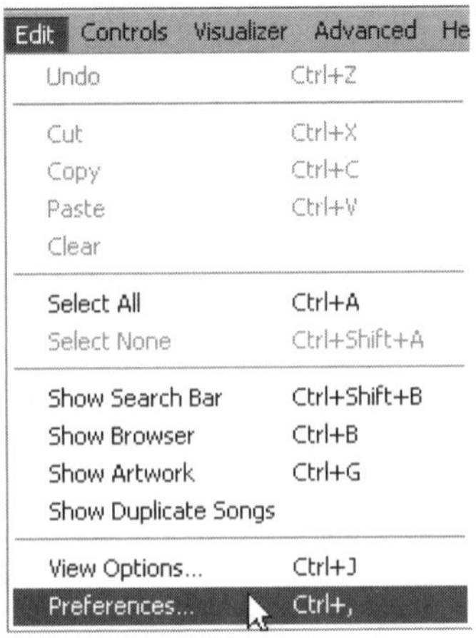

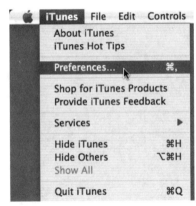

Figure 1.20 (Windows) From the Edit menu, choose Preferences to open the Preferences window.

Figure 1.21 (Mac) From the iTunes application menu, choose Preferences to open the Preferences window.

Figure 1.22 The Preferences window lets you set preferences for importing music from CDs, sharing music over a network, displaying special effects, buying music from the iTunes Music Store, and much more.

Preferences tabs overview:

◆ The **General** tab offers miscellaneous settings, most affecting what's shown in the iTunes window but one regarding checking for updates.

◆ The **iPod** tab lets you specify all sorts of options for how your computer and iPod interact. Most of what's found on this tab is covered in Chapters 4, 10, and 11.

◆ The **Podcasts** tab lets you specify your preferences for handling episodes of the podcasts to which you've subscribed (covered in Chapter 9).

◆ The **Playback** tab lets you make choices that affect song playback (most of which we cover in Chapter 8).

◆ The **Sharing** tab is where you'll select your preferences for sharing your music and accessing other people's shared music (covered in Chapter 3).

◆ The **Store** tab allows you to tailor your shopping experience in the iTunes Music Store (covered in detail in Chapter 7).

◆ The **Advanced** tab offers miscellaneous options as well as options for importing music from audio CDs (covered in Chapter 8) and Burning CDs (covered in Chapter 6).

◆ The **Parental** tab (Mac) or **Parental Controls** tab (Windows) gives you a few controls over what can be seen in your copy of iTunes. To lock the settings, you'll need to use the user name and password for your computer.

About iPods

Odds are that you already have an iPod if you're reading this book, but if not, let us give you a quick introduction.

Choosing an iPod

Currently, Apple is offering three iPods:

◆ **iPod:** This is the largest iPod in physical size and capacity, currently coming in 30 GB or 60 GB models (**Figure 1.23**). It comes with a color screen. It's the first iPod to be able to play video, and, as such, is referred to by most everyone except Apple as the "video iPod"— a term we'll stick to for the rest of this book. Besides being a portable music and video player, it serves as a portable hard drive and is useful for importing, storing, and showing photographs (including displaying photos on a television); keeping an address book; acting as an alarm clock; and more (see Chapter 11). These iPods come in black or white.

◆ **iPod nano:** Smaller in both size and capacity (2 and 4 GB) than the standard iPod, it's also less expensive (**Figure 1.24**). It functions in much the same way as a standard iPod, however, and has nearly the same features except for the number of songs (or other files if you're using it as a hard drive) that it can store and the fact that it can't play video. It also can't show photos on TV or import photos directly from a camera.

Figure 1.23 The iPod comes in 30 and 60 gigabyte versions. (Image Courtesy of Apple)

Figure 1.24 The iPod nano comes in 2 and 4 gigabyte versions. (Image Courtesy of Apple)

Figure 1.25
The iPod shuffle only comes in 512 megabyte or 1 gigabyte versions. (Image Courtesy of Apple)

How Many Songs?

You may not care about the size of your iPod in gigabytes (GB); you just want to know how many songs will fit. Of course, since songs vary in length, it's tough to say, but if we use the assumption that Apple does in its estimates ("....4 minutes per song and 128-Kbps AAC encoding") you end up with approximately 250 songs per gigabyte. That means 15,000 songs for the highest capacity (60 gigabyte) iPod and only 125 songs for the lowest capacity (512 megabyte) iPod shuffle. (Apple actually estimates a conservative 120 songs for the iPod shuffle.)

Just so you know, the 128 Kbps (kilobits per second) AAC encoding that Apple bases its estimates on is what you can count on when you import from audio CDs (as long as you don't change iTunes' default preferences) and when you purchase from the iTunes Music Store. It's not necessarily what you get if you purchase MP3s, which are often more than 128 kilobits per second—50 to 100 percent more—for music files. (We'll explain lots more about different audio bit rates and formats in Chapter 8.)

◆ **iPod shuffle:** This tiny white iPod is quite different in that it has no screen so you can't locate specific songs to play (**Figure 1.25**). It plays the songs randomly or in an order you've created in iTunes, depending on how you've set a switch on the back of the device. The only other controls are those that you use to play, pause, fast-forward, rewind, and control volume. It can be used as a hard drive but doesn't have the other features that the iPod and iPod nano have, since those features require a screen.

No longer being sold retail by Apple, you may find other models as refurbished units being sold by Apple, in the second-hand market, or at online discounters:

◆ **iPod** (pre-October 12, 2005): This was the iPod that Apple sold for just a few months before they came out with the newest, video-capable iPod. It came in 20 or 60 GB versions. It's got a smaller screen and a slightly larger body than the current iPod, can't play video, and came only in white (although there were some "special edition" versions, such as the U2 iPod, that came in black).

◆ **iPod photo:** This was the first iPod to come with a color screen, larger capacity (60 GB), and output to TV; it's essentially the same as the pre-October 2005 iPod. It came, however, with a dock (a cradle to hold the iPod for connecting to your computer).

◆ *iPod mini:* The physical size of this device falls in between the nano and the standard iPod, as does its capacity (4 to 6 GB). No color screen, and no photo features, it otherwise has essentially the same functionality as the current crop. It does come in different colors!

◆ **Various older iPods:** All of them white, none with a color screen, ranging in size from 5 to 40 GBs, with some having a slightly different layout of the controls.

Getting the Latest iPod Software

To make sure you can take advantage of all your iPod's bells and whistles, you want your iPod to have the most current version of iPod software. Windows users will also need to have iPod software installed on their computer; this is merely behind-the-scenes software that enables the computer and the iPod to communicate.

Getting iPod software from the Apple Web site is the first step toward ensuring an updated iPod for all iPod users and, for Windows users, a computer that can communicate with an iPod.

To get the latest version of the iPod software:

1. Visit the iPod download page at www.apple.com/ipod/download/ and download to your computer the iPod Software Update appropriate for your computer. (You'll need to supply identifying information.)

2. Run the downloaded installer.

   This will entail choosing a language and then going through the standard installation screens. In most cases you'll need to restart your computer.

3. Connect your iPod to your computer.

   You'll be prompted to update your iPod's software (**Figure 1.26**). Follow the onscreen instructions.

✔ Tip

■ A software installer comes on the CD that's bundled with your iPod. We recommend, however, that you get the software from the Web site instead, because it's likely to be more current.

You'll see this on a Mac computer.

You'll see this on a Windows computer.

Figure 1.26 When you connect your iPod after installing the iPod Software Update on your computer, you'll see this window. (The Windows and Mac versions are slightly different.)

Of Cables and Docks: Connecting Your iPod

For most users with most iPods, you'll take the cable that came with your iPod, plug the large end into your iPod and the smaller USB (or FireWire for some older iPods) end into your computer where you normally plug in those cables; look for the appropriate symbol on the cable.

Lucky users with slightly older iPods that shipped with a Dock (or those that have purchased or been given a Dock), get to plug the Dock in once, and then just set the iPod into the Dock whenever they want to connect.

The shuffle also lets you connect without a cable: You can plug the shuffle directly into your USB port on your computer (but not the USB port on the keyboard because it's not powered). This is especially convenient with many laptops. (On the other hand, with some computers, the shuffle's housing may not fit the USB port and you may need to purchase an additional cable or Dock to make it work.)

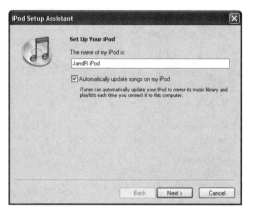

Figure 1.27 This window allows you to initially define how your iPod should be updated.

Setting Up Your iPod with iTunes

The first time iTunes opens with your iPod connected (with all the necessary software installed), iTunes displays a window in which you specify how you want iTunes and the iPod to interact.

To set up your iPod for use with iTunes:

1. Connect your iPod to your computer.

   iTunes opens automatically. (In the rare case that iTunes doesn't open automatically, you may need to open it yourself.)

2. In the iPod Setup Assistant window that appears (**Figure 1.27**), enter a name for your iPod.

   This is the name that will appear in the iTunes Source pane when the iPod is connected.

continues on next page

Connecting Your iPod to a PC for the First Time

Got a brand new iPod? As of this writing, all iPods (except for the iPod nano and iPod shuffle), straight out of the box, are formatted for use on a Mac. Or do you have an iPod (any iPod) that previously had been used on a Mac? If the iPod software has been installed on your Windows system and the system has been restarted, the first time you connect your iPod, you'll see a message that the iPod is not readable and that it needs to be formatted for use on a PC (**Figure 1.28**). If you click Update, the iPod Software Updater opens. Click Restore and then follow the onscreen instructions to reformat the iPod's hard drive; this ensures that your iPod will play nicely with your PC. (Warning: This also erases the contents of your iPod, something you only have to worry about if it previously had been used on a Mac.)

Figure 1.28 If you have an iPod that's never been used on a Windows system and connect it to a Windows computer, you'll see this window. You must update if you want to use the iPod on your Windows computer.

3. Leave "Automatically update songs on my iPod" checked. (Or in the case of an iPod shuffle leave "Automatically choose songs for my iPod" checked.)

This sets your iPod so that any songs in your iTunes library will be put on the iPod. We're assuming that, since you're just getting started, the music (if any) stored in your iTunes library will fit on your iPod. Things get a little trickier (and you can always change this preference) when you have a good collection of songs; we get into the details in Chapter 4 and beyond.

4. If you see "Automatically copy photos to my iPod," we recommend you leave this choice unchecked. We'll show you how to get your photos on your iPod in Chapter 11.

5. Click Next.

6. On the next screen, register your iPod if you like.

7. Click Finish (Windows) or Done (Mac) to close the window.

Your iPod is now set up to work with iTunes, and if there were songs in your iTunes library, some or all of them have been copied to your iPod. Make sure not to disconnect your iPod if it displays "Do not disconnect"; if it says this, you should first eject it by clicking the eject icon next to the entry for the iPod in the Source pane (**Figure 1.29**). Also, you should leave the iPod connected until it's fully charged. (See the sidebar "Charging Your iPod.)

✔ Tip

■ No music in your iTunes Library, yet? Never fear. We cover all the methods for adding music to your library in the next chapter.

Figure 1.29 To eject an iPod, click the eject icon.

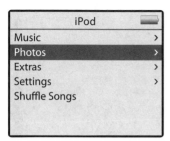

Figure 1.30
The iPod's main menu.

iPod Quick Overview

The iPod, with its tiny screen, isn't very complicated at all, and that's the beauty of it. (Here, we're of course not talking about the iPod shuffle, which has no screen.)

When you first turn an iPod on you'll see a simple list of choices (**Figure 1.30**). This is your main menu.

We'll go into all those items on the iPod main menu eventually, but here's a quick overview:

◆ **Music** is where you'll access all your music. Select this and you'll find more menus that help you navigate to any item you want to hear. We'll spend time here when we get to playing music in Chapter 4.

continues on next page.

Charging Your iPod

There has been talk about iPod batteries and the need to condition the battery by charging, discharging, charging again—or some such urban myth.

There's been so much talk about this that Apple has a whole Web page devoted to the topic http://www.apple.com/batteries/ipods.html. But here's the summary: You should fully charge your iPod battery before the first use or you may not get the maximum playback time for the rest of its life. Since all iPods charge when connected to your computer, the first time you connect your iPod, just leave it plugged in until it is fully charged. This takes about 4 hours for an iPod or a shuffle and 3 for a nano. The iPod display indicates when it is fully charged; when charging it displays an icon that looks like a lightning bolt on a battery, and when charged it looks like a plug on a battery. (The shuffle's battery indicator light will be solid green.)

Thereafter, you'll want to charge your iPod as much as you need. It's not crucial that it be fully charged unless you need it to be: The shuffle gives you up to 12 hours fully charged, the iPod nano and the 30 GB iPod give you 14 hours, and the 60 GB iPod gives you 20 hours of music playback (but less—more 3 to 4 hours—if you're showing slide shows with music and only 2 to 3 hours for video.)

Warning: iPods charge only when plugged into ports that provide power. Your keyboard won't do this.

iPod Quick Interface Overview

◆ **Photos** lets you import photos directly from a digital camera and view photos in a variety of ways, as we'll cover in Chapter 11. You won't see this in your main menu if you don't have a color iPod.

◆ **Extras** provides access to all the non-music and non-photo features: the clock (with alarm clock features), address book, calendar, a way to view text files, and even a few games. In addition, on the video iPod and nano, you'll find a stopwatch and a way to lock the screen. Chapter 11 also covers how to use most of these.

◆ **Settings** is the equivalent of Preferences in most applications, letting you customize your iPod to meet your needs. We'll cover many of the options here when we get to Chapter 10.

◆ **Shuffle Songs** randomly plays the music on your iPod.

To choose from among these or any list of items in a menu, you'll simply use the wheel on your iPod: move your finger or thumb clockwise to highlight items lower on the list, counterclockwise to highlight items higher on the list. Once your choice is highlighted, press the Select button (the one in the middle of the wheel). If you want to return to the menu from which you just left, press Menu (**Figure 1.31**).

Slide your finger or thumb along the wheel to change the line that's highlighted.

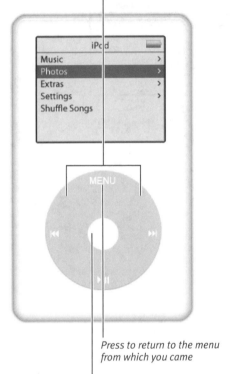

Press to return to the menu from which you came

Press to select the highlighted item

Figure 1.31 Basic controls on the iPod for navigating the menus.

POPULATING YOUR LIBRARY

2

If you want to listen to music or any other audio (which is what it's all about, right?), you'll need to start by populating your iTunes library. This is a prerequisite for getting audio onto your iPod, too. (If you already have items in your iTunes library and are in a rush to get it on your iPod, skip right ahead to Chapter 4.)

Once we provide a quick explanation of the iTunes library, we'll show you what is probably the simplest and cheapest method of adding music: importing (also known as *ripping*) songs from a CD. It's the cheapest (for most of you) because you already own CDs. And it's simple because importing an audio CD is basically a one-step process.

Some of you may already have audio files, such as MP3s or WAVs, on your computer, so we'll show you several methods for importing stand-alone audio files into iTunes. We'll then introduce you to your options for getting music and other forms of audio from the Internet; the iTunes Music Store will likely be your primary source but we'll also cover other options.

Finally, we'll show you how to delete songs from the library.

About the Library

Your iTunes library is the central repository of your music. Everything you add to iTunes is listed there. This includes music imported from audio CDs, copied from hard disk (or any other computer media, such as a USB Flash drive), or downloaded over the Internet. Your iTunes library can even include links to streaming audio on the Internet.

As you'll see in upcoming chapters, even if your library becomes one huge bin of songs— the number can easily mushroom into the thousands—it's still easy to find specific items in it, because you can browse, search, and sort the library in a variety of ways.

The library provides the source for all songs in iTunes playlists. (Chapter 5 covers playlists in depth.) Songs in playlists are merely pointers to songs in the library.

Everything in the library points to an actual file somewhere—usually on your hard drive, but it could also be on the Internet.

To view a list of everything in your library:

◆ Click the library entry in the Source pane.

All items in your library are listed in the Detail pane (**Figure 2.1**).

Source pane —   — Detail pane

Figure 2.1 When you click Library in the Source pane, all of the songs in your collection are listed in the Detail pane.

Figure 2.2 Double-click to make the name of your library editable.

Figure 2.3 Type a new name, and then click away from the text to set the name.

✔ Tips

- To see everything in your library, be sure nothing is typed in the Search field and that you are not using the Browser. This caveat is important (as we discuss in the next chapter), since both searching and browsing limit what appears in the Detail pane.

- You can rename your library. Just double-click the text of the library entry to make the text editable (**Figure 2.2**). Type a new name for your library, and then click anywhere other than on the text you just edited to make the name change take effect (**Figure 2.3**).

ABOUT THE LIBRARY

Importing an Audio CD

You'll love how easy this is. Grab an audio CD from your shelf and start ripping.

To import all the songs on a CD:

1. Insert the CD into your computer's CD drive.

   The CD icon appears in the iTunes Source pane (sometimes it takes a few seconds, so be patient); the songs on it are likely listed by name, along with additional information such as album and artist (**Figure 2.4**).

2. Click the Import CD button (refer to Figure 2.4).

   iTunes begins to import each song in the list, showing the progress of your import in the status display as it goes (**Figure 2.5**). When iTunes is in the process of importing a song, you'll see an orange circle with a moving wave. Once a song has been imported, you'll see a green circle with a white checkmark.

CD icon and name

Click to eject CD

Click to import all checked songs from selected CD

Figure 2.4 When you insert a CD, its icon and name appear in the iTunes Source pane; its songs appear in the Detail pane, and the Import button becomes available, as does the Eject button.

Shows progress of the import

Indicates song currently being imported

Indicates song that has finished importing

Indicates how quickly (compared with normal playback speed) song is being imported

Click here to stop importing

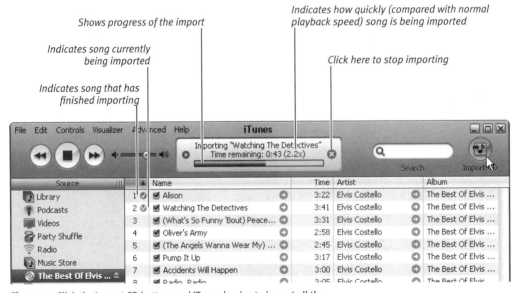

Figure 2.5 Click the Import CD button, and iTunes begins to import all the

IMPORTING AN AUDIO CD

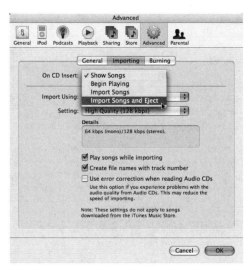

Figure 2.6 If you'll be importing a lot of CDs, you can save time by changing your On CD Insert option to Import Songs and Eject.

Ways to stop an import in progress:

◆ Click the Import CD button again.

◆ Click the tiny "x" icon in the status area (refer to Figure 2.5).

✔ Tips

■ Songs are encoded as AAC, a highly efficient encoding technology; see Chapter 8 if you're interested in learning more about how iTunes encodes audio and how you can change this default.

■ To eject a CD from within iTunes, do any of the following: click the Eject icon to the right of the CD name in the Source list (refer to Figure 2.4); click the Eject Disc button at the bottom of the iTunes window; click the Controls menu and choose Eject Disc; Press Command-E (Mac) or Control-E (Windows); Control-click (Mac) or right-click (Windows) and choose Eject Disc from the contextual menu that appears.

■ If you're using an operating system that allows you to do *fast user switching*—a way of logging out of the operating system so that one user's files and programs can remain open while another user logs on—don't switch during a CD import. (Fast user switching is a feature of Mac OS X 10.3 and later and Windows XP.)

■ If you import a lot of CDs in quick succession, you'll save time if you set iTunes to automatically import the songs from a CD once it's inserted and eject the CD when the import is done. To do this, open your Preferences window, click the Advanced tab, click Importing and, from the On CD Insert pop-up menu, select Import Songs and Eject (**Figure 2.6**).

continues on next page

IMPORTING AN AUDIO CD

- If iTunes isn't already open when you insert an audio CD, you may find that iTunes opens automatically. On a Windows computer this occurs only if iTunes is set as the default audio player. On the Mac, you can change this setting in the CDs & DVDs pane of your System Preferences.

- You can monitor how quickly iTunes is importing by checking in the status area (refer to Figure 2.5); the figure in parentheses indicates how much faster the import speed is than the normal speed of play. (For example, if the figure here averages around "2.0 x", a 2-minute song will be imported in 1 minute.)

- While it's nice that you get a green check box icon that tells you when a song has finished importing from a CD, iTunes unfortunately won't remember what you've imported from a particular CD the next time you insert it, so you won't see those icons; in other words, when you pop in a CD, iTunes doesn't immediately tell you that you've already imported a particular song. Instead, iTunes will warn you that the song you're trying to reimport is already in your library.

How Does It Know?

When you insert an audio CD with iTunes, iTunes normally connects to a special CD database on the Internet (called the *CDDB*, for Compact Disc Database), retrieves information about that CD and the songs on it, and places that information in the list of songs that appears in the Detail pane. (If you're connected to the Internet, and if you pay attention when you first insert a CD into your computer, you'll see a message in the status area for a few seconds, stating "Accessing Gracenote CDDB.")

If you're not connected to the Internet, iTunes obviously can't access CDDB. If you are seeing songs listed only as Track 1, Track 2, and so on, it is likely that you were not connected to the Internet when you first inserted the CD. If you later reconnect, you can manually retrieve information about a CD by clicking the Advanced menu and choosing Get CD Track Names (**Figure 2.7**). If that still doesn't work, it may be one of the rare situations where the CD is not listed in the CDDB; you can enter the track names yourself (see "Editing Song Information" in Chapter 9) and then, from the Advanced menu, choose Submit CD Track Names.

Figure 2.7 If you aren't connected to the Internet when you first insert a CD, you can later (when you connect) download album and song information by choosing Get CD Track Names from the Advanced menu.

▲	Name		Time	Artist
1	☑ Take My Word For It	◉	4:14	Mare Winninghar
2	☐ Train Song	◉	3:00	Mare Winninghar
3	☑ That Night	◉	4:22	Mare Winninghar
4	☐ Einstein	◉	3:30	Mare Winninghar
5	☐ He's Coming	◉	4:24	Mare Winninghar
6	☑ Where Are You Come Get Me	◉	4:28	Mare Winninghar
7	☑ Camera	◉	3:28	Mare Winninghar
8	☐ What Might Be	◉	4:57	Mare Winninghar

Figure 2.8 Only checked songs get imported when you click the Import button.

Figure 2.9 Alternatively, you can select songs and drag them to your library.

Importing Individual Songs from CD

Sometimes you don't want every song on an audio CD to be imported into your iTunes library. Rather than simply click the Import button after you insert a CD, try one of the following.

To import individual songs from a CD (I):

1. Click the check box to the left of each song you *don't* want to import, so that only the songs you want to import are checked (**Figure 2.8**).

2. Click the Import CD button.

To import individual songs from a CD (II):

1. Select the song(s) you want to import by clicking on them.

   Shift-click to select multiple contiguous songs. Command-click (Mac) or Ctrl-click (Windows) to select multiple songs that are not contiguous.

2. Click on any of the selected songs and drag to the library in the Source pane (**Figure 2.9**).

   As you drag, you'll see a ghosted version of the song(s); a plus-sign icon appears when you mouse over the Library entry (refer to Figure 2.9), indicating that you've dragged to a source that can receive the songs.

3. Release the mouse button.

   The songs are added to your library.

Problems Reading a CD? (Windows only)

If you're having trouble reading a CD, choose Help > Run CD Diagnostics. Don't be concerned by the technical-looking text that appears. Click the Help button at the bottom of the CD Diagnostics window. You'll be taken to a page on Apple's Web site, where you can read information and paste in all that technical-looking text to submit to Apple so they can help you.

✔ Tips

- (Mac only) When you drag multiple songs to the Source pane, along with the plus sign you'll see a red circle with a number to show how many songs are selected.

- To quickly add or remove all the check-marks, Command-click (Mac) or Ctrl-click (Windows) any one of the check boxes.

- Don't confuse the two methods for importing individual songs. Be aware that when you import songs by clicking the Import CD button, what's *selected* (high-lighted in blue) is not necessarily what gets imported—only checked items are imported. If you import songs by dragging them to the Source pane, it doesn't matter what's checked, only what's selected.

- If you opt for the latter method (drag-ging selected songs), you can drag your selected songs to the white area below your sources (the plus-sign icon will appear when you do) and then release your mouse button to create a new play-list containing those songs. You can also drag to an existing playlist, if you have any. We'll explore these topics in more depth in Chapter 5.

Joining Songs

Some albums contain songs that are meant to be played without pausing, even though they are divided into separate tracks. (The Beatles' *Abbey Road* is one well-known example.) If you want iTunes to import a number of tracks from a CD as one song, select the songs you want joined and, from the Advanced menu, choose Join CD Tracks (**Figure 2.10**). The tracks appear linked (**Figure 2.11**). You'll end up importing a single song, with a name consisting of the names of all the joined songs, separated by hyphens.

(If you don't join songs, you may not notice the pause between tracks if you have "Crossfade playback" checked on the Playback tab of your iTunes Preferences window; see "Adjusting Sound Settings" in Chapter 8.)

Figure 2.10 When you want contiguous songs on a CD imported as a single song, select the songs and choose Advanced > Join CD Tracks.

Figure 2.11 iTunes shows that it knows you want the selected songs joined. When you import, you end up with a single long song.

Figure 2.12 Drag audio files directly from Explorer (Windows) or the Finder (Mac) to your library.

Figure 2.13 Alternatively, you can pull down your File menu and choose an Add option.

Check this box.

Figure 2.14 You can change whether or not iTunes makes a copy of files.

Adding Audio Files from Your Computer

If you've got audio files on your hard drive, a Zip drive, a CD-ROM, or any other type of media that is recognized by your computer, you can add those songs to your library. While some songs may have been automatically added when you set up iTunes, this page describes how to add those files that are not yet in your library. (You can add a large variety of audio formats; see the table "Audio File Formats iTunes Can Import.")

Ways to add audio files to your iTunes library:

◆ Select a file(s) or folder(s) in the Finder (Mac) or Windows Explorer (Windows) that you want to add, and then drag it to your iTunes Library in the Source pane (**Figure 2.12**) or to the Detail pane.

◆ From the File menu, choose Add to Library (Mac), Add File to Library (Windows, **Figure 2.13**), or Add Folder to Library (Windows). Then locate the file(s) or folder(s) you want to add and click Choose.

The files you've selected are added to your library as long as they are music files that iTunes can recognize. If iTunes can't recognize them, it ignores them.

✔ Tips

■ When you add audio files to iTunes, the program may make copies of the files, depending on your iTunes preferences. For Windows users, the default is that files are *not* copied; iTunes points to the file in its original location. For Mac users, iTunes makes a *duplicate* of the file and copies it to your iTunes music folder by default. You can change the default on the General tab of the Advanced tab of the Preferences window (**Figure 2.14**).

continues on next page

- If you or iTunes has set your preferences so that files are copied, but you occasionally don't want a file to be copied (if it's very large, for example), you can hold down the Option key (Mac) or Alt key (Windows) when you drag the file, and it won't be copied.

- If you drag to the Source pane, but miss the Library listing or if you drag to the Detail pane when something other than your library is selected, you may end up putting the songs in a playlist in addition to your library. (See Chapter 5 for more on playlists.)

- Unlike songs imported from an audio CD, most audio files on your computer are *not* encoded into a different format when you add them to your iTunes library. For an exception, see "What about Windows Media Audio Files?" later in this chapter.

Adding Video Files

You can drag a QuickTime video file into your iTunes library. iTunes recognizes it as a video clip: it has a special icon next to it and it appears in a special Videos playlist that you'll see in your Source pane. You'll be able to watch the video play in the Artwork pane, located in the lower-left of the iTunes window, or a separate larger window; see "Accessing and Playing Video" in Chapter 3.

Only some video files, however, will be copied to the video-capable iPod; you'll learn more about this in Chapter 11.

You can convert the *audio* portion of a QuickTime video file to a format that will play on all iPods; see "Converting Songs to a Different Audio Format" in Chapter 8.

Table 2.1

Audio File Formats iTunes Can Import

FILE FORMAT	EXTENSION	DESCRIPTION
MIDI	.mid	Musical Instrument Digital interface
Karaoke	.kar	A variation on MIDI with text of lyrics; displays as QT movie
MPEG Layer III	.mp3	Popular audio format; includes MPEG-1 Layer III and MPEG-2 Layer III
MPEG Layer II	.mp2	A less popular MPEG-1 format; includes MPEG-1 Layer II and MPEG-2 Layer II
MPEG-4	.m4a	MPEG-4 AAC audio created with iTunes
MPEG-4	.m4b	MPEG-4 AAC audio for books from iTunes Music Store; copy-protected
MPEG-4	.m4p	MPEG-4 AAC audio for music from iTunes Music Store; copy-protected
MPEG-4	.mp4	MPEG-4 files created by applications other than iTunes
Audible Book	.aa	MP3 Format for Audible.com books
Audio Interchange File	.aif, .aiff, .aifc	Standard audio file format for Mac
Wave	.wav	Standard audio file format for Windows
QuickTime Movie	.mov	Cross-platform media file format; besides audio can contain video, text, and other types of data
Nomad Voice File	.nvf	Format for files recorded on some Creative Nomad Audio devices
Playlist	.pls, .m3u	MP3 playlist
Windows Media Audio*	.wma	Popular web audio file format

* iTunes can import only on Windows; files get converted to default iTunes import format

Buying from the iTunes Music Store

The iTunes Music Store provides a legal way to purchase music (and more) online at reasonable prices. We'll go into much more detail about the iTunes Music Store in Chapter 7, but we want to give you a quick introduction here.

You can explore the store as much as you want without an account, but to download anything (even the few free songs that are usually there), you'll need an account. Buying is simple once you have that account.

Getting Spoken Word Content from Audible.com

Yet another source of online audio is Audible.com (www.audible.com), where you can download audio files of entire books from all sorts of genres, including fiction, nonfiction, business, biography, and children's literature, to name a few. Audible.com also makes it easy to subscribe to audio versions of periodicals, such as the *New York Times,* and get daily (or weekly or monthly) content in digest form. You can even subscribe to radio shows, such as NPR's "Car Talk."

On both Mac and Windows, you can make sure that Audible content gets put right into your iTunes library. If you're a Mac user, you have to make sure iTunes is set to handle Internet audio. (If you didn't set it this way originally, as in Figure 1.17, you can change it in your Preferences window on the Advanced Tab: click General and then click the Set button to the right of the words "Use iTunes for Internet music playback".) Windows users need to download Audible DownloadManager from the Audible.com site; this software ensures that Audible content gets put in your iTunes library. On either platform, the first time you download from Audible, iTunes prompts you for your Audible account name and password.

You may be wondering about the difference between purchasing at Audible.com and the iTunes Music Store. The most significant difference is that Audible.com has subscription plans: Currently there's a $15 per month plan, which allows for one book download and one periodical subscription, and a $22 per month plan, which allows for two books. If the books you wish to purchase cost more than $15, this might be a more economical route. (Audible calls these plans their AudibleListener plans.)

While Audible.com has lots of great content and good plans, their Web site is one of the most poorly designed we've ever seen. For example, when we first tried, there was no way to sign up for the less expensive subscription plan from the home page; the Web site "forced" us to sign up for the more expensive plan, and then we had to dig around for a way to change it. When we did change it, the account information displayed didn't correctly reflect the change. If you've tried hard to find something (a way to sign up for a particular subscription plan, a particular item you want to purchase, information on how to do something), or if your account information doesn't reflect what you think it should, trying calling their toll-free support line. They're very helpful!

To explore the store:

1. In iTunes, click Music Store in the Source pane.

iTunes connects to the iTunes Music Store and displays the Music Store home page (**Figure 2.15**), where you can click on links or icons that interest you. Or you can use the Search field; see Chapter 7 for detailed info about searching.

Music Store is selected in Source pane.

Account sign-in

Back and forward buttons. These work just like the back and forward buttons in your Web browser.

Home button. Click to go to the Music Store home page. (When you have moved further into the store, additional items will be listed here that show your path.)

Search field is for searching the Music Store.

Click to pick a genre.

Click to go directly to the 1st, 2nd, 3rd, or 4th subset of albums in the full set.

Click to scroll to the next set of albums in this category. What you can see in this scrolling field may be a featured subset of the full set of albums in this category.

Click to switch to a view that shows all of the albums in this category, which may be more than what's in the scrolling field.

Figure 2.15 The iTunes window, as it appears when you've selected Music Store as your source. (Like any good, dynamic Web site, the iTunes Music Store is constantly updated with new content, so what you'll see when you visit probably won't be exactly what you see in these pages.)

2. Peruse or search the store until you are shown a page with a list of songs (**Figure 2.16**) or videos to buy.

continues on next page

Click to go to genre page, if it exists.
If no page exists for this genre,
clicking this button will just take you
to the home page.

Click to go the
page for this artist.

Songs by this artist that have
been downloaded most. Click
any of these to select the song
in the song list.

Click the artist's
name to go the
page for that artist.

Click to buy all
the songs on the
album.

Double-click any
row to play a
preview of the
song.

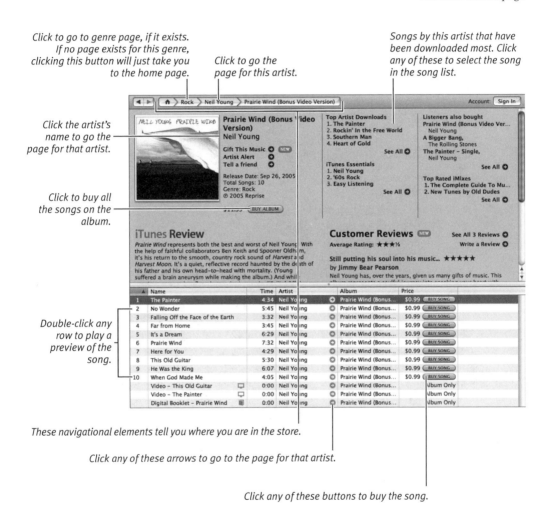

These navigational elements tell you where you are in the store.

Click any of these arrows to go to the page for that artist.

Click any of these buttons to buy the song.

Figure 2.16 A page on which you can buy items.

If you find yourself on a page with no individual songs or videos listed, you may be on an Artist page (**Figure 2.17**) in which case you can buy albums by that artist or click one of the album icons to go to the corresponding Album page. Or you may just want to click the Music Store Back button to retrace your steps.

3. Preview songs or videos by double-clicking the entry in the list.

Songs by the artist that have been downloaded the most. Click any of these to go to the page for the album on which the song is found. The song will be selected in the song list.

Click to go to the genre page if it exists. If no page exists for that genre, clicking this button will take you to the home page.

Choose how you want to sort the list of albums.

Click to buy the whole album.

Click the album name to go to the album.

Click the album cover to go to the album.

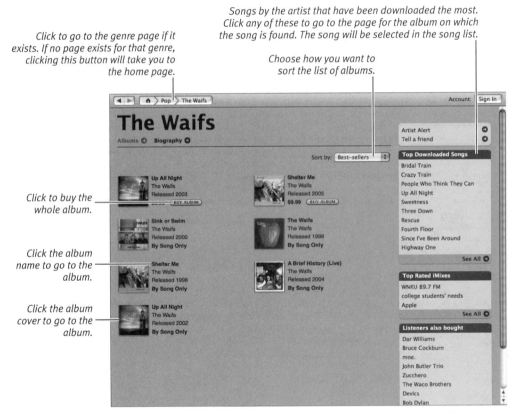

Figure 2.17 An artist page with only a core set of elements. (Some artist pages have lots more information and links than this.)

Figure 2.18 Click the Sign In button to start the process of creating an account.

Figure 2.19 In the Sign In window, click Create New Account if you have no existing Apple or AOL account. (If you do have an account, enter your Apple ID or AOL screen name and password and click Sign In.)

To get an account at the iTunes Music Store:

1. If you're not already in the store, click Music Store in the Source pane.

2. Click the Sign In button on the right side of the window (**Figure 2.18**).

3. Click Create New Account (**Figure 2.19**) and enter the information for which you are prompted: You'll need to agree to the "Terms and Conditions" for the store on the first screen; fill in identifying information on the second; and provide credit card information on the third. When you finish entering your information, you'll see a screen with a message that says you're ready to buy music from the iTunes Music Store.

To purchase music you've located in the iTunes Music Store:

1. Simply click the appropriate Buy button. This may be Buy Song, Buy Album, Buy All Songs, Buy Book, or Buy Work. (Refer to Figures 2.16 and 2.17).

   If you're not currently signed in, you'll be prompted to do so (refer to Figure 2.19); provide your account info or create an account if you haven't already done so.

2. Click Buy when prompted to confirm that you actually do want to purchase, or enter your password if asked.

   The item or items purchased are downloaded to your Library. (If you purchased an album that came with a video or booklet, the video or booklet will be listed in your library, as well.) You'll also see them listed in a special Purchased Music playlist. A receipt will arrive via e-mail.

BUYING FROM THE iTUNES MUSIC STORE

✔ Tips

- If you have an Apple ID or are an AOL member, you can use those accounts to sign in; there's no need to click Create New Account.

- It's a good idea to put some serious thought into your password, because if somebody else guesses it, they can buy lots of music on your credit card.

- By default, iTunes is set for 1-Click shopping. If you prefer to collect items in a shopping cart and pay for all the items at a later time, you can change this on the Store pane of the Preferences window. (We cover this in detail in Chapter 7.)

- In the screen that asks if you're sure about your purchase, you can check an option to have iTunes skip the warning in the future. Unless you wish to throw caution to the wind, don't check this. If you do check it, however, you can later tell iTunes that you actually do want to see the warning; see "Managing Your Account" in Chapter 7.

- Don't want the iTunes Music Store to be a temptation? Open your Preferences window, and in the Parental or Parental Controls tab, check Disable Music Store. Or you can simply check "Restrict explicit content" if you don't want to be quite so heavy-handed.

Fun Ways to Discover New Music

Don't necessarily know exactly what you want to buy? Try these other ways to discover new artists or albums:

- **Celebrity Playlists**—accessible from the home or genre pages, as well as some artist pages—are pages in the store with lists of songs chosen by selected artists and often with additional commentary by those artists.

- **iTunes Essentials**—also accessible from the home or genre pages—are lists of songs that define a category of music, an artist, or a mode. If you're trying to impress your future in-laws with your knowledge of Classical music, you might want to spend some time with the Classical 101 Essentials.

- **Billboard charts**—are lists of top songs from various Billboard charts going back to 1946. Go check out songs from the year your Dad graduated high school! Radio Charts let you look at what certain radio stations around the U.S. are currently playing.

- **Free Downloads**—usually listed in the lower right corner of the home page—are a risk-free way to listen to a complete song of an artist you may never have heard before. You'll still need to have an account, but your account won't be charged.

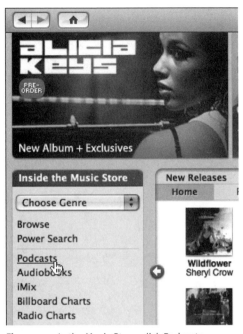

Figure 2.20 In the Music Store, click Podcasts...

Shows you're in the Podcasts section

Figure 2.21 ...to browse the Podcasts section.

Subscribing to Podcasts

A podcast is an audio or video show, something like a radio broadcast or a cable-channel show, that is published on the Internet. You can subscribe to a podcast so that you can receive regular updates (called *episodes*) of the program.

iTunes offers full support for podcasts. In the iTunes Music Store you'll find thousands of podcasts to which you can subscribe (all free). iTunes handles the automatic download of new episodes as they become available. And, as it does with all other items in your library, iTunes gets each new episode onto your iPod; if you have a video iPod, you can watch the video podcasts, too. It's all amazingly seamless. All you need to do is subscribe, so give it a try!

To find and subscribe to a podcast:

1. Click Music Store in the Source pane.

2. Click Podcasts (listed in the Inside the Music Store area; see **Figure 2.20**).

   The navigation bar shows that you're in the Podcast section of the store. You see a standard Music Store graphical interface for you to browse around in, whether by clicking icons or links (**Figure 2.21**). The Search field is also available.

   continues on next page

SUBSCRIBING TO PODCASTS

3. Search for a topic in which you're interested, or let those icons or links entice
you to a page for a podcast to which you'd
like to subscribe. (See **Figure 2.22** for an
example of such a page.)

If you want to preview an episode, double-
click the line that lists that episode. (Find
other methods for previewing work, too;
see "Previewing Songs" in Chapter 7.)

To return to the main Podcasts page, just
click Podcasts in the navigation bar (refer
to Figure 2.21).

4. Once you've found a podcast that you
think you want, click the Subscribe button
at the top of the page (refer to Figure 2.22).

5. When asked if you're sure, click
Subscribe.

iTunes will download to your library the
most recent episode and set your system
to automatically download future episodes
when they become available. Once subscribed, iTunes makes it easy for you to get
past episodes, customize and manage how
your podcasts are handled both by iTunes
and the iPod, and cancel the subscription.
See "Managing Podcasts" in Chapter 9 for
more information.

Click to subscribe to podcast

Double-click
any line to
preview before
downloading
or subscribing

Click to
download only
this episode

Click to get details about the specific episode

Figure 2.22 A Podcast page is like an Album page with a few differences.

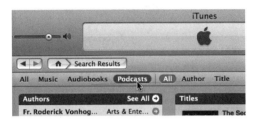

Figure 2.23 Click the Podcasts button in the Search bar to search the store only for podcasts.

Podcasts Begone

Do you fear that evil lurks in some of these podcasts? Want to make it difficult for your kids to access them? Open your Preferences window, and in the Parental tab, check Disable Podcasts. This prevents users from subscribing to podcasts, downloading episodes, or even previewing episodes in the iTunes Music Store. It also removes Podcasts from the Source pane in the main iTunes menu, eliminates the Podcast tab on the iPod tab of the Preferences window, and even hides the Podcasts tab in the iPod tab of the Preferences window. It does not, however, remove or hide podcast episodes from your library (at least as of this writing).

✔ Tips

■ Podcasts will not automatically be moved to the iPod shuffle. You can manually do this. (We'll cover how to manually move songs and podcasts to the shuffle in Chapter 10.)

■ If you are interested in getting a specific episode without subscribing, simply click Get Episode (refer to Figure 2.22). Only that episode will be downloaded to your library. It will also be placed in the Podcasts list, with a Subscribe button so you can choose to subscribe later without having to refind the podcast in the Store. For the few podcasts that are "Subscribe only," you may have to subscribe and then cancel your subscription. See "Managing Podcasts" in Chapter 9 for more information.

■ If you enter a term in the Search field and hit return, the entire iTunes Music Store is searched. Click the Podcasts button that appears in the Search bar (See **Figure 2.23**) to narrow the search to podcasts. (For more about searching in iTunes, see "Searching the Store" and "Power Searching the Store" in Chapter 7.)

■ On the Podcasts page, if you click a category name in the Categories area, the Music Store interface changes to a hierarchical listing, a browser in which you can click a category and subcategory to get to a list of podcasts you can subscribe to. (See "Navigating with the Browser" in Chapter 7.)

■ Click the "i" button in the Description column to read a full description of the contents of that episode. (If all that is provided is a URL, select and copy it, and then paste it into the address bar of your Web browser to get the information.)

Getting Audio Files from Other Online Sources

As you're probably well aware, there are numerous Internet sources for downloading audio files. But before you start downloading songs from these sites, it's important to know which sources provide files that are compatible with iTunes and the iPod.

Files You Download for a Fee

If you want to add purchased songs to your library, the songs need to be in a format that iTunes understands. Virtually all online music stores other than the iTunes Music Store sell MP3 or Windows Media Audio (WMA) files. In the iTunes world, MP3 is good and WMA usually is bad. (See the sidebar "What About Windows Media Audio?")

EMusic (www.emusic.com) is an example of a store that sells MP3 files; you can add its songs to your iTunes library without a hitch.

But Napster (www.napster.com), BuyMusic (www.buymusic.com), and MusicNow (www.musicnow.com) sell WMA files, and iTunes won't be useful with these.

What About Windows Media Audio Files?

Windows Media Audio, or WMA, is a Microsoft-developed audio file format, designed to work seamlessly with Windows Media Player. You'll find WMA audio files available for download in many online music stores (such Napster), and these files can be played on many portable digital music players (such as the Creative Zen Touch). iTunes and the iPod, however, do *not* support this format.

iTunes on Windows *will* convert *unprotected* WMA files into compatible formats. So if you've got WMA files ripped from CDs in the days before you started using iTunes, you can import them into iTunes and put them onto your iPod. This won't work, however, for most purchased music because those files are protected.

To convert unprotected WMA files, add them as you would other files from your hard disk (see "Adding Audio Files from Your Computer," earlier in this chapter) but be aware that (unlike other audio files) what gets put in your library isn't in the same format as the original file. Just as when you import from a CD, the songs are typically changed to the AAC format. (You can change to a different format; see Chapter 8.)

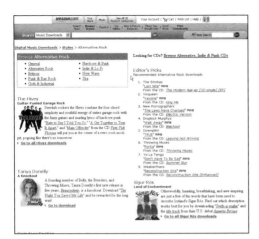

Figure 2.24 Amazon.com offers a free downloads area where you can download MP3s for your iTunes library. At Amazon's main page, click the Music tab and then the Free Downloads subtab to see what is available.

Files You Download for Free

You'll also come across audio on the Web in a variety of places—on artists' Web sites, educational sites, or personal sites. If the site provides a download button, it's most likely that the format is MP3. For example, Amazon.com's Free Downloads area in their Music Category offers lots of MP3s from independent artists that you can download (**Figure 2.24**).

On many sites, you'll just find a link that you click to play the audio. Sometimes, such links point to audio *streams* in the WMA format or the Real Media format (another major streaming format); in these cases, there's no file to download. Many of these links, however, point to audio *files*—often MP3s— that you *can* download. (See the second tip in this section if you don't know how to do this.) The files you download may be full songs or may only be segments of songs. And, while downloadable files (rather than streams) are not the norm for well-known, established bands, it's worth checking the Web sites of artists you like, especially if they are not yet famous.

✔ Tips

- If you download free audio from an artist's Web site, and you like it enough to keep it in your library, make sure you support their work by *purchasing* some of their music, too.

- Not sure how to download an audio file for which you find only a link? Windows users typically do this in Internet Explorer by right-clicking the link for the file and choosing Save Target As (**Figure 2.25**). Macintosh users typically do this in Safari by Control-clicking the link and choosing Download Linked File (**Figure 2.26**). The technique will likely be similar in other browsers.

- Two additional types of files you may come across are those with .m3u or .pls extensions. These files contain pointers to MP3 files on the Internet. You can download them and add them to your library, but they don't actually contain any music.

- As we'll cover later in the chapter, you can add the Internet address (the URL) of an audio file to your iTunes library as an alternative to downloading and adding the actual file.

Figure 2.25 Windows Internet Explorer users need to right-click the link to an audio file and select Save Target As.

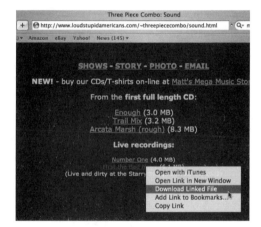

Figure 2.26 Macintosh Safari users need to Control-click the link to an audio file and select Download Linked File.

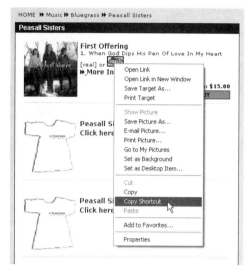

Figure 2.27 To get the URL for an audio file or stream, right-click (Windows) or Ctrl-click (Mac) and choose the option that copies the address. (This is Internet Explorer on Windows; other browsers have such terms as Copy Link to Clipboard or Copy Link Location.)

Figure 2.28 From the Advanced menu, choose Open Stream.

Adding Links to Audio on the Internet

It's not always necessary to download an audio file in order to add it to your library. If you come across a Web page (such as a favorite musical artist's Web site) that contains a link—textual or graphical—that plays audio when clicked, you can opt to add the Internet address (the URL) of the song to your library, effectively adding the same link to your iTunes library. (Links don't get copied to iPods, of course.)

You can include links to streams of live or recorded music as well as to download-able files on the Internet. The usual caveat applies, however: the link must be pointing to audio that's in a format that iTunes understands, most likely MP3. (Typically, MP3 *streams* have a .pls or .m3u extension and MP3 *files* have a .mp3 extension.)

To add a link to audio on the Internet:

1. Right-click (Windows) or Control-click (Mac) the link that you normally click to play the music, and choose the option that copies the URL for that link.

   Different browsers label this differently; examples include Copy Shortcut, Copy Link to Clipboard, and Copy Link Location (**Figure 2.27**).

2. In the iTunes Advanced menu, choose Open Stream (**Figure 2.28**).

continues on next page

3. Paste in the URL (**Figure 2.29**), and click OK.

A new item is added to your library (**Figure 2.30**).

What's added is not the actual music but a *pointer* to its location on the Internet. If you lose your Internet connection, or the owner of the stream shuts the stream down, you won't be able to play it anymore.

✔ Tip

■ Mac users browsing with Safari can Control-click a link to an MP3 file and choose "Open with iTunes." This also adds the link to your library in one step.

Figure 2.29 Paste in the URL you copied from the browser.

Broadcast icon

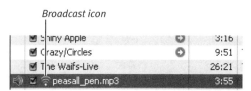

Figure 2.30 Links added to your library have a broadcast icon as part of their song name.

Figure 2.31 To delete a song, Control-click (Mac) or right-click (Windows) to access this contextual menu, and then choose Clear.

Figure 2.32 iTunes asks if you're sure you want to remove the items from your library.

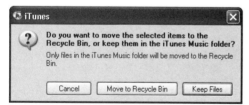

Figure 2.33 iTunes asks if you want to delete the file from your hard drive, too. (This occurs only if the file is stored in your iTunes Music folder.)

Deleting Songs

It's not always about *adding* songs to iTunes. You may decide you want to delete some songs from your library. Deleting a song from your iTunes library is permanent; so proceed with caution.

To delete songs from the library:

1. *Do one of the following:*
   - ▲ Select the song(s) you want to delete, and press the Delete key.
   - ▲ Select the song(s) you want to delete, and from the Edit menu choose Clear.
   - ▲ Control-click (Mac) or right-click (Windows) the song you want to delete, and choose Clear from the contextual menu that appears (**Figure 2.31**).

2. If iTunes asks whether you're sure you want to remove the selected items from your library (**Figure 2.32**), click Remove.

3. You will likely be asked whether you want to move the files to the Trash (Mac) or Recycle Bin (Windows) (**Figure 2.33**). Click Move to Trash or Move to Recycle Bin, as long as you won't ever want the song in your library again. Click Keep Files if you want the song removed from your library but still want its file to remain on your hard disk. (See "How iTunes Organizes Files on Your Hard Drive" in Chapter 9 to understand why iTunes might not ask you this question.)

✔ Tips

- If you don't want to be asked if you're sure that you want to delete the file, hold down the Command key (Mac) or Ctrl key (Windows) when you delete.

- Songs deleted from your library are also deleted from any playlists they're in. The opposite is not true: see Chapter 5 for more on playlists.

- Mac users can drag the song(s) from the iTunes window to the Trash icon on the Dock, but Windows users can't drag songs to the Windows Recycle Bin.

PLAYING MUSIC AND MORE IN iTUNES

3

Once you've added some songs to your library, you'll want to know how to locate specific songs and how to play them.

Of course, you've probably already started poking around in iTunes; it's just too hard not to jump in and start playing your favorite music.

iTunes gives you multiple ways to locate and play songs. You may already know some of them; if you read this chapter, however, you'll likely pick up some new tricks, as well as grasp some nuances of iTunes that may save you confusion and frustration.

We also provide information about things you may want to do while playing—controlling volume, viewing artwork, playing video, and rating songs.

Finally, we end the chapter with coverage of playing music over a network via iTunes sharing capabilities.

Browsing Through Your Library

Just as you navigate through the file system on your computer to get to specific files, you'll need to navigate through the songs in your iTunes library to find the ones you want to listen to. One of the easiest ways to do this is to use the iTunes Browser. When the Browser is hiding, and your library is selected, you see one long list of songs, as in **Figure 3.1**. When the Browser is showing, however (**Figure 3.2**), it's much easier to locate songs by genre, artist, and album.

Ways to hide and show the Browser:

◆ Click the Browse button at the top right of your iTunes window (refer to Figure 3.1).

◆ From the Edit menu, choose either Show Browser or Hide Browser. (Or use keyboard shortcuts: Mac users can press Command-B; Windows users can press Ctrl-B.)

The Browser appears in the upper portion of the Detail pane, displaying columns listing genres, artists, and albums (refer to Figure 3.2).

Click to show the Browser

Figure 3.1 If you're looking at your library with the Browser hidden, you see one long list of songs.

Click to hide the Browser

Figure 3.2 Once you show the Browser, you can select a specific genre, artist, and album to view.

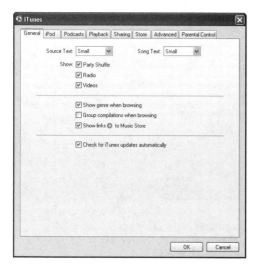

Figure 3.3 Open the Preferences window, and on the General tab, uncheck "Show genre when browsing" to remove the Genre column from the Browser.

To browse for songs:

◆ With the Browser showing, click a genre, artist, album, or any combination of these.

Only songs that match the item(s) you clicked appear in the song list.

✔ Tips

■ You can select multiple genres, albums, or artists. Shift-click to select contiguous items; Command-click (Mac) or Ctrl-click (Windows) to select items that are not adjacent.

■ If you don't care about genre when browsing, you can get rid of that column in the browser: On the General tab of the Preferences window, click to uncheck "Show genre when browsing" (**Figure 3.3**).

BROWSING THROUGH YOUR LIBRARY

Searching for Songs

Sometimes browsing just doesn't get you where you want to go fast enough. What if all you know, for example, is that either the song title or the album title has the word *Wheels* in it or that the artist's name starts with *Al*? iTunes has a search feature that will help.

Also, if you have a very large library and you know the exact title of the song you want, the fastest way to get to that song is by using iTunes' search feature.

To search for a text string:

1. In the Source pane, click the source you want to search.

   Most likely this source will be your library, although you can search other items in your Source pane in the same way.

2. In the Search field, located in the top right corner of the iTunes window, type the text you want iTunes to locate.

   As you type, the song list changes to reflect what you've typed so far. The song list displays the songs that contain—in the Song Name, Artist, Album, Genre, or Composer columns—the text you've typed in the search field. The more you type, the more you narrow the search results (**Figures 3.4** and **3.5**).

   Also, as soon as you start typing in the Search field, the Search bar appears if it wasn't already visible (refer to Figure 3.4).

To limit a search:

◆ Click the appropriate button in the Search bar (refer to Figure 3.4) to have iTunes search only a specific type of item (Music, Audiobooks, Podcasts, Videos, or Booklets) or to have it search in only a specific column (Artist, Album, or Name).

Search bar   *Search field*

Figure 3.4 As soon as you start to type in the Search field, iTunes shows only songs that have those characters in the Song Name, Artist, Album, Composer, or Genre column.

Figure 3.5 As you type, the songs that match your search criteria are narrowed down further.

✔ Tips

■ You can also search the iTunes Music Store, but the search function doesn't work in exactly the same way; see Chapter 7.

■ iTunes searches for your text string in the Comments column but only if that column is visible. To learn how to hide and show columns, see "Hiding and Showing Columns" in Chapter 9.

Figure 3.6 Click any column head to sort by that column. Songs are sorted in alphabetical order, since this triangle points up. Click the triangle to reverse alphabetical order.

Figure 3.7 After clicking the column head so the arrow points down, the songs are in reverse alphabetical order.

Hate Mousing?

You'll find that you can navigate to and play any song in your iTunes collection using just the keys on your keyboard. Using the Tab key, you can jump to different panes and fields: the Search field, each of the columns in the browser (if showing), the song list in the Detail pane, and the Source pane.

When you're in the Search field, it's bordered in blue, and you can just start typing. When any of the other elements are active, the selected row is highlighted in blue with white text (in Figure 3.2, earlier in this chapter, The Beatles is highlighted, though you'll just have to imagine the blue color); you can move in the list using your arrow or alpha keys. Once you've selected the song you want to play, press the Return (Mac) or Enter (Windows) key.

Also, you can press Option-Command-F (Mac) or Ctrl-Alt-F (Windows) to jump directly to the Search field.

Sorting Songs

If browsing or searching yields many songs (or if you're viewing your entire library), it helps to be able to sort the songs that appear in the song list. You may also want to sort your songs in a particular way, since the order they appear in the song list is the order in which they'll play.

To sort by a particular column:

◆ Click the column name (**Figure 3.6**).

The column head becomes highlighted, so you can tell that it's the column by which the entire list is sorted. If the triangle on the right side of the column name points up, everything is sorted in alphabetical or numeric order.

To reverse the order of the sort:

◆ Click the column head again.

The column is now sorted in the reverse order (**Figure 3.7**).

✔ Tip

■ There are many additional columns available for you to sort on that may not be currently visible. (Date Added, for example, is a column that we find helpful to sort on to easily find the most recent additions to our music collection.) In Chapter 9, we cover the additional columns and how to show them.

Playing and Pausing Songs

Once the songs you want to play are visible in your song list, you have numerous ways to play them. (You've surely discovered some of them by now.)

It gets a little tricky, however, depending on whether or not there's a *current* song. A current song is one that is playing or was just playing; it has a speaker icon next to it (**Figure 3.8**).

Ways to play songs:

◆ Press the Play button (**Figure 3.9**) to play the current song.

◆ If there's no current song, press the Play button to play whatever song is selected or to play the first song in the list, if nothing is selected.

◆ Double-click any song's line to play it.

◆ Click a song's line in the song list to select it, and press the Return key (Mac) or Enter key (Windows) on your keyboard.

◆ Double-click a line in the Browser pane to put the songs in that category in the song list and start playing the first of these.

The song that plays becomes the current song; the speaker icon appears next to it with lines emanating from the speaker.

As the song plays, the diamond in the progress bar moves to the right. The elapsed time appears on the left side of the bar in the Status display, and the remaining time appears on the right side.

Figure 3.8 Use different techniques to play depending on whether songs are selected or current. In this example, *Maxwell's Silver Hammer* is the current song; press the space bar (or click the Play button or choose Controls > Play) to play it. Press Return (Mac) or Enter (Windows) to play *Come Together*, the selected song. Double-click to play any song even if it's not selected or current, such as *Oh! Darling*.

Figure 3.9 Click the Play button to play the current song (the one with the speaker icon) or the selected song if no song is current, or the first song in the song list if no song is current or selected.

Figure 3.10 Click the Pause button to pause playback of the current song. (When you click the Play button again, playback resumes where you've stopped it.)

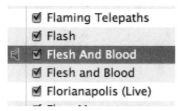

Figure 3.11 Notice that the speaker icon no longer has lines emanating from it, indicating that this song is paused. It still shows that the song is current, however.

Figure 3.12 Click the Skip Forward button to make the next song in the list the current song. (Or click the Skip Backward button, the one with the double arrows pointing left, to make the previous song in the list the current song. You may have to click twice if the song is playing.)

To pause a song:

◆ Click the Pause button, the button with the parallel lines (**Figure 3.10**).

The speaker icon next to the playing song changes so that there are no sound waves emanating from the speaker (**Figure 3.11**). This song is still the current song, however.

Ways to make the next or previous song current:

◆ Press the right or left arrow key.

◆ From the Controls menu, choose Next Song or Previous Song.

◆ Click the Skip Forward or Skip Backward button (**Figure 3.12**).

The speaker icon appears to the left of the new current song. If iTunes is playing a song at the time you do any of the above, the new current song begins playing from the beginning; otherwise, use one of the previously described methods to play the new current song.

✔ Tips

- You can also play or pause a song by pressing the spacebar or choosing Play or Pause from the Controls menu.

- If a song is playing when you try to make the previous song current, you'll usually have to press the left arrow key twice, or choose Controls > Previous Song twice, or click the Skip Back button twice. Taking these actions only once will return you to the beginning of the playing (current) song.

- If you're playing your own music in iTunes and go to the iTunes Music Store, the Pause button turns into a Stop button (a solid square); if you click the Stop button, you'll find that you can't resume playback of the song—you'll have to go back to your library and start playing the song over again.

- If you want to make current the next song in the list that's from a different album than the current song—in other words, you want to skip over all the songs from the album you're now listening to—hold down the Shift, Ctrl, and Alt keys (Windows) or the Option key (Mac) while you click the right arrow key. (Doing the same with the left arrow key goes up the song list to find a song that's on a different album.)

- The keyboard shortcuts listed in iTunes' Controls menu say that you need to add the Ctrl or Command key to the right and left arrow key to make the next or previous song current. This hasn't been our experience—using the arrow keys on their own has worked fine—but it's possible that Apple may change this in a future release.

What's Selected Isn't Necessarily What Plays

It can be confusing that one song can be selected (highlighted) while a different song is "current" (has the speaker icon next to it); see Figure 3.8.

Since the highlighting is so much more prominent than the speaker icon, one might think that clicking the Play button (or choosing Controls > Play or pressing the spacebar) would play the selected song. Not so: The song that gets played is the one that has the speaker icon next to it.

You can, however, make the selected song and the current song one-and-the-same: From the File menu, choose Show Current Song (**Figure 3.13**) to select the current song. Or you can click the little curving-arrow button that shows on the right side of the Status display. This is particularly useful when you've been browsing around your iTunes library while listening to a song and you want to get back to that song.

Figure 3.13 From the File menu, choose Show Current Song to select the current song.

PLAYING AND PAUSING SONGS

Click here to change what's displayed.

Drag the diamond to move around in the song.

Figure 3.14 The Status display provides several types of information about the current song.

Figure 3.15 Click and hold the Skip Forward or Skip Backward button to fast forward or fast rewind.

Chapter Jumping

Most audiobooks and some podcasts purchased at the iTunes Music Store provide a *chapter menu*; this gives you another way to access specific points in the audio. To see how this menu operates, see Figures 3.23 and 3.24 in "Accessing and Playing Podcasts" later in this chapter. When playing items with chapters (whether from the iTunes Music Store or another outlet, like Audible.com) you can also jump to the next chapter or previous chapter using the Next Chapter or Previous Chapter commands in the Controls menu.

Moving Around in a Song

How do you move around in a song—say, to skip the first 15 seconds or to jump to that cool guitar riff near the end that you want your best friend to hear? Try these techniques.

To randomly access portions of a song:

1. Start playing the song.

2. If the Status display doesn't show a rectangular bar with a diamond in it as in **Figure 3.14,** click the tiny triangle on the left side of the display until it looks like Figure 3.14.

3. Drag the diamond to the right or left in the bar to get to the portion of the song you want to hear.

   As you drag, the times displayed (amount played and remaining time) update.

To fast forward or fast rewind:

◆ Click and hold the Skip Forward or Skip Backward button (**Figure 3.15**).

✔ Tip

■ When you want to fast forward or fast rewind in a song, it won't work to simply click (that is, press your mouse button down and immediately release) the Skip Forward or Skip Backward button. If you do this, you'll simply make the next or previous song in the list current.

Options for Playing Multiple Songs

If iTunes is providing the background music for an activity—working, partying, cooking, whatever—you probably want it to keep playing song after song, just as if you were playing a CD. This it does automatically, playing the next song in the list—be it your full library or a subset of it—until it reaches the last song in the list.

You can control how iTunes plays music in several ways: repeating, shuffling, and picking particular songs that you don't want to play.

To set iTunes so it repeats the songs in the song list:

◆ Click the Repeat button (located in the lower left of the iTunes window) until it is highlighted blue (**Figure 3.16**).

To set iTunes to play all the songs in the song list and then stop:

◆ Click the Repeat button until it's not highlighted (that is, is gray only).

To set iTunes to play the current song repeatedly:

◆ Click the Repeat button until it's highlighted blue and displays the number 1 (**Figure 3.17**).

That little number 1 can be hard to see, but once you've seen it, you'll recognize it when you see it again.

To set iTunes to play the songs in the song list in random order:

◆ Click the Shuffle button so that it's highlighted blue (**Figure 3.18**).

Figure 3.16 Click the Repeat button so it is highlighted in blue if you want the current list of songs to repeat. (Click it so it is gray to turn the repeat function off.)

Figure 3.17 Click so the Repeat button looks like this—notice the little number 1—to repeat only the current song.

Figure 3.18 Click the Shuffle button so that it's highlighted in blue if you want the songs to play in random order.

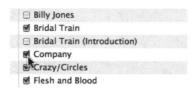

Figure 3.19 Songs that are not checked won't play.

To specify individual songs that you don't want to play:

◆ Click to remove the checkmark for each song you don't want to play (**Figure 3.19**).

✔ Tips

■ If Shuffle mode is on, clicking the Skip Forward or Skip Backward buttons (or using any other method for making the next or previous song current) switches the current song to the next or previous one in the shuffled order, which is not necessarily the song immediately below or above the current song.

■ You can put checkmarks next to all the songs in the list or remove them all at once by Command-clicking (Mac) or Ctrl-clicking (Windows) any one check box.

■ You can add or remove checkmarks on a number of songs at once by selecting them all, right-clicking or control-clicking any one of the selected songs, and choosing Check Selection or Uncheck Selection.

■ To play all the songs on an album, by a particular artist, or in a particular genre, just double-click the name of the album, artist, or genre in the Browser. (This won't work in all circumstances. For example, it won't work if you've already selected an album by the artist or in the genre that you double-click.)

■ If a song is playing when you select a new category from the Browser, iTunes is smart enough to finish playing that song and then stop; it doesn't move on to the song that would have been next. It doesn't, however, start playing your newly selected album, artist, or genre automatically; you need to manually start play.

continues on next page

- You can use the Browser to select multiple albums, artists, or genres. The combined songs from the selected categories appear in your song list, ready to play.

- You can Command-click (Mac) or Ctrl-click (Windows) an artist, album, or genre to add to the list of songs even while a song is playing.

- Another cool way to get a random selection of songs is to use the Party Shuffle playlist. See Chapter 5.

- If there are certain songs you never want to appear when you're playing randomly, do this: Select the song, choose File > Get Info, Click the Options tab, and check "Skip when shuffling." Podcasts and audiobooks are set this way automatically (and can't be changed).

- iTunes song playing behavior is somewhat different when you're playing from the Podcasts or Videos playlists. See "Accessing and Playing Podcasts" and "Accessing and Playing Video" later in this chapter.

Shuffling Preferences

If you've turned Shuffle on, iTunes' default behavior is to randomly play all the songs appearing in the Detail pane. However, you can tell it to shuffle by album, in which case it plays all the songs from an album in the order they appear before randomly going to another album, and playing all those songs in the order they appear. If you choose to shuffle by groupings, it will play all the songs from a grouping (a collection of the movements of a classical work) before randomly going to another grouping.

You can switch the Shuffle mode on the Playback tab of the Preferences window (**Figure 3.20**).

You'll also find a Smart Shuffle slider that allows you to specify how "random" you want the shuffling to be (refer to Figure 3.20). The further to the left you set the slider, the more likely it is that you'll get repeats of songs by the same artist or on the same album. The further right, the less likely to get repeats.

Figure 3.20 On the Playback tab of the Preferences window you can specify shuffling preferences.

Blue dot indicates there are
new episodes to listen to

Click the disclosure triangle
to see specific episodes

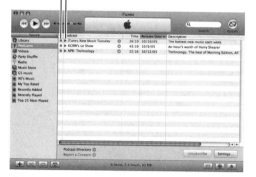

Figure 3.21 When you select Podcasts in your Source pane, all podcasts you've subscribed to or have downloaded an episode from appear.

Figure 3.22 Specific episodes of podcasts appear when the disclosure triangle is turned down.

Accessing and Playing Podcasts

While the ways you find and play podcast episodes are the same as those you use to find and play songs in your library, iTunes gives podcasts special status and provides you with smarter ways to access them, via a special Podcasts playlist.

To see your Podcasts playlist:

◆ Click Podcasts in the Source menu.

You'll see a list of all the podcasts to which you've subscribed or from which you've downloaded specific episodes (**Figure 3.21**).

A blue dot appears in the far left column of any podcasts that have unlistened-to episodes.

If you select a podcast and play it (using any of the techniques for playing songs), the most recent episode that you haven't yet listened to will play.

To access specific podcast episodes:

◆ Click the disclosure triangle (refer to Figure 3.21).

All the available episodes of that podcast appear in the list (**Figure 3.22**).

✔ Tips

■ You can get rid of the Podcasts playlist in your Source pane: on the Parental or Parental Controls tab of the Preferences window, check the Disable Podcasts option.

■ You can further manage podcasts (changing how often you want iTunes checking for new episodes, unsubscribing, and so on). We cover this in Chapter 9.

Playing Enhanced Podcasts

Enhanced podcasts are those that contain more than audio; they are divided into chapters and usually include synchronized graphics. They may also have links you can click to open a Web page or page in the iTunes music store.

You'll recognize an enhanced podcast in your library because, once you start playing it, a Chapter button appears between the Status display and the Search field (**Figure 3.23**).

You can click the Chapter button to view the Chapter menu (**Figure 3.24**), from which you can select a chapter to jump to.

If there are graphics associated with the items in the menu, larger versions of them appear in your Artwork pane at appropriate times (see "Viewing Artwork" later in this chapter to learn about the Artwork pane). Links also appear in the Artwork pane (refer to Figure 3.24).

Chapter button

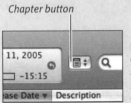

Figure 3.23 This Chapter button appears once you start playing an enhanced podcast.

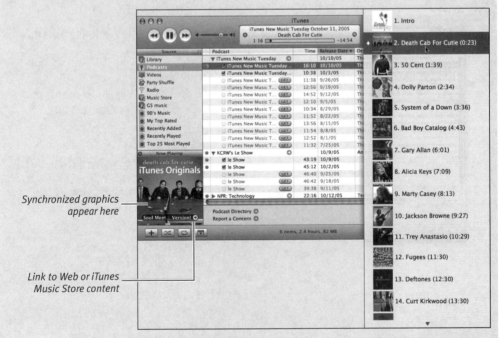

Synchronized graphics appear here

Link to Web or iTunes Music Store content

Figure 3.24 Click the Chapter button to view and select from the Chapter menu.

Figure 3.25 Change iTunes' volume using the volume slider.

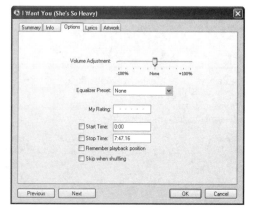

Figure 3.26 Change the default volume for a song in the song's Info window, on the Options tab. (Select the song and choose File > Get Info to open this window.)

Controlling Volume

You can change the volume for the iTunes application as a whole, or you can change the default volume of specific songs.

Ways to change the volume for all songs:

◆ Click and drag the volume slider in the iTunes window (**Figure 3.25**).

◆ Hold down the Command key (Mac) or Ctrl key (Windows) and press the up or down arrow keys on your keyboard.

Setting the default volume for a single song:

1. Click the song in the song list to select it.

2. From the File menu, choose Get Info. The Info window for the song appears.

3. Click the Options tab.

4. Select the default volume by adjusting the Volume Adjustment slider (**Figure 3.26**).

5. Click OK to close the window.

Setting the default volume for multiple songs:

1. Shift-click to select multiple contiguous songs or Command-click (Mac) or Ctrl-click (Windows) to select multiple noncontiguous songs in the song list.

2. From the File menu, choose Get Info.

3. If you're asked whether you want to edit information for multiple items, click Yes.

4. Move the Volume Adjustment slider in the lower left corner of the window to adjust the volume (**Figure 3.27**).

5. Click OK to close the window.

✔ Tips

■ Your system sound level affects the playback volume, too.

■ Volume control works logarithmically. You'll find that you have finer control of volume at the low end; in other words, to hear much of a change requires a greater adjustment. At the high end, small adjustments result in relatively large changes in volume.

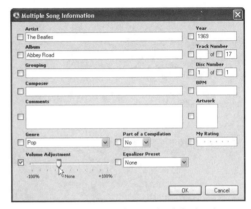

Figure 3.27 You can also change the default volume for a number of songs by selecting them, choosing File > Get Info, and then adjusting the Volume Adjustment slider in this window.

Figure 3.28 Click Radio in the Source pane to get a list of the categories of streams available to you.

Listening to Radio Streams

The first thing both of us ever used iTunes for (oh so many years ago!) was listening to Internet radio streams while working, largely because all we needed to gain access to a reasonable selection of music was iTunes and an Internet connection. This is still the case.

iTunes provides access to a fairly large collection of streams. Some of these streams are offered by radio stations that also broadcast over the airwaves; others operate like radio stations (playing one song after another) but are Internet-only.

To listen to a radio stream:

1. Click Radio in the Source pane (**Figure 3.28**).

2. Click the disclosure triangle to the left of one of the categories.

   The triangle turns downward. After a second or so, a list of available radio streams appears (**Figure 3.29**).

   Below the Detail pane, the number of streams available to you is listed.

3. Play any of the radio streams listed by double-clicking one (or by using any of the other methods for playing a song described in "Playing and Pausing Songs" earlier in this chapter).

   Sometimes it takes a while to contact the server that's providing the streams.

What's the URL, Kenneth?

You can get the URL for any radio stream: Select the stream, choose File > Get Info, and on the Summary tab click the Edit URL button; in the Edit URL window that appears, you'll see the stream's URL, which you can then copy and paste into other applications such as QuickTime Player (in which you'd use the File > Open URL command) or e-mail to a friend.

Disclosure triangle   Number of streams   Refresh button

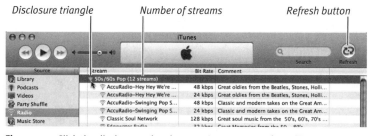

Figure 3.29 Click the disclosure triangle next to a category to have iTunes contact the tuning service and return a list of streams available in that category.

Ways to stop radio play:

◆ Click the Stop button (the square), located where the Pause button would normally be (**Figure 3.30**).

◆ Press the spacebar.

◆ From the Controls menu, choose Stop.

To view the latest list of categories:

◆ Click the Refresh button at the top right of the iTunes window (refer to Figure 3.29), and iTunes will recontact the tuning service.

✔ Tips

■ Dial-up-modem users should pick stations that are listed at 56 kbps or less.

■ On the Advanced tab of the Preferences window, you can select a streaming buffer size of Small, Medium, or Large (**Figure 3.31**). The buffer size is a reflection of how much audio data should be downloaded before iTunes will play. If you request a small buffer, the stream will start more quickly, as long as you have a fast connection. If you have a slow connection (such as a dial-up modem), you'll want a large buffer, so enough music will be available for playback without stuttering.

■ Once you locate a favorite radio stream, drag it to your library or to a playlist so you can access it quickly (**Figure 3.32**). This also lets you search for it, since iTunes can't search the Radio source. You'll be able to tell which are radio streams by the broadcast icon and by the fact that the time is listed as "Continuous."

■ To open all or close all of the Radio categories, Command-click (Mac) or Ctrl-click (Windows) any one disclosure triangle.

Figure 3.30 When you listen to an Internet radio stream, there's no Pause button— only a Stop button.

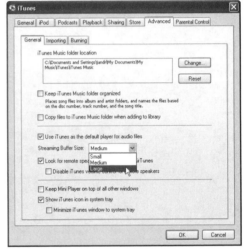

Figure 3.31 If you have a slow Internet connection (such as dial-up), pick a larger buffer size.

Figure 3.32 Radio streams you've added to your library look like the selected listing above. Notice the broadcast icon and the fact that time is listed as "Continuous."

■ Not ever going to use the iTunes Radio? You can get rid of it in the Source list. Open the Preferences window, make sure you're on the General tab, and, in the first group of checkboxes (labeled "Show") uncheck Radio.

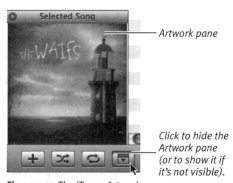

Artwork pane

Click to hide the Artwork pane (or to show it if it's not visible).

Figure 3.33 The iTunes Artwork pane is visible by default. If you find it distracting, simply click it to hide it.

Figure 3.34 When you click a graphic in the Artwork pane, it opens in its own window at full resolution.

Figure 3.35 Clicking the bar at the top of the Artwork pane switches the artwork between that for the playing song and that for the selected song. (Notice that the bar in Figure 3.33 says "Selected Song.")

Viewing Artwork

Any graphics or video associated with an item appear in the Artwork pane. (Artwork comes with most songs you purchase at the iTunes Music Store; we'll also show you how you can add your own artwork to songs in Chapter 8.) You can do more than just stare at that little pane, however.

Ways to hide or show the Artwork pane:

◆ Click the rightmost of the buttons at the bottom left of the iTunes window (**Figure 3.33**).

◆ From the Edit menu, choose Hide Artwork or Show Artwork.

To show the image at full resolution:

◆ Click the image in the Artwork pane. The full-resolution version opens in a separate window (**Figure 3.34**).

To switch between artwork for the selected song and for the playing song:

◆ Click the bar above the Artwork pane. The text on the bar tells you whether you are looking at the artwork for the selected song (refer to Figure 3.33) or for the currently playing song (**Figure 3.35**).

✔ Tips

■ The window containing the full-resolution version of the graphic is titled by the name of the song; it is listed in the iTunes Window menu (Mac) or the Windows taskbar (Windows).

■ Right and left arrow buttons appear at the top of the Artwork pane if there is more than one graphic associated with the song that's not synchronized in time with the audio (as with enhanced podcasts). Click the arrows to show the different graphics.

Accessing and Playing Video

We mentioned in Chapter 2 that you can have video files in your iTunes library; you can purchase video from the iTunes Music Store, and you can also add your own video content.

Videos are listed in your library just like songs, although you'll see a video icon to the right of the name of the file (**Figure 3.36**).

You'll also find a special Videos playlist in your Source pane that displays thumbnails of the video items in your library (**Figure 3.37**); you can change it to a normal list view by clicking the icon in the upper right of the window.

You can play the video (regardless of source or display method) using any of the techniques described earlier in this chapter for playing songs; the video plays in the Artwork pane by default (refer to Figure 3.36), but you can also see it in a separate window.

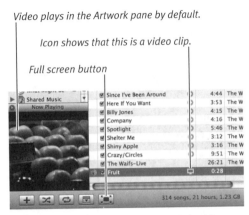

Video plays in the Artwork pane by default.

Icon shows that this is a video clip.

Full screen button

Figure 3.36 Your iTunes library may include video items you can play just like other items.

You can also use the Search bar to show subcategories of videos.

Change to a normal list view by clicking here.

This one is a QuickTime movie with audio only.

Figure 3.37 When you choose Videos as your source, the Detail pane shows video items in thumbnail view.

To play the video in a separate window with a controller:

1. Play the video, and make sure the Artwork pane is showing (methods are covered in "Viewing Artwork"; previously in this chapter).

2. Click the Artwork pane.

   The video appears in a separate window with a standard movie controller (**Figure 3.38**).

Use the Volume Control button to adjust the volume of a movie: Hold it down until an image that looks like a thermometer appears. Then drag the indicator up to increase the volume or down to decrease the volume.

Move the indicator to change the current time in the movie.

Click the Pause button to pause a playing movie. Click the Play button to start playing a paused movie.

Right and left step buttons move you one frame forward and back.

Figure 3.38 If you click the Artwork pane when a movie is playing, the movie shows in a window with a standard movie controller.

ACCESSING AND PLAYING VIDEO

To resize the video or play it full screen:

◆ Right-click (Windows) or Control-click (Mac) the video playing in a separate window and choose Half Size, Normal Size, Double Size, or Full Screen (**Figure 3.39**).

◆ Click the Full Screen button (refer to Figure 3.36) when the video is playing in the Artwork pane.

◆ When a video is playing full screen, press the escape key or the space bar to return the video to its previous size.

To change the thumbnail image:

1. Open the video in a separate window and show the image in the video you want as a thumbnail.

2. Right-click (Windows) or Control-click (Mac) the video playing in a separate window and choose Set Poster Frame (refer to Figure 3.39)

✔ Tips

■ You can change the default method for how videos play. In the Playback tab of the Preferences window, there's a "Play videos" pop-up menu: you can choose to have all video play back full screen, in a separate window (as in Figure 3.38), or in the main window (which means playing in the Artwork pane, as in Figure 3.36).

■ When you play videos from the Videos playlist (rather than from your library), the next item in the list does not automatically play.

■ Some QuickTime movies may contain only audio. Currently, the Videos playlist includes even QuickTime movies with no video. Your clue that a "video" has no video is the QuickTime icon (refer to Figure 3.37) in the Videos playlist.

Figure 3.39 Right-click (Windows) or Control-click (Mac) to display this menu in a movie playing in a separate window.

Figure 3.40 Click in the My Rating column to assign a rating.

Figure 3.41 Or choose a rating from the contextual menu that appears when you Control-click (Mac) or right-click (Windows) a song.

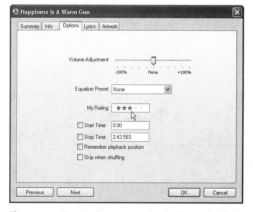

Figure 3.42 Or rate the song on the Options tab of the information window for the song.

Rating Songs

One thing you may want to do when you're playing your songs is to rate them. Song ratings come in handy when you want to sort your library in order of rating (see "Sorting Songs" earlier in this chapter) or when you want to create a playlist of your favorite songs (see Chapter 5 for more about playlists). You can rate songs between 1 and 5 stars. iTunes provides a variety of ways to do this, either one song at a time or as a group.

Ways to rate a single song:

◆ In the My Rating column, click at the position of the number of stars you want to assign (**Figure 3.40**).

◆ Right-click (Windows) or Control-click (Mac) in any column of the song you want to rate, choose My Rating, and then choose the number of stars you want to assign (**Figure 3.41**).

◆ Select the song and choose File > Get Info. On the Options tab, assign a rating by clicking at the position of the number of stars you want to assign; in other words, to assign a three-star rating, click the third star (**Figure 3.42**).

continues on next page

◆ To rate the current song (the one with the speaker icon next to it), click and hold the iTunes icon in the Dock (Mac; **Figure 3.43**) or right-click the iTunes icon in the system tray (Windows; **Figure 3.44**); then choose the number of stars from the My Rating submenu.

Figure 3.43 Mac users can rate the currently playing song by clicking and holding the iTunes menu in the Dock, choosing My Ratings, and selecting the desired star rating. (This is useful when iTunes is providing background music and is not the frontmost application.)

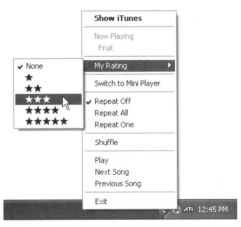

Figure 3.44 Windows users can rate the currently playing song by right-clicking the iTunes icon in the system tray, choosing My Ratings, and selecting the appropriate number of stars.

Click in this field to rate multiple songs.

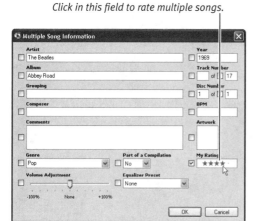

Figure 3.45 If you select more than one song and choose Get Info, this Multiple Song Information window appears, letting you rate all the selected songs at once.

To assign the same rating to multiple songs:

◆ Select the songs, choose File > Get Info, and in the Multiple Song Information window, click in the My Rating field (**Figure 3.45**).

✔ Tips

■ In the My Rating column or in the rating fields in the Info windows, you'll find that once you press the mouse button down, you can drag to change the number of stars assigned.

■ It's great that you don't have to painstakingly rate each song in your iTunes library one by one. Do you adore every track on *Abbey Road*? If all the songs on the album are in a playlist, select the playlist in the Source pane; if not, use the browse or search feature to show them all in the song list. Then select them all, choose File > Get Info, and give all the songs on the album five stars.

■ The My Rating column may not be visible; see Chapter 9 for details on hiding, showing, and moving columns.

Sharing Your Music

iTunes lets you do more than just listen to your favorite songs. You can actually *share* your iTunes music library over a small local network. This might mean your home, a small business, or a segment of a large corporate network (otherwise known as a *subnet*). Sharing over a network is an easy way for family members or office mates to listen to your music collection.

If you want to make your music available to others on your network, you need to enable sharing in iTunes.

To turn on sharing:

1. Open your Preferences window and click the Sharing tab.

2. In the Sharing tab, click to check "Share my music" (**Figure 3.46**).

AirTunes

AirTunes, part of Apple's AirPort Express wireless network base station, enables wireless music playing. This means, for example, that you can plug the AirPort Express base station into a wall outlet and plug your home stereo (or powered speakers) into the audio output jack on the base station. If your network is set up properly, iTunes will automatically (like sharing between iTunes users) "see" the base station and, via a pop-up at the bottom of your iTunes screen, let you select that base station; iTunes (perhaps running on a computer in your home office) then plays the music through to the base station and in turn to your stereo (which may be in your living room). Kinda cool!

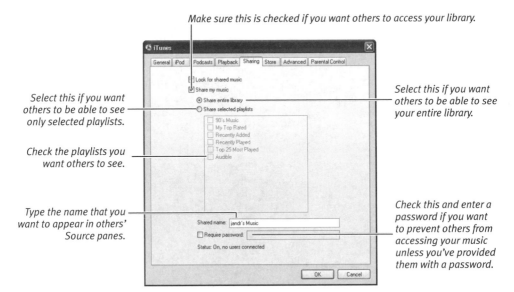

Make sure this is checked if you want others to access your library.

Select this if you want others to be able to see only selected playlists.

Check the playlists you want others to see.

Type the name that you want to appear in others' Source panes.

Select this if you want others to be able to see your entire library.

Check this and enter a password if you want to prevent others from accessing your music unless you've provided them with a password.

Figure 3.46 The Sharing tab of the Preferences window.

3. If you want to share only selected playlists, select "Share selected playlists," and then check the playlists you want to share.

4. If you want to change the way your shared music is listed when it appears in someone else's Source pane, type the name you prefer in the "Shared name" field.

5. If you want people to have to type a password before they can connect to your library, select "Require password" and type a password.

6. Click OK to close the Preferences window and save your settings.

Once you turn on sharing, all computers on your local area network—or on your subnet if you're part of a large network—can see an item from your shared library in their iTunes Source pane. (See "Playing Music from Others' Libraries" next in this chapter.)

To turn off sharing:

◆ In your Preferences window, in the Sharing tab (refer to Figure 3.46), uncheck "Share my music."

✔ Tips

■ If you need to be able to determine if you're on the same subnet as another computer, check your TCP/IP settings; if the first three sets of numbers are the same (for example, 192.168.12.43 and 192.168.12.135), you're on the same subnet.

■ Only five computers can share your music in any one day.

■ If you want to know whether anyone is connected to your library, look at the bottom of the Preferences window's Sharing tab (refer to Figure 3.46).

■ You can't disconnect individual users or determine which users are connected.

What Won't Be Shared

Not everything in your library will be accessible to others on your local network.

iTunes skips over songs and audiobooks purchased from the iTunes Music Store when playing via iTunes sharing, unless the computer is authorized to play music from the account under which the item was purchased. If you try to play a shared purchased item by double-clicking it, iTunes prompts you to authorize the computer. (See "Authorizing Multiple Computers to Play Your Songs" in Chapter 7.)

You won't even *see* audiobooks purchased from Audible in a shared library (at least as of this writing), regardless of whether the computer accessing the share has been appropriately authorized. (The method for playing audiobooks is covered in "Authorizing a Computer to Play Audible. com content" later in this chapter.)

Videos also don't appear. As a matter of fact, anything that iTunes considers a QuickTime movie file (including karaoke and MIDI files), as well as various obscure audio formats (such as Sound Designer and Nomad Voice File), don't show up in a shared library, either (even though they work just fine when played in iTunes on the computer on which they reside).

Booklets (such as the ones that come with certain albums in the iTunes Music Store) also don't appear.

Playing Music from Others' Libraries

Turning on sharing so that others can access your music is nice, but iTunes is much more fun when you can play other users' shared music libraries.

Shared libraries show up in an iTunes song list, so the person accessing the shared music can browse, search, and sort the songs, as well as view the full range of information associated with each song.

To view shared libraries:

1. Look in your Source pane.

   Any shared libraries should already be visible. (The icon for a shared library is similar to that for your iTunes library and the Music Store except that it's blue.)

   If there's one shared library on your network, you'll see it listed in your Source pane (**Figure 3.47**).

   If multiple people on your network are sharing, you'll see a Shared Music entry in your Source pane, with the different libraries listed below that (**Figure 3.48**).

2. If you don't see any shared libraries, and you know there are people on your local network who are sharing, open the Preferences window, and on the Sharing tab, make sure that "Look for shared music" is checked (**Figure 3.49**). (This is the default setting.)

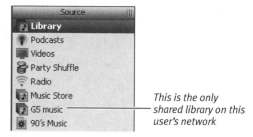

This is the only shared library on this user's network

Figure 3.47 A single shared library on your network appears like this.

As you can see, multiple shared libraries are available on this network.

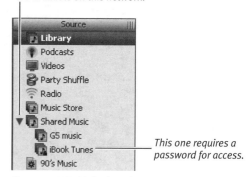

This one requires a password for access.

Figure 3.48 Multiple shared libraries on your network make your iTunes experience much more exciting.

This needs to be checked to see others' shared libraries.

You don't have to share your music to see others' shared libraries. (But it would be a little selfish to not reciprocate if you're taking advantage of others' shared libraries, don't you think?)

Figure 3.49 If you see no shared libraries, make sure that your Sharing preferences are set to "Look for shared music."

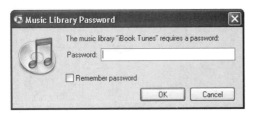

Figure 3.50 When you try to connect, you may be asked for a password. The owner of the shared library will give this to you if they want you to have access.

Disclosure triangle

Figure 3.51 A disclosure triangle indicates that you've connected to a library with playlists. (The songs listed in the song list are all those that the owner of the shared library wants to share and that are shareable.)

Figure 3.52 When you click the disclosure triangle, you see the playlists that the owner of the library has shared.

To connect to a shared library:

1. Click the name of a shared library in the Source pane.

2. If the owner of the shared library has required a password, you are prompted to enter it (**Figure 3.50**). (Without the password you won't be able to get any further.)

After a second or so, the songs in the shared library appear in your Detail pane; you can play them as you play the songs in your own library.

Assuming the shared library has playlists, a disclosure triangle appears to the left of the shared library entry (**Figure 3.51**).

To access playlists in a shared library:

1. Click the disclosure triangle next to a shared library entry in the Source pane to show the playlists in that library that are shared (**Figure 3.52**).

2. Click a playlist name to see what's in that playlist.

✔ Tips

■ You can browse, search, and sort a shared library and its playlists just as you can your own songs.

■ Playing songs is pretty much the same as playing from your own library except that when you try to change the current time in the song by dragging the diamond indicator, the time displays (elapsed and remaining time) don't update until you release the mouse button; this makes it difficult to find a precise time in the song.

■ You can't drag any songs from a shared library or its playlists to your own iTunes library.

continues on next page

PLAYING MUSIC FROM OTHERS' LIBRARIES

- If there are already five users that have connected to a shared library on the day you click it, a window appears telling you that the shared library is not accepting connections at this time (**Figure 3.53**).

- If the owner of a shared library requires a password, the icon for their library in the Source pane will have a tiny graphic of a locked icon (refer to figure 3.48).

- If you really don't want any sharing to go on, you can, in the Parental or Parental Controls tab of your Preferences window, select "Disable shared music" and lock that setting.

- Sometimes, you'll have problems seeing or connecting to a shared library because of firewall issues. See the last section of this chapter for more information on firewalls and iTunes.

- When you're browsing someone's shared iTunes library, you can select any song and get information about it (File > Get Info), but you can't change anything: You can't rate songs or edit information or even access the Artwork tab.

- You *can* view and access streams that have been placed in a shared library.

- The Search bar doesn't work correctly when looking at a shared library, at least as of this writing. If you ask it to show anything but All or Music (Podcasts, for example), it shows nothing, even though items that belong in the category selected appear when you choose All.

- To disconnect from a shared library, click the eject icon next to the shared library name in the Source pane or click the eject icon in the lower right of the iTunes window (**Figure 3.54**).

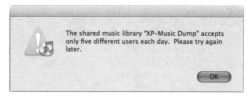

Figure 3.53 If you try to connect to a shared library but five users have already connected today, you'll see a message like this.

Figure 3.54 Click the Disconnect button at the lower right of the iTunes window to disconnect from a shared library.

Authorizing a Computer to Play Audible.com Content

Although you can't currently share content purchased at Audible.com via iTunes sharing, it's still possible to authorize another computer to play the content. To do so, you'll need to copy the file for the audiobook to the computer you want to authorize. (You can do this by burning the file to a data CD or putting it on removable media, such as a flash drive, and bringing the media to the computer you want to authorize. Or you can copy the file over a network, or e-mail it.)

Once you've placed a copy of the file on that computer, drag it to your iTunes library, or from the iTunes File menu choose Add to Library (Mac) or Add File to Library (Windows). (On a Mac, you can also double-click the file in the Finder to have iTunes try to open it.) A window appears in which you are requested to enter your user name and password; if you do as requested, the audiobook will be playable in your library.

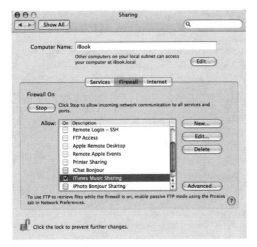

Figure 3.55 Mac OS X system preferences are usually set to allow iTunes traffic through the firewall.

Dealing with Firewalls

Due to the increased incidence of bad behavior on the Internet (that is, by hackers accessing computers other than their own), it's a good idea to set up a *firewall,* a set of programs that protects your computer from unauthorized network access. This firewall, however, may prevent you from sharing your library with others.

If sharing is important to you, you can set up a port that will let iTunes traffic through, without unduly compromising your security.

Fortunately Mac OS X is set up by default to let iTunes traffic through. And when iTunes is installed on a Windows XP system, it adds an exception to the Windows Firewall software to let iTunes traffic through. Windows XP users that have opted not to use Windows Firewall, and Windows 2000 users, may be using other firewall software.

To ensure that iTunes can get through your firewall (Mac):

◆ In the Sharing pane of your System Preferences, click the Firewall button and make sure iTunes Music Sharing is checked (**Figure 3.55**).

To ensure that iTunes can get through Windows Firewall (Windows XP only):

◆ In the Windows Firewall control panel, on the Exceptions tab, make sure iTunes is checked (**Figure 3.56**).

To let iTunes traffic through other firewalls (Windows):

◆ You need to open up port 3689 for TCP traffic and port 5353 for UDP traffic.

If you have a system administrator, pass this information on to them and let them do it.

If it's all up to you, you're going to have know (or learn) how to configure your own firewall. You can read a tech note that Apple provides at http://docs.info. apple.com/article.html?artnum=93396.

✔ Tip

■ After you configure your firewall to let iTunes traffic through, sharing may still not work until you close iTunes and reopen it.

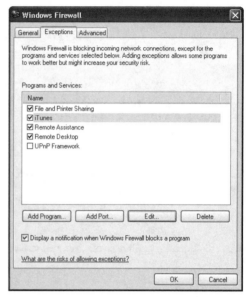

Figure 3.56 iTunes also sets up an exception in Windows Firewall.

PLAYING MUSIC ON YOUR IPOD

4

Now that you've got some music in your iTunes library (and maybe some audiobooks, podcasts, and videos as well), you're ready to move it to your iPod and hit the road. Getting audio and video from iTunes to the iPod is called *synchronizing*. In this chapter we'll cover the synchronization process and then give you an introduction to using the iPod so you can locate and play what you want. We end with some troubleshooting tips. Our intent is to give you enough information to get started. If at the end of this chapter, you still want to know more about your iPod, you may want to jump ahead to Chapters 10 and 11.

For the most part, we'll continue our tradition of referring to many forms of audio as "songs" and "music." Since video has special characteristics, and since only some of you own video-capable iPods, we'll wait until Chapter 11 to cover using your iPod to play videos. (iTunes will, however, copy videos to your iPod during the normal synchronization process.)

A note is in order here for iPod shuffle owners: Your device has no screen, so much of what's in this chapter doesn't apply to you. You'll want to read the two shuffle-specific sections near the beginning of the chapter. Then, skip right to the end of the chapter to read about troubleshooting.

Transferring Songs to Your iPod

Assuming that you've followed the instructions in Chapter 1 to set up your iPod, you've actually already synced your iPod once. Syncing it again—now that you've added to your library—is a breeze. (The following assumes that you left the automatic updating option selected during set up and that you haven't changed it since. It also assumes you're not using an iPod shuffle; if you are using a shuffle, go to the next section.)

To sync an iPod (other than an iPod shuffle):

1. Connect your iPod to the computer that has your iTunes library.

    iTunes opens (if not already open) and begins transferring songs automatically (**Figure 4.1**).

Shows status of update

Click here if you can't wait for the update to finish.

These icons indicate songs that still need to be copied.

This icon indicates that you can't change the contents of the iPod yourself; it's set for automatic updating.

This indicator is continually updated during the syncing process.

Figure 4.1 The iTunes window during an automatic update of an iPod. All the songs in the iPod library are dimmed while the update takes place.

If your iPod displays "Do not disconnect," click here to eject it first.

All you can do is scroll to see the entire list of songs in your library.

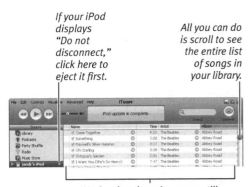

Notice that these items are still grayed out, indicating that you can't select them or play them.

Figure 4.2 The iTunes window after an automatic update. The Status display tells us that the update is complete.

2. When the update is complete (as indicated in **Figure 4.2**), you can disconnect your iPod, assured that you've got music to play on the road.

✔ Tips

- If your iPod display reads "Do not disconnect," you'll need to use iTunes to eject it first. One method for doing this is to click the eject icon next to the iPod's entry in your Source pane (refer to Figure 4.2). Other methods are covered in Chapter 10.

- What if you've already got more music in your library than can fit on your iPod? iTunes handles this by asking if you want to create a new playlist consisting of songs selected from your library and then copy that to your iPod. If you agree, iTunes tells you it will name this playlist so that it is the same as the name of your iPod with the word "Selection" appended; for example, our iPod is "JandR's iPod," and the playlist iTunes created is "JandR's iPod Selection." (This is most common on iPod nanos and minis.)

- When you do decide that you want control over what goes on your iPod—you don't want it *all* and you don't want a random selection—you'll switch to having the iPod copy only selected playlists (we cover this in Chapter 5) or you'll opt to manually drag songs to the iPod (we cover this in Chapter 10).

continues on next page

■ Can't wait for updating to finish? (Gotta run, gotta take the iPod *now*!) You can click the little *x* icon on the right side of the Status display (refer to Figure 4.1). You'll need to eject the iPod if it reads "Do not disconnect" (see first tip) before removing it. You'll have, on the iPod, as many files as iTunes was able to copy before you interrupted it. When you reconnect, copying will continue where it left off.

■ iTunes alerts you of any specific songs that can't be copied to your iPod (see **Figure 4.3** for an example), whether because they're not a valid file format, or because files for those songs are missing, or because you're not authorized to play them. (See Chapter 7 for more on authorization issues.)

■ If you don't disconnect your iPod after updating, you can scroll through the song list using the vertical scroll bar, but you won't be able to change anything in that list.

■ After iTunes has automatically updated your iPod, you may continue to make changes in iTunes while the device is still connected. Before you disconnect the iPod, however, you can update the iPod to reflect these latest changes: Control-click or right-click the iPod icon in the Source pane and, in the contextual menu that appears, choose Update Songs (**Figure 4.4**). (You can also choose File > Update Songs.)

Figure 4.3 iTunes lets you know if songs from your library won't end up on your iPod.

Figure 4.4 If you change your library after it automatically updates, but when your iPod is still connected, you can force an update.

The Monogamous iPod

An iPod set for automatic updating wants to have a relationship with only one computer. If you connect to a second computer, you'll see a window (**Figure 4.5**) announcing that your iPod is linked to another iTunes library and giving you the option of changing the link to this second computer's iTunes library. *Don't* agree to this unless you're willing to have what's currently on your iPod erased and replaced with the contents of the library to which you're about to link. If you want your iPod to "play the field" (that is, to receive songs from more than one computer), you'll need to change your updating mode; see the sidebar "Copying Music from Multiple Computers to Your iPod" in Chapter 10.

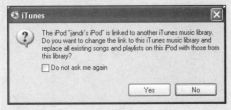

Figure 4.5 iTunes displays this window if an iPod set to do automatic updating is connected to a computer other than the one it was updated from previously.

What Can Be Transferred to an iPod?

Luckily, you can copy the majority of audio files in your iTunes library to your iPod without a hitch. These files include WAV, MP3, AAC (including the protected ones purchased from the iTunes Music Store), and Audible (.aa) files. iPods other than the shuffle handle AIFF files, too, as well as those compressed with the Apple Lossless Encoder. (See Chapter 8 for more info on all these formats.)

The audio file types that *won't* be copied to any iPod include various obscure audio formats (such as SoundDesigner 2, Nomad Voice Files, and various MPEG audio files other than MP3.) It also skips any audio-only file that iTunes recognizes as a QuickTime movie (those having an .mov extension, as well as MIDI and Karaoke files). As you'll see in Chapter 8, you can convert audio and video files to formats recognized by the iPod. Use this option if it's important to copy audio that's in a nonsupported format.

Finally (and unsurprisingly), any item in your library that's a stream or a pointer to something on the Internet—in other words, anything that doesn't have a file on your hard disk—won't be transferred.

A smaller set of video files can be transferred. See Chapter 11 for more on this.

Transferring Songs to Your iPod Shuffle

As with other iPods, the shuffle is synced the first time you connect it. When you connect from then on, doing an automatic sync—where you don't need to make any decisions—is simple, although it does require a button click.

To sync an iPod shuffle:

1. Connect your shuffle to the computer that has your iTunes library.

   iTunes opens if it's not already open, the iPod shuffle is selected in the Source pane, and an additional pane appears at the bottom of the Detail pane.

2. Click the Autofill button at the bottom of the iTunes window (**Figure 4.6**).

   iTunes randomly selects enough songs from your library to fill your iPod and lists them in the Detail pane. It then transfers those songs to the shuffle. The song list looks much like on other iPods, although the songs are not dimmed (**Figure 4.7**).

3. When the update is complete (refer to Figure 4.2), disconnect your iPod.

✔ Tips

- (Windows only) When the shuffle is first connected, Windows may open a dialog saying that it can "perform the same action each time you connect this device." Don't worry that "Manage the device with iTunes" isn't one of the choices. The device still appears in iTunes.

- In Chapter 10, we cover the other options in the pane in which you see the Autofill button as well as how you can manually add and delete individual song files.

- Podcasts don't get automatically copied to a shuffle, so if you want podcasts on one, you'll need to manually add those.

Figure 4.6 With an iPod shuffle, you'll see these options below your song list. Click the Autofill button to fill your shuffle with a random selection of songs.

Figure 4.7 The songs picked through Autofill are listed.

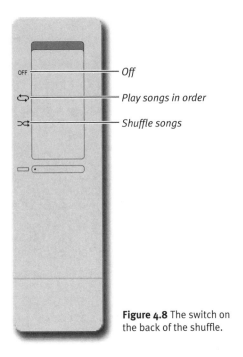

Off

Play songs in order

Shuffle songs

Figure 4.8 The switch on the back of the shuffle.

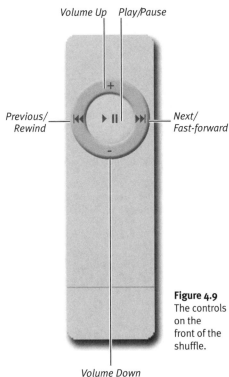

Volume Up   *Play/Pause*

Previous/ Rewind   *Next/ Fast-forward*

Figure 4.9
The controls on the front of the shuffle.

Volume Down

Listening to Music on Your iPod Shuffle

Like all iPods, the interface on the shuffle is pretty straightforward.

To turn your shuffle on and switch between random or ordered playback:

◆ Push the switch on the back of your shuffle downwards all the way (**Figure 4.8**) to have the songs on the iPod play back randomly.

◆ Push the switch down only partially to have songs play in the order in which they were copied to the shuffle.

To play or pause a song:

◆ Press the Play/Pause button (**Figure 4.9**) to play a song.

A song begins to play, and the green status light comes on for 2 seconds.

◆ Press the Play/Pause button to pause a playing song.

The green status light blinks for one minute as a reminder that you have paused.

To raise and lower volume:

◆ Press the Volume Up (+) or the Volume Down (-) buttons (refer to Figure 4.9).

To skip around:

◆ Press the Next/Fast-forward button once to skip to the next song (refer to Figure 4.9).

◆ Press and hold the Next/Fast-forward button to fast-forward in the song.

You'll hear bits of the song (fractions of a second at a time) as the iPod jumps ahead. If you fast-forward to the end of a song, the next song plays normally even if you're still pressing the button.

◆ Press the Previous/Rewind button once to start playing the current song from the beginning.

◆ Press the Previous/Rewind button twice to go the beginning of the song that played just before the currently playing song.

You click once to go to the beginning of the current song and once more to go the beginning of the previous song.

◆ Press and hold the Previous/Rewind button to rewind in the current song.

When the iPod gets to the beginning of the current song it stops and then plays normally forward.

✔ Tip

■ A Quick Reference card comes with the shuffle. If you've lost it, you'll find it here: www.apple.com/support/ipodshuffle/reference/.

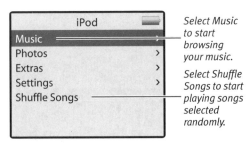

Select Music to start browsing your music.

Select Shuffle Songs to start playing songs selected randomly.

Figure 4.10 This is the iPod main menu.

Figure 4.11 If you picked Music, you then have to pick a method to browse your music.

Figure 4.12 Continue picking from the menus until you've found what you want to hear.

Browsing on Your iPod

Once you have music (or podcasts or audiobooks) on your iPod, you'll want to locate it. All this takes is being comfortable navigating iPod menus and using the basic controls (see "iPod Quick Overview" in Chapter 1).

This, of course, doesn't apply to the shuffle; you can't locate any specific songs on an iPod shuffle with any precision, since you have no screen.

To browse music on your iPod:

1. When you first turn your iPod on, you'll see the main menu (**Figure 4.10**). Make sure Music is highlighted, and press the Select button.

    You are presented with a list of ways to browse the music on the iPod: by Playlists, Artists, Albums, Songs, Podcasts, Genres, Composers, or Audiobooks. (Older iPods may not show Podcasts.)

2. Scroll to highlight a method to browse (**Figure 4.11**), and press the Select button.

3. If the method by which you chose to browse was Songs, you will see a list of all the songs on your iPod. Otherwise, continue to make selections until you reach a list of songs (**Figure 4.12**).

4. Scroll to highlight the song you want to hear, and click the select button.

✔ Tips

■ If you don't feel like browsing and just want to start listening, choose Shuffle Songs from the main menu (refer to Figure 4.10). The iPod will immediately start playing, randomly picking from all the songs on your iPod, except (on iPods made after January 2004) for those that had been marked "Skip when shuffling" on the Options tab in the song's Info window in iTunes. (Select the song and choose File > Get Info to open the Info window.)

■ If you choose Podcasts from the Music menu, you'll find only podcasts to which you've subscribed. If you've only downloaded single episodes, you'll find the episodes via the other choices (Songs, for example) in the Music menu.

■ On the newest iPods (the nano and the video iPod, as of this writing), when you view a list of podcasts in the Podcasts area, you'll see a blue dot next to any podcasts that have episodes you haven't yet played (**Figure 4.13**). If you select one of those podcasts, the specific episodes that you haven't played have a blue dot.

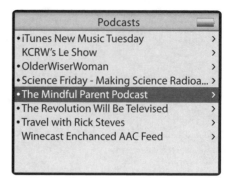

Figure 4.13 On nano and video iPods, dots indicate which podcasts haven't been played.

Play icon   Progress bar

Figure 4.14
When you select a song to play, the iPod displays a screen like this.

Elapsed   Remaining
time   time

Figure 4.15
Press the Play/Pause button.

Play/Pause Button

Pause icon

Figure 4.16
The music pauses if it was playing.

Pausing and Playing Songs

When you select a song on your iPod, it begins to play automatically. Visual clues that the song is playing are the Play icon displayed on the top left side of the display, the advancing progress bar and the changing display of elapsed time and remaining time (**Figure 4.14**).

To pause a song:

◆ Press the Play/Pause button on your iPod's wheel (**Figure 4.15**).

The Play icon changes to a Pause icon (**Figure 4.16**), and the music stops.

To play a paused song:

◆ Press the Play/Pause button again.

The Pause icon changes back to a Play icon and playback resumes.

✔ Tips

■ On some iPods—any that display color, for example, as well as the shuffle—you can unplug the headphones to pause playback.

■ When a song is playing (or even paused) you can continue to browse through the menus on your iPod. If you forget what you're listening to, return to the main menu and select Now Playing (**Figure 4.17**). The iPod displays the screen that shows the song that's currently playing (refer to Figure 4.14).

■ Playback of one song stops automatically when you play another one. With audio-books and podcasts, however, your iPod remembers where you stopped listening, so when you next play the audiobook or podcast—even days later and no matter how many other things you have listened to in between—it picks up exactly where you left off. It's just like a bookmark!

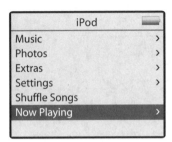

Figure 4.17 If you continue browsing, you can always find out what's playing by going back to the main menu, and choosing Now Playing.

Figure 4.18
When a song is playing, simply spin the iPod's wheel right to increase volume and left to decrease volume.

Controlling Volume

Changing the volume on an iPod is one of those tasks that's not obvious to everyone at first, but once shown you never forget.

To change the volume:

◆ Once you've started playing a song (even if it's currently paused), simply spin the wheel: clockwise raises the volume, and counter-clockwise lowers it.

As soon as you start spinning, the iPod knows you're trying to control volume and switches to a graphic representation of the volume (**Figure 4.18**).

Preventing Inadvertent Button Pushes

The hold switch is on top of all iPods. By switching it on (so you can see the red and toward the word *Hold*), you lock the controls on the iPod. This prevents you from pushing any button by accident, so for example, you don't skip a song or turn the volume way up. For the same reasons, this is also a good way to save your battery; you really don't want your iPod accidentally turned on and playing all night without you, do you?

The iPod shuffle doesn't have the same Hold switch as the other iPods. To use Hold on a shuffle, you press and hold the Play/Pause button for 3 seconds and the orange light blinks. Now all the controls on the front are locked out. To turn off hold, press and hold the Play/Pause button for 3 seconds and the green light blinks and all holds are off.

Fast-forwarding and Fast-reversing

There are two methods for fast-forwarding and fast-reversing when a song is playing. Try them both, and see which you prefer. (One of us prefers using the latter method, because of her preference for using the wheel—it's just so smooth. The other doesn't like having to take multiple steps.)

To fast-forward or fast-reverse using the Forward and Back buttons:

◆ Press and hold down the Forward button (**Figure 4.19**) to fast-forward the song.

◆ Press and hold down the Rewind button to fast-reverse the song.

To fast-forward or fast-reverse using the wheel:

1. Making sure the normal progress bar is showing, press the Select button.

   The scrubber bar appears. This bar is a bit different from the normal progress bar (**Figure 4.20**); rather than being partially filled in, it contains a diamond at the point of the bar representing the current time. (Below the bar you'll still see how much time in the song has played and how much time remains.)

2. Immediately (in less than 5 seconds) spin the wheel clockwise to move to a later point in the song or counterclockwise to move to an earlier point in the song.

   If you wait 5 seconds or more, the normal progress bar reappears, and scrolling the wheel affects volume. You'll need to press the Select button again to see the scrubber bar.

Rewind   *Fast-forward*

Figure 4.19
The iPod controls.

Scrubber bar

Figure 4.20
Access this screen by pressing the select button when a song is playing. Scroll right to fast-forward, left to rewind.

Figure 4.21
Vertical lines in the scrubber bar indicate chapters if your audiobook or podcast is divided into chapters.

Figure 4.22
Chapter names appear above the scrubber bar for enhanced podcasts.

✔ Tips

- If, when listening to music, you press the Select button more than once, you'll find yourself on a different screen; the iPod rotates through a series of three, four, or five screens with each press of the Select button when playing a song. Other screens include album art (only with a color iPod for items that have artwork), the rating screen (you'll see five dots), speed adjustment (for audiobooks), and description (for podcasts) or lyrics (for songs to which you've added lyrics). You may have to cycle through the screens to get back to the one you want.

- Almost all audiobooks and some podcasts are divided into chapters and thus show chapter marks (**Figure 4.21**) to help you locate portions of the media. Enhanced podcasts even have chapter marks with labels (**Figure 4.22**).

Skipping to the Next or Previous Song

When you found the song you wanted to play, it was in a list, right? It might have been a list of all your songs or all the songs by a particular artist, or, well, you get the idea. Your iPod treats that list as a playlist and assumes you want to play each song in the list one after another. (Have you noticed the numbering that appears in the upper left of the Now Playing display, reading, for example, 7 of 12?) Since it treats the songs as a list, you can skip to the next or previous one quite easily.

To jump to the next or previous song in the list:

◆ Press the Forward button to go to the next song (**Figures 4.23** and **4.24**).

Do not hold the button down or you'll just fast-forward through the current song.

◆ Press the Back button twice to go the previous song in the list.

You click once to go to the beginning of the current song and once again to go the beginning of the previous song.

✔ Tips

■ Whenever a song is the last in the list (*12 of 12*, for example) pressing the Forward button ends playback and puts you back at the iPod's main menu.

■ Pressing the Back button twice when you're on the first song in the list also puts you at the iPod's main menu.

■ When going to the previous song, that second press needs to happen within two seconds of the first.

Tells you which song in the list is playing

Figure 4.23
When you press the Forward button, the iPod switches from one song...

Changes to the next song in the list

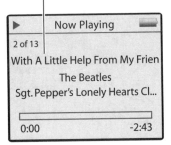

Figure 4.24
...to the next.

■ Podcasts, although you may find them in a list of other podcasts, are almost always displayed as *1 of 1*. So when you press the Forward button in a podcast, you end up at the iPod's main menu.

Figure 4.25
When a song is playing on your iPod, press the Select button to show this Rating screen. (It will probably take two or three presses.)

Figure 4.26
Then use the wheel to rate the song.

Rating Songs on Your iPod

There's another important task you can accomplish when you're on the road with your iPod: You can rate your songs. iTunes will transfer the rating to your library when it next does an automatic update.

To rate songs on your iPod:

1. When a song is playing (or paused), press the Select button until you see a screen with gray bullets in roughly the position of the song progress bar (**Figure 4.25**).

2. Use the wheel to turn the bullets into stars (**Figure 4.26**).

To transfer song ratings to iTunes:

◆ Connect your iPod to your computer. You'll find that the song in iTunes now has the rating you applied on your iPod (**Figure 4.27**).

Figure 4.27 The rating is transferred to your iTunes library during the next automatic update.

iPod Troubleshooting

For the most part, our iPods have been trouble-free. Nothing is perfect, however. Here we'll provide some basic tips for helping with an iPod that is not behaving as you think it should.

Troubleshooting suggestions:

◆ If iTunes doesn't recognize your iPod, try quitting iTunes and reopening it.

◆ If your iPod doesn't seem to be responding, make sure the hold switch is not on.

The hold switch is on the top of your iPod (unless it's a shuffle) and labeled Hold. Red indicates that the switch is on, so slide it so the red disappears.

On the iPod shuffle, if you see the orange light blink when you press any control button, Hold is on. To turn Hold off, press down on the Play button for 3 seconds; the orange light will come on solid and then the green light will blink three times to indicate that Hold is off.

◆ If you're seeing nothing on the screen, try charging your iPod.

Plug in your iPod to a computer, and be sure that you see that it is charging. On an iPod with a screen, you should see a lightning bolt on a battery and some type of animation that the battery is filling; the indicator stops animating when it's charged. On the shuffle, the orange light on the front will be on solid when it's charging and will turn to green when done.

◆ If your iPod is generally misbehaving—its battery seems to be going dead too quickly, you're unable to play back purchased music, or some other unexplainable behavior— make sure the iPod software is up to date. See Chapter 1.

◆ If your sure your software is up to date, reset (or restart) the iPod.

This will not affect anything already on the iPod; all your music, photos, and so on will remain as they were. The process you'll follow on each iPod is slightly different. See http://docs.info. apple.com/article.html?artnum=61705 for iPods other than the shuffle. See http://docs.info.apple.com/article. html?artnum=300595 for the shuffle.

◆ If all else fails, restore the iPod. (Warning: This will delete everything on the iPod!)

Run the software updater as described in Chapter 1, but instead of choosing Update choose Restore (refer to Figure 1.28).

Turning On and Off Your iPod

One of the most often-asked iPod questions is, "Where's the on/off switch?" The iPod shuffle is the only iPod with an off switch (refer to Figure 4.8).

With other iPods, you don't actually turn it off but you do put it to sleep. To put the iPod to sleep, hold down the Play/Pause button until the screen goes dark. To wake up the iPod, press any button or plug in your headphones.

CREATING AND USING PLAYLISTS

Playlists—customized lists of songs—are a great way to group songs, whether for playback in iTunes, for creating audio CDs, for transferring to or from an iPod, or for sharing with others over a network.

We'll use this chapter to teach you how to create playlists and mold them to your liking (by reordering and deleting songs in them).

We'll cover both kinds of playlists that you create in iTunes: regular playlists (which you create yourself) and *Smart Playlists* (which iTunes creates automatically based on predefined criteria you set).

At the end of the chapter, we'll cover how you put specific playlists on your iPod and how you create playlists on your iPod that can be transferred back to iTunes.

Special Playlists: Videos and Podcasts

The Podcasts and Videos items in iTunes' Source pane are called "playlists" but are somewhat different than the playlists we cover in this chapter: you don't create them, you don't pick and choose what goes in them in the same way, and if you delete items from them, you delete those items from your library. Chapter 3 talked about your Videos playlist. We go into detail about managing your Podcasts playlist in Chapter 9.

About Playlists

You create two kinds of playlists in iTunes: regular ones (which we'll generally refer to simply as *playlists*) and *Smart Playlists*. Both show up as sources in your Source pane, though each has a different icon (**Figure 5.1**). You add songs to regular playlists yourself. For Smart Playlists, you set up criteria defining the kinds of songs that you want, and iTunes automatically adds any songs that meet those criteria.

It's important to understand that both kinds of playlists contain *pointers* to songs in your library, not copies of the songs themselves. Songs in playlists don't take up any additional space on your hard disk. A single song can be in as many playlists as you want. And if you delete a song from a playlist, it remains in your library. (On the other hand, if you delete a song from your library, it *does* get removed from any playlists that it's in.)

Anything you can do to the list of songs in your library, you can do to the set of songs in a playlist. As long as the playlist is the selected source, you can use the Browser to limit the songs that appear in the song list, you can search the playlist, and you can sort it in any of the ways covered in Chapter 3. You'll find this useful when you have very long playlists.

✔ Tip

- You won't see a Browse button in the iTunes window when a playlist is selected as the source. To show the Browser, you'll have to use the menu option (Edit > Show Browser) or its keyboard equivalent (Ctrl-B in Windows; Command-B on the Mac).

These are Smart Playlists.

These are regular playlists.

Figure 5.1 iTunes lets you create two kinds of playlists: Smart Playlists and the regular kind. Both help you organize your music collection.

Playlist Ideas

There are as many reasons to make playlists as there are CDs in your library. As a matter of fact, many people create a playlist whenever they import songs from a favorite CD; then they can click the playlist for that CD in their Source pane anytime they want to listen to it. Or would you rather group songs by artist? If you like to listen nonstop to Elvis Costello, for example, just find all his songs and put them in a playlist. Think also about creating different playlists for different tasks, such as working, playing, cooking, exercising, or going to sleep. Or consider putting together playlists to match the tastes of different friends or family members that may visit. You can create playlists of your favorite songs or songs by a single artist or songs about a certain topic. The possibilities are endless.

Figure 5.2 To create a new playlist, click the plus-sign (+) button.

Figure 5.3 A new, untitled playlist appears.

Figure 5.4 You should name the playlist so it describes what you will put in it.

Creating a Playlist and Adding Songs to It

We'll start with regular playlists, the kind to which you add songs manually.

To create a playlist:

1. Click the button with the plus sign (+) in the lower left of the iTunes window (**Figure 5.2**), or choose File > New Playlist.

   A new playlist is added with the name "untitled playlist" highlighted (**Figure 5.3**).

2. Type a name for your playlist (**Figure 5.4**).

To add songs to a playlist:

1. In the Source pane, click the name of the source that contains the song(s) you want to add.

   The source can be your library, Radio, an audio CD, or another playlist.

2. If the number of songs in the selected source is very large, you may want to limit the number of songs showing in the song list.

   Use whatever method works best for you—browse, search, or simply sort—to ensure that the songs you want to add are visible in the song list.

3. Select the songs you want to add.

4. Drag the songs from the song list to the playlist (**Figure 5.5**).

✔ Tips

■ You may find it convenient to use the keyboard shortcut Command-N (Mac) or Ctrl-N (Windows) to create a new empty playlist.

■ After creating your first untitled playlist, each subsequent untitled playlist you create since you opened iTunes will be numbered sequentially (that is, untitled playlist 2, untitled playlist 3, and so on).

■ If you try to put videos and songs in the same playlist, iTunes shows a window asking if you're sure you want to mix videos and music. If you have a reason for doing this—say because you want all media about a certain topic grouped— go ahead and click OK. On a video iPod, however, playlists with mixed media appear in both Videos and Music areas of the iPod; this will seem a little odd.

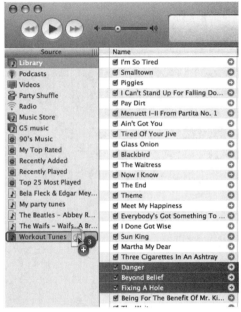

Figure 5.5 To put songs in a playlist, drag them from the song list to the playlist.

Including Streams in Your Playlists

A reminder: You can add streams (whether from iTunes radio or other sources) to your playlists, too. It may seem odd to put streams in a playlist: After all, while you often group songs in playlists so that they'll play one after another, iTunes will never play the item after a stream in a song list—the stream will play until you actively choose another item to play. You also can't burn a CD containing a stream or copy a stream to your iPod. However, adding a stream to a playlist offers the convenience of having it in an easily accessible and logical location. Do you want to have a ready source for anything and everything rockabilly-related? Create a Rockabilly playlist, and make sure to include Rockabilly Radio.

Figure 5.6 If songs are selected, you can choose File > New Playlist from Selection to create a playlist that contains the selected songs.

Figure 5.7 You can also drag selected songs to the area below existing playlists to create a new playlist containing those songs.

Ways to create a playlist and add songs to it at the same time:

◆ Select songs, and then choose File > New Playlist from Selection (**Figure 5.6**).

◆ Select songs, and then drag them from the song list to the empty area at the bottom of your Source list (**Figure 5.7**).

If the selected songs are all from the same album or by the same artist, or both, iTunes names the playlist by artist name, album name, or both. (For example, if all the songs happen to be by Emmylou Harris, the resulting playlist will be called "Emmylou Harris.") Otherwise, the newly created playlist will be named "untitled playlist."

To import songs from a CD and create a playlist at the same time:

◆ Insert a CD, select some or all of the songs, and drag the selected songs from the song list to the empty area at the bottom of your Source list (**Figure 5.8**).

iTunes imports the songs and creates a playlist containing the imported songs. It also automatically names the playlist according to the artist and album (or just the album, if the songs are by different artists).

✔ Tips

■ (Mac only) You can select songs from your library or a playlist and then Shift-click the plus-sign button to both create a new playlist and add the selected songs to it.

■ To create a playlist, you can select any item(s) from the Browser (genre name, artist name, or album name) and then drag the item(s) to the empty area at the bottom of your Source pane. The new playlist will contain all songs from the selected genre(s), artist(s), or album(s).

■ If you drag a single song to the Source pane below the existing sources, iTunes creates a new playlist containing only that song, with a name identical to the song name.

Figure 5.8 If you insert a CD and drag selected songs to the area below your playlists, iTunes creates a playlist containing the selected songs.

Selecting Songs

Since a preliminary step for creating playlists is selecting songs, we'll go over the various methods for selecting them:

◆ Click a song to select it.

◆ Shift-click to select multiple contiguous songs (that is, songs that are next to each other in your library).

◆ Command-click (Mac) or Ctrl-click (Windows) to select multiple songs that are not contiguous.

◆ From the Edit menu, choose Select All to select all the songs in the song list.

◆ To select the currently playing (or most recently played) song, choose File > Show Current Song. (Remember from Chapter 3 that the selection does not necessarily correspond to the current song.)

◆ To select the song above or below the selected song, click the up or down arrow on your keyboard.

◆ To add to the selected song(s), hold down the Shift key and click the up arrow or down arrow key.

Figure 5.9 Choose New Smart Playlist to show the Smart Playlist window.

Creating a Smart Playlist

Smart Playlists are playlists that iTunes automatically builds based on criteria you set. As long as the playlist exists, iTunes can continue to add to it whenever a song meets the specified criteria. For example, if you like old blues songs, you can create a Smart Playlist that consists of all songs in the blues genre recorded between 1920 and 1950. Are you a longtime Nick Lowe fan? Create a Smart Playlist with Nick Lowe as the specified artist, and iTunes will update it every time you add new Nick Lowe songs to your library.

To create a Smart Playlist:

1. From the File menu, choose New Smart Playlist (**Figure 5.9**) to open the Smart Playlist window.

continues on next page

CREATING A SMART PLAYLIST

2. If you want iTunes to match a specific condition, select a type of information—such as Artist, Genre, or Time—from the leftmost pop-up menu at the top of the window and then specify your criteria by choosing from the second pop-up menu (**Figure 5.10**) and filling in a value or values (**Figure 5.11**).

Once you've done this, you'll find you've created a nice little sentence that describes what you're looking for.

3. If you'd like to specify additional conditions, click the plus-sign button to add a new line (**Figure 5.12**) and then repeat step 2.

Once you have more than one condition, the first line reads, "Match all of the following rules." The word *all,* however, appears in a pop-up menu and can be changed to *any.* This allows you to specify, for example, that you want any songs for which the artist is The Who or Pete Townshend.

4. Uncheck the "Match the following rule" check box if you don't want to specify any conditions.

Pick the type of information here.

Pick a verb phrase here.

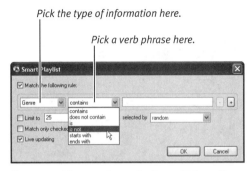

Figure 5.10 After you choose the type of information you want iTunes to look at, specify a verb phrase...

Type a value here.

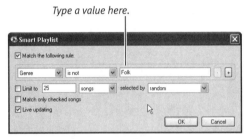

Figure 5.11 ...and a value. Here, we're making sure that no folk songs make their way onto this playlist.

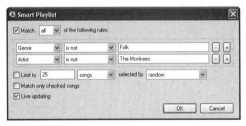

Figure 5.12 Click the plus-sign button to add a new row for specifying a condition, and the minus-sign button to remove the condition in that row. Here, we've already added a second condition—no Monkees, either.

You can select minutes, hours, MB, GB, or songs here.

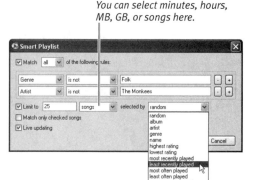

Figure 5.13 Specify limitations on time, file size, or number of songs here. You can have iTunes pick randomly or by the top songs (alphabetically, numerically, or temporally) in a variety of information types.

Figure 5.14 Type a name for the Smart Playlist.

5. If you want iTunes to limit the amount of music (whether by song length, number of songs, or disk space used), select the second check box and specify how you would like it limited (**Figure 5.13**).

6. If you've unchecked songs in your library, you may want to check "Match only checked songs" (refer to Figure 5.13).

7. If you want iTunes to continually add to the playlist, leave "Live updating" checked.

8. Click OK.

The new playlist shows in your Source pane. It is selected and editable.

9. Type a new name for the playlist, if desired (**Figure 5.14**).

If you've set criteria that match any songs in your current collection, those songs are added to the playlist. If you have left "Live updating" checked, iTunes continues to add to the playlist as you add new songs to your library, edit song information, or play songs.

To edit a Smart Playlist:

1. Select the Smart Playlist in the Source pane.

2. From the File menu, choose Get Info (or its keyboard equivalent: Command-I for Mac, Ctrl-I for Windows).

3. In the Smart Playlist window, make changes and click OK (refer to Figures 5.10 through 5.13).

CREATING A SMART PLAYLIST

✔ Tips

■ A quick way to create a new Smart Playlist is to hold down the Option key (Mac) or the Shift key (Windows) so that the icon on the Add Playlist button changes to a Smart Playlist icon (a gear); click it to create a new Smart Playlist.

■ If you make a choice other than random for the "selected by" pop-up menu (refer to Figure 5.13), iTunes selects the top songs from a sort of your library by that attribute. (For example, if you choose album, you are likely to get only albums that start with the letters at the beginning of the alphabet.)

■ As you fill in the fields in the Smart Playlist window, iTunes types ahead to match the first name (alphabetically) in your library that matches what you've typed so far.

■ If you rely on play count to help you organize your library, but someone else uses your library and the play count no longer reflects how many times *you* played the song—maybe drunken guests at your holiday party played "Jingle Bell Rock" 25 times—you may want to reset the play count for that song to 0. To do so, select the song, Control-click (Mac) or right-click (Windows), and choose Reset Play Count.

■ iTunes may do some intelligent naming of your Smart Playlists. If you specify a single textual criterion as your Smart Playlist criteria (for example, the artist Elton John), the playlist name will be the same as the value you choose—in this case, Elton John. Otherwise, it will be named "untitled playlist," followed by a number, to indicate how many untitled playlists have been created.

■ You'll typically want to set time or space limitations for a playlist when you plan to burn a CD. (See Chapter 6.)

■ (Mac only) You can Option-click a Smart Playlist to edit it.

Smart Playlist Ideas

You'll get some ideas for Smart Playlists by looking at the ones that come with iTunes (90's Music, My Top Rated, Recently Played, Recently Added, and Top 25 Most Played). Here are some others:

◆ If you accidentally delete your Purchased Music playlist, you could regenerate the same list by building a Smart Playlist that looks for "Kind is Protected AAC."

◆ If you tend to sit in front of your computer for too long, make a Smart Playlist that you "Limit to 90 minutes selected by random"; when the music stops, it's time to take a break. Then just delete all the songs in the playlist, and iTunes will pick a new set of random songs. (This assumes you've left Live Updating checked.)

◆ Create a Smart Playlist of the radio streams you like to listen to: Specify "Time is greater than 300000" (which translates to 3 days, 11 hours, 20 minutes, and 0 seconds); iTunes will choose files that are continuous.

◆ Want to know which songs you haven't played recently? Try "Last Play is not in the last 6 months" (or whatever time period you'd like).

Click here.

Figure 5.15 To change the order of songs in a playlist, start by clicking the column head on the left so that the songs are not sorted by any other column.

Figure 5.16 Shuffle mode has to be turned off; click the Shuffle button so it's not highlighted blue.

This indicator line shows that if you release the mouse button now, the selected song will become the 6th song in the list.

	Name		Time	Artist
1	☑ Sink Or Swim	●	2:01	The Waifs
2	☑ When I Die	●	2:55	The Waifs
3	☑ A Brief History...	●	3:51	The Waifs
4	☑ Service Fee	●	4:41	The Waifs
5	☑ Taken	●	3:53	The Waifs
6	☑ Love Serenade	●	2:42	The Waifs
7	☑ The Haircut	●	3:30	The Waifs
8	☑ Without You	●	3:31	The Waifs
9	☑ Danger	●	2:30	The Waifs
10	☑ Lies	●	4:15	The Waifs
11	☑ The Waitress	●	2:19	The Waifs
12	☑ When I Die (Introduction)	●	0:40	The Waifs
13	☑ Bridal Train (Introduction)	●	0:35	The Waifs

Figure 5.17 Drag a song up or down to reposition it.

Reordering the Songs in a Playlist

In many ways, working with the songs in a playlist is much like working with them in the library: You can browse, search, and sort. One key difference, however, is that you can reorder songs in a playlist any way you want. This is especially useful when you're creating a playlist that you plan to burn to CD.

To reorder songs in a playlist:

1. With the playlist selected, click the empty column head of the leftmost column (**Figure 5.15**) of the song list.

2. If the Shuffle button is highlighted blue (indicating that Shuffle mode is on), click it to turn it off (**Figure 5.16**).

3. Click any song and drag up or down in the list.

4. Release your mouse button when the indicator line appears in the position you would like the song to be (**Figure 5.17**).

5. Repeat steps 3 and 4 until your songs are in the order you want them to play.

✔ Tips

- If you click the Shuffle button to let iTunes randomly reorder the songs in the playlist, you can see the new order as long as the songs are sorted by the leftmost column.

- If you happen to really like the way iTunes has randomly shuffled your songs, so much that you want them to stay that way, tell iTunes to keep this new order as your preferred order (just as if you had dragged the songs that way yourself): Control-click (Mac) or right-click (Windows) the playlist name and, from the contextual menu, choose Copy To Play Order.

Sharing a Playlist Through the Music Store

Have you put together the absolutely perfect collection of songs? So perfect that you absolutely *must* share it? If the songs in your playlist are available in the iTunes Music Store (even if that's not where you got them from originally), you can publish the playlist as an *iMix* in the iTunes Music Store. It costs you nothing to publish, and other shoppers can view, preview, rate, or purchase your collection (**Figure 5.18**). Or you can give the playlist as a gift to a friend; this lets you pay the iTunes Music Store for songs that your friend gets in her iTunes library.

To publish your playlist as an iMix or give it as a gift:

1. In your Source pane, click on the playlist you want to publish or give.

2. Click the Link arrow for that playlist (**Figure 5.19**).

3. Click Create iMix or Give Playlist in the dialog that appears (**Figure 5.20**).

   You'll be asked to sign into the store if you're not signed in, and you may be asked to provide your password again even if you are signed in.

   The Music Store shows a form at the top of the screen, and below that a list of the songs in your playlist that are available in the store.

4. If you're publishing an iMix, you can write a description and change the title (by default it's the name of your playlist) and then click Publish.

5. If you're giving the playlist to a friend, provide the recipient's name and e-mail address, type a message, and then click Continue to go on to a screen where you can confirm or cancel your purchase.

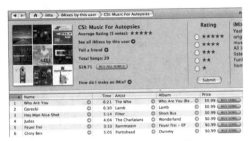

Figure 5.18 Here's what an iMix—created by someone like you—looks like in the iTunes Music Store. (Find iMixes by clicking iMix on the Store's home page.)

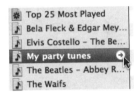

Figure 5.19 Click the Link arrow next to the playlist name.

Figure 5.20 Pick Create iMix or Give Playlist. After this, you'll have a form to fill out.

✔ Tips

■ See "Managing your Account" in Chapter 7 if you want to know how to remove an iMix.

■ If you publish your Purchased Music playlist as an iMix, please be sure to give it a new name on the form that's provided; when last we checked there were over 100 iMixes at the iTunes Music Store called "Purchased Music."

Figure 5.21 To delete a song from a playlist, Control-click (Mac) or right-click to access this contextual menu, then choose Clear.

Figure 5.22 iTunes asks if you're sure you want to remove the items from your playlist.

Deleting Songs from a Playlist

Eventually, you'll want to *delete* some songs from playlists, too—perhaps you dragged the wrong song to a playlist, or maybe you want to subtly change the focus of particular playlists. Remember, deleting a song from a playlist doesn't normally delete the song from your iTunes library; see the first Tip if you want the song permanently gone from your library.

To delete songs from a playlist:

1. *Do one of the following:*

▲ Select the song(s) you want to delete, and press the Delete key.

▲ Select the song(s) you want to delete, and from the Edit menu choose Clear.

▲ Control-click (Mac) or right-click (Windows) the song you want to delete, and choose Clear from the contextual menu that appears (**Figure 5.21**).

2. If iTunes asks whether you're sure you want to remove the selected items from the list (**Figure 5.22**), click Remove.

✔ Tips

- If, when deleting a song from a playlist, you also want it deleted from the library, hold down the Option key (Mac) or Shift key (Windows) while you press Delete or choose Clear.

- If you don't want to see any warnings, hold down the Command key (Mac) or Ctrl key (Windows) when you delete.

Finding Out Which Playlists a Song Is In

Wondering what playlists a particular song is in? Control-click (Mac) or right-click (Windows) the song, and in the contextual menu that appears select Playlists (**Figure 5.23**). You'll see the playlists (other than the one you're currently looking at) that contain this same song. If Playlists isn't a choice in the contextual menu, then the song isn't in any playlists.

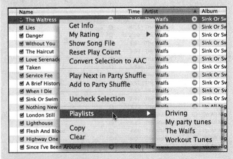

Figure 5.23 You can check to see what other playlists the song is part of. (Windows users right-click and Mac users Control-click on the song to see this contextual menu.)

Figure 5.24 In the Source pane, double-click a playlist icon...

Figure 5.25 ...to open the playlist in its own window. (Notice that there's just a Detail pane; no Source pane.)

Figure 5.26 You can drag a whole playlist to another playlist's window.

Figure 5.27 You can also drag selected songs from one window to another.

Organizing Multiple Playlists

As you create more playlists and the number of songs in those playlists grows, you may find that you need to reorganize them in various ways: merging two playlists into one, or taking selected songs out of one playlist and putting them into another, or even grouping playlists into folders (perhaps "mellow playlists" or "Judy's playlists" if you share a computer). One convenient touch is that you can see each playlist in its own window.

To view a playlist in its own window:

◆ Double-click the icon for playlist (**Figure 5.24**).

A new iTunes window opens, showing only a Detail pane (**Figure 5.25**).

To merge playlists:

◆ Drag one playlist from the Source pane to the window for the other playlist (**Figure 5.26**).

To copy selected songs from one playlist window to another:

◆ Open the playlists in their own windows, select the songs you would like to copy in one playlist window, and drag to the other playlist window (**Figure 5.27**).

To group playlists into folders:

1. From the File menu, choose New Folder (**Figure 5.28**)

2. A new folder is created in your Source pane, called "untitled folder" (**Figure 5.29**).

3. Type to rename the folder.

4. Drag playlists into the folder (**Figure 5.30**).

✔ Tips

■ To open a playlist in its own window, you can also double-click the blank space to the right of the playlist name in the Source pane. (It won't work to click the text itself, however; doing so allows you to edit the playlist name.) Still another method is to Control-click (Mac) or right-click (Windows) and select Open from the contextual menu.

■ If you don't need to see what's in your playlists when you merge them, simply drag one playlist in the Source pane on top of another one in the Source pane.

■ You can't manually add songs to a Smart Playlist, but you can copy songs from one of them to a regular playlist.

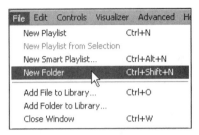

Figure 5.28 Choose File > New Folder to create a folder for holding playlists.

Figure 5.29 The new folder will be called "untitled folder" to start with. (You should rename it.)

Figure 5.30 Drag playlists to the folder.

Figure 5.31 You can delete a playlist by selecting it and Control-clicking (Mac) or right-clicking (Windows) and then choosing Clear.

Figure 5.32 If you try to delete a playlist, iTunes asks if you're sure. Click Yes unless you've had second thoughts.

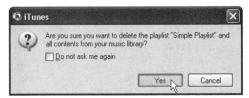

Figure 5.33 If you hold down the Shift key (Windows) or Option key (Mac) and choose Edit > Clear, iTunes asks if you really want to remove both the playlist and its contents from your library.

- If you'd rather not see the warnings shown in Figure 5.32 or 5.33, hold down the Ctrl key (Windows) or Command key (Mac) when you delete.

- You can't select multiple playlists in the Source pane, so you can't delete more than one playlist at a time.

Deleting Playlists

Eventually, you may want to remove some of your playlists. Think carefully before deleting a playlist, as there's no way to undo the action.

Ways to delete a playlist:

◆ Select the playlist in the Source pane, and press the Delete key.

◆ Select the playlist in the Source pane, and from the Edit menu, choose Clear.

◆ Control-click (Mac) or Right-click (Windows) the playlist in the Source pane, and choose Delete (**Figure 5.31**).

  If you have songs in the playlist, you'll be asked if you really want to remove the playlist (**Figure 5.32**). Click Yes.

To delete a playlist and all the songs it contains from your library:

◆ Hold down the Shift key (Windows) or Option key (Mac), and use either of the first two methods above for deleting a playlist.

  You'll be asked if you want to delete the playlist and all contents from your music library (**Figure 5.33**). If you click Yes and the file is stored in your iTunes Music folder (see "How iTunes Organizes Files on Your Hard Drive" in Chapter 9), you will then be asked if you want to move the contents to the Trash (Mac) or Recycle Bin (Windows).

✔ Tips

- All methods above work to delete a folder of playlists, too. If you need to move a playlist out of the folder before deleting the folder, drag it to the area below all your playlists in the Source pane.

- (Mac only) To delete a playlist, you can also drag it from the Source pane to the Trash icon in your Dock.

Party Shuffle

In your Source list is Party Shuffle (**Figure 5.34**), which is a playlist of sorts but one that continually updates when the songs in it are playing. You need only tell it what playlists (or your entire library) to draw from.

For a party, it's better than using the Shuffle button, because it clearly shows you what it's played and what it's about to play, and it also can take into account song ratings. It also never comes to the end of the list, since it adds a new song each time one is done playing.

If you want to take a more active, DJ-like role, you can reorder the upcoming songs by dragging them up or down. For your convenience you may also want to change the number of recently played songs and upcoming songs to display (refer to Figure 5.34). You may also want to check "Play higher rated songs more often."

Note that you can remove Party Shuffle from your source list if you don't think you'll use this feature; in the General tab of the Preferences window, simply uncheck Party Shuffle.

What's been played.

What's coming up. (You can reorder these or delete any you don't like.)

The playlist songs are being selected from.

Figure 5.34 Party Shuffle lets you pick a playlist from which it will randomly select songs to add to the list of what will play next.

Figure 5.35 Click the iPod Options button if you want to change your updating preferences.

If you select this, you need to check the playlists you want iTunes to copy to the iPod. Songs not in the selected playlists won't be copied and will be erased from the iPod.

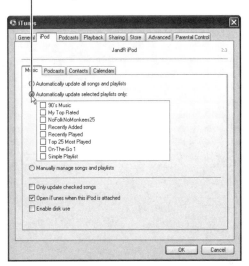

Figure 5.36 The iPod tab of the Preferences window.

Putting Specific Playlists on Your iPod

Now that you know how to create playlists, you may want to put only specific playlists on your iPod when it syncs. If you have an iPod with a display, you can access the playlists on the iPod. In the case of an iPod shuffle, you transfer the songs from playlists you specify.

To specify the playlists that should be transferred to an iPod other than the shuffle:

1. Select the iPod in the Source list.

2. Click the iPod Options button at the bottom right of the iTunes window (**Figure 5.35**).

   You can also Control-click (Mac) or right-click (Windows) the iPod icon in your Source pane; from the contextual menu that appears, choose iPod Options.

3. In the iPod Preferences tab that appears (**Figure 5.36**), select "Automatically update selected playlists only."

4. Click to put checkmarks next to those playlists you want updated. It's important to understand that after the update, your iPod will contain only the selected playlists; songs not in those playlists will be erased from the iPod.

5. Click OK.

   As soon as you click OK, iTunes starts the update.

   As long as you don't change your preferences, the same playlists will be transferred to your iPod each time you connect your iPod.

Ways to transfer songs from specific playlists to an iPod shuffle:

◆ Pick a playlist as a source (**Figure 5.37**), and then click Autofill. If there are songs in additional playlists you want to include, uncheck "Replace all songs when Auto-filling," choose another playlist and click Autofill again. You can repeat this process until the shuffle is filled.

◆ Create a folder and put the playlists you want in that folder (See instructions for grouping playlists into folders earlier in this chapter). Then select the folder in the "Autofill from" menu (refer to Figure 5.37).

Figure 5.37 With the iPod shuffle you can pick a playlist to Autofill the iPod from.

Figure 5.38 An On-The-Go playlist is always in your iPod's Playlists menu. (To add a song to it, select the song and press down on the Select button for several seconds, until the selection blinks.)

Using Your iPod to Create On-The-Go Playlists

If you have a relatively new iPod (one built after April 2003), you can create playlists directly on your iPod that you can later transfer to iTunes. This is handy if you suddenly have the time or find the inspiration to create a spontaneous song playlist when you're not near your computer.

The method for creating playlists on your iPod, however, is not completely intuitive. If you scroll to the bottom of the iPod's Playlists screen, you'll see an On-The-Go playlist (**Figure 5.38**). You add songs to this playlist using your iPod, and then transfer the playlist back to iTunes, *as long as your iPod is set for automatic updating.*

To add songs to your On-The-Go playlist on your iPod:

1. On your iPod, browse to a list (Songs or Artists, for example) and highlight a song you want to add.

2. Press and hold the Select button for several seconds, until the selection blinks.

   If you check your On-The-Go playlist, you'll see that it contains the song(s) you've added.

To save an On-The-Go playlist so you can create another playlist:

1. In your Playlists menu, select On-The-Go playlist (refer to Figure 5.38).

2. Select Save Playlist (**Figure 5.39**).

3. In the Save menu, select Save Playlist (**Figure 5.40**).

   In your Playlists menu, you'll now see New Playlist 1 listed (**Figure 5.41**) (or New Playlist 2, and so on).

To delete a song in your On-The-Go playlist:

◆ In your On-The-Go playlist (refer to Figure 5.39) highlight the song you want to delete, and press and hold the Select button for several seconds until the selection blinks.

   The song disappears from the playlist.

To delete all the songs in your On-The-Go playlist:

1. In the On-The-Go menu, scroll to the bottom of the list and select Clear Playlist.

2. In the Clear menu, select Clear Playlist.

✔ Tips

■ iPods that can create playlists are those with a Dock Connector port (the port on the bottom of the iPod). iPods with no port on the bottom were built prior to this.

■ You don't have to grow old while you laboriously add songs to your iPod's On-The-Go playlist, one by one. If you like, you can add entire lists of songs to an On-The-Go playlist at one time. On your iPods' Artists, Albums, Composers, Genres, or Playlists menus, scroll to an item and then press the Select button for several seconds to add all the songs from the selected artist, album, composer, genre, or playlist to the On-The-Go playlist.

Figure 5.39 If you select On-The-Go in your playlists menu after you've added a song, you'll see this. Select Save Playlist

Figure 5.40 Select Save Playlist again.

Figure 5.41 Once you save your On-The-Go playlist, it's called New Playlist 1. (Subsequent lists will be New Playlist 2, New Playlist 3, and so on.)

This contains pointers to the same songs that were in the On-The-Go playlist on the iPod.

Figure 5.42 When you connect the iPod to your computer, the On-The-Go playlist is transferred to iTunes.

To transfer an On-the-Go playlist to iTunes:

◆ Simply connect your iPod to your computer.

After iTunes does its automatic updating, you'll see in your Source pane an On-The-Go 1 playlist (**Figure 5.42**). If you created multiple playlists, you'll also see an On-The-Go 2 playlist, On-The-Go 3 playlist, and so on. These are numbered in the order you created them, so the On-The-Go 1 playlist is the first one you created; if you saved it, it's now called (confusingly) New Playlist 1 on the iPod.

continues on next page

On your iPod, you'll find that its On-The-Go playlist is empty, but that there's an On-The-Go 1 playlist (as well as On-The-Go 2, On-The-Go 3, and so on if you created more than one) (**Figure 5.43**).

Each time you repeat the process of creating On-The-Go playlists on your iPod and then syncing to iTunes, you'll find additional On-The-Go playlists in your Source pane. These are numbered sequentially (On-The-Go 2, On-The-Go 3, and so on) as long as you haven't deleted or renamed the previous ones.

As with any playlists, you can rename these and add or delete songs. We highly recommend renaming to something more descriptive, so they'll be more useful both in your iTunes library and on your iPod when they get copied back to it during the next sync.

✔ Tip

■ If you have specified "Automatically update selected playlists only" (see "Putting Specific Playlists on your iPod" earlier in this chapter), when you connect your iPod to your computer, it adds an On-The-Go 1 or On-The-Go 2 (or higher) to your list of playlists (as you would expect). Since these new playlists, however, couldn't possibly be in your list of selected playlists—they're brand new—iTunes is not going to copy them back to your iPod unless you open the iPod Preferences window (refer to Figure 5.36) and check these latest On-The-Go playlists to ensure they get copied back to the iPod.

Figure 5.43 On your iPod, the playlists match what they're called in iTunes. On-The-Go is now empty.

BURNING CDS AND OTHER DISCS

One of the coolest things you can do with iTunes is to *burn,* or create, your own CDs. You can create your own greatest hits compilation of your favorite songs, burn it to a CD, and then listen to that CD anywhere—take it to a party, or listen to it in your car. Unlike the commercial CDs you purchase, the CDs you burn contain only the music *you* want. It's downright liberating.

iTunes makes this process extremely easy. Essentially, you add the songs you want to a playlist, and then click the Burn Disc button. Of course, as is the case with most iTunes features, you should know about various options and techniques that will ensure a smoother process.

In this chapter, we'll start by giving you some pointers to help you decide what type of disc to burn (iTunes can actually burn not only regular audio CDs and also MP3 CDs as but also data CDs and DVDs. For simplicity, we'll refer to all discs as CDs.).

The bulk of the chapter contains instructions and tips for preparing to burn the different types of CDs—and then actually burning them.

We end the chapter with a bunch of tips that apply to all the different kinds of CDs you may want to burn with iTunes.

Deciding on a CD Format

You have a choice of three types of CDs that you can burn with iTunes, depending on what you ultimately want to do with that CD.

◆ **Audio CD.** This is a CD that plays in audio CD players (the kind that's part of your stereo system). When iTunes burns an audio CD, it converts songs in the selected playlist to an uncompressed format; the audio data is virtually identical in structure to that on commercial audio CDs. The sound quality, however, may not be quite as good as on the original CD from which you ripped the songs; see the sidebar "About CD-Quality Audio."

◆ **MP3 CD.** This is a CD that will play only in MP3-enabled audio CD players. While many newer CD players have this feature, you can't count on it; thus, this choice is appropriate only when you are creating CDs to play on specific devices that you know can play MP3 CDs. The major advantage to an MP3 CD is the amount of music that will fit on it: You can fit about 10 hours on an MP3 CD versus the slightly more than 1 hour that will fit on an audio CD.

◆ **Data disc.** This type of disc is not designed to play in any audio CD player. Instead, it's a CD-ROM or a DVD-ROM designed to be accessed by a computer; the song files burned to a data disc remain in their initial format. A song file on a data disc is just like a file on a computer hard drive; you can open and play it with any application that can handle files of that format, iTunes included. Data discs provide a good method for backing up your song collection or for copying songs from one computer to another.

What Type of Blank Discs Should I Buy?

It's usually best to buy name-brand discs, such as Sony, TDK, or Memorex. These almost always work, whereas the off-brands that you can sometimes find for bargain prices have a higher incidence of failed burns.

If you're trying to decide between CD-R (CD-Recordable) and CD-RW (CD-Rewritable) discs, know that both may work, but CD-R discs are likely to play in more audio CD players. CD-R discs are cheaper, anyway. On the other hand, you can erase and reuse CD-RWs, so you may want to try them, especially if you're just experimenting with making CDs.

When shopping, you may find both 74-minute (650 MB) and 80-minute (700 MB) blank CDs (though 74-minute discs are becoming harder to find). Either is fine; the latter will let you burn slightly more music to the CD.

If you plan to archive songs to DVD, you have a choice of DVD+R, DVD-R, DVD+RW, or DVD-RW. Since the DVDs created in iTunes only play back on a computer, you don't need to be concerned with playback in audio players (as with CDs); however, you should check the specifications for your individual burner to find out what type of discs it will burn.

✔ Tip

- If you know that you want to burn an audio CD and you're anxious to get going, skip to the section "Burning Audio CDs" later in this chapter. iTunes is set up by default to do this reasonably well. The text on the pages between here and there goes into your many options and may help you avoid problems.

About CD-Quality Audio

Have you heard the term *CD-quality sound*? This is actually a euphemism for audio that is encoded at 44.1 kHz, the rate for the songs on an audio CD.

When you burn an audio CD with iTunes, the files that you copy to the CD are encoded at 44.1 kHz, too. Does this mean you get audio quality as good as that of commercial audio CDs? Not necessarily.

Files you import (or rip) from CD are compressed as AAC, unless you've changed your importing preferences (as we'll cover in Chapter 8). No matter how good a job is done during compression, some audio data is lost; the file is just not as good as it originally was. When converted back to a CD audio file, the resulting file is as large as the original but doesn't have all the data or all the quality of the original.

When the song is played through a typical home stereo, most people can't hear the difference between a cleanly compressed AAC file and the original uncompressed file. It may matter to you, though. If it does, the trick is to import as AIFF, WAV, or Lossless (see Chapter 8) and then burn an audio CD (not an MP3 CD). The imported files take up much more space on your computer than if you had imported as AAC or MP3, but you'll have true CD-quality audio on the audio CD you burn from those files.

Preparing to Burn Audio CDs

Before you can burn any audio CDs, you'll want to set your preferences appropriately and you'll also need a playlist to burn.

To prepare to burn an audio CD:

1. In iTunes, open the Preferences window.

2. Click the Advanced tab and then click Burning.

3. Make sure Audio CD is selected (**Figure 6.1**).

4. If you want to alter the amount of silence between songs, make a selection from the Gap Between Songs pop-up menu.

   The 2-second default is usually fine, however, and is what you'll often find on commercial audio CDs.

5. Select Use Sound Check if you want iTunes to raise the volume of songs that are considerably more quiet than the rest of the songs or to lower the volume of songs that are much louder than the rest.

6. Click OK to close the Preferences window.

7. If you don't already have a playlist created containing the songs you want to burn, create one. (We covered creating playlists in Chapter 5.)

   These songs can be in almost any format. (See the Sidebar "What Can and Can't be Burned.")

8. Select the playlist, making sure all the songs are checked.

Make sure Audio CD is selected.

You can change the amount of silence between songs (but 2 seconds is usually fine).

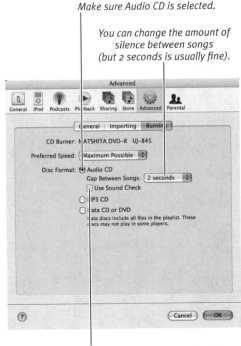

You can tell iTunes to make all the songs on the CD play at approximately the same volume.

Figure 6.1 iTunes' default burning preferences are usually fine for burning audio CDs.

What Can and Can't Be Burned

You can burn just about all audio files in a playlist to an audio CD. (iTunes does the job of converting them to the right format.) If you have video files in the playlist you're trying to burn, the audio portion of them will burn, unless the file is a video purchased from the iTunes Music Store. Radio streams also can't be burned, of course.

Number of songs. (Multiply this by the gap amount, and divide by 60 to determine the number of minutes the gaps will require.)

Amount of time required for songs

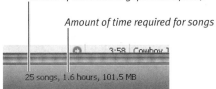

Figure 6.2 To determine the number of minutes for which you need to provide CD space, take the time required for the actual songs and add to it the amount required to account for the gap. (By the way, there's too much audio in this playlist to fit on a single audio CD.)

A Smart Playlist for Creating an Audio CD

A Smart Playlist, such as that in **Figure 6.3**, can help you quickly put together a playlist for a single audio CD. In the Smart Playlist window, specify "Limit to 72 minutes" if you're using 74-minute discs or "limit to 78 minutes" if you're using 80-minute discs. To pick the music you want on this CD, try setting different conditions (such as "Artist is Bruce Springsteen" if you want a random collection of songs by the Boss), selecting by different criteria (such as "selected by highest rating"), or limiting the playlist to a specific musical genre, such as folk or blues.

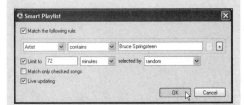

Figure 6.3 Here's an example of a Smart Playlist that will provide a playlist ready to burn to a single 74-minute, blank CD. (We've asked for only 72 minutes to account for the gap between songs.)

9. Check at the bottom of the iTunes window (**Figure 6.2**) to see how many minutes of audio you have, and make sure you have a blank CD for each 74 or 80 minutes (depending on which type of blank CDs you've purchased) you want to burn.

When determining how many minutes of audio you have in your playlist, you'll also need to account for the amount of time in the gaps between songs (refer to Figure 6.1), though 2 minutes per CD is usually a safe estimate.

✔ Tips

- Use Sound Check is a good option to pick if you don't want to startle your listeners. For example, if you're creating an audio CD that veers from a quiet Nick Drake ballad to a raucous Screamin' Jay Hawkins song, you'll definitely want to enable this option.

- If you click the text at the bottom of the window, iTunes toggles between showing the time in hours or minutes (for example, 1.1 hours) and showing it in an hours:minutes:seconds format (for example, 1:10:36).

- iTunes doesn't list times over an hour in minutes. So 74 minutes is listed as 1:14:00 or 1.2 hours, and 80 minutes is listed as 1:20:00 or 1.3 hours.

- If iTunes lists the length of a playlist in days (rather than hours or minutes), you probably don't want to be burning it to CDs!

- If you're burning an audiobook that's split into multiple items, you'll probably want the gap between "songs" to be set to 0.

- If you want to burn music that you've purchased from the iTunes Music Store, the computer you're working on must first be authorized to play that music. See "Authorizing Multiple Computers to Play Your Songs" in Chapter 7 for more information.

Burning Audio CDs

There's nothing quite so satisfying as burning your own audio CD. The process is simple and requires little input from you. Feel free to wander away to fix a snack once the CD burning commences.

To burn an audio CD (when your playlist has one CD's worth of audio):

1. Follow the steps in "Preparing to Burn Audio CDs" (in order to ensure your preferences are set appropriately and prepare a playlist).

2. Make sure the correct playlist is selected in your Source pane.

3. Click Burn Disc (**Figure 6.4**).

4. If directed in the Status display to insert a blank CD, do so.

   If you had previously inserted a blank CD, iTunes won't ask you to do so now.

5. Sit back, and let iTunes burn.

   The actual burning process commences after a few seconds of checking the media and checking the playlist. (You'll be warned if the playlist contains items that can't be burned; see **Figure 6.5**)

   When the entire playlist has been burned, iTunes emits a "ding" sound and mounts the CD, just as if you had just inserted any commercial audio CD.

6. Eject the CD, and try it out in an audio CD player.

   If the CD doesn't play, try some of the suggestions we provide at the end of this chapter and repeat the steps for burning.

Figure 6.4 When you're ready to burn, click Burn Disc.

Click the disclosure triangle to hide or show the problem descriptions. (Only applies if there's more than one problem.)

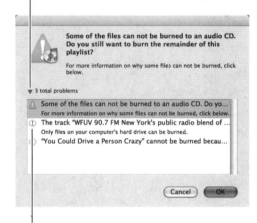

Click the visible text for each problem to read the full description.

Figure 6.5 iTunes lets you know if there are problems with the songs on your playlist.

Figure 6.6 If you have more audio than will fit on one CD, iTunes gives you the option of creating multiple CDs.

To burn multiple CDs (because your playlist has more than one CD's worth of audio):

◆ Follow the steps on the previous page, but when iTunes offers to create CDs with the playlist split across them, click the Audio CDs button (**Figure 6.6**). iTunes will burn each disc in turn, prompting you to insert another blank disc when it's ready for it.

✔ Tips

■ If you're listening to music while iTunes is burning, you can click the little right-pointing arrow on the left side of the Status display to cycle between showing the status of the burn, information about the current song, and a mini graphic equalizer.

■ Wondering how long it's going to take for your audio CD to burn? If you know the speed rating for your drive, divide the number of minutes of audio by that number to approximate how long it will take to burn the actual data. (For example, 72 minutes of music burned on a 24x CD burner will take 3 minutes; 80 minutes of music burned on a 4x CD burner will take 20 minutes.) Then add a couple of minutes for initializing the disc before writing the songs and for finalizing the disc after writing the songs.

■ If iTunes tells you it can't find the disc burner, but you're sure it's there and has been recognized by iTunes before, try quitting iTunes and reopening it.

■ If iTunes reports errors at any time during the burning process, you may want to try some of the suggestions we provide at the end of this chapter.

Burning Limits on Purchased Music

If you've purchased music from the iTunes Music Store, you may encounter a minor restriction when it comes to burning: iTunes limits to seven the number of times you can burn a playlist containing purchased music. After the seventh burn, iTunes tells you that you're licensed to burn only 7 CDs of that playlist. You need to change the playlist slightly—add or subtract at least one song—and you'll be able to burn that playlist seven more times.

Preparing to Burn MP3 CDs

To create an MP3 CD, you'll need to have a playlist containing MP3-encoded songs and you'll need to set your burning preferences appropriately. Remember, MP3 CDs differ significantly from audio CDs. Although you can fit ten times as many songs on an MP3 CD, it can only be played on MP3-enabled audio CD players.

To prepare to burn an MP3 CD:

1. Create a playlist that contains only MP3 files (**Figure 6.7**).

   If you're not sure if the files you want to include are MP3, or if you need to convert songs to MP3, refer to the next section.

   Check the bottom of your iTunes window to determine the amount of data in the playlist.

This indicates that these are probably MP3 files.

Since this is less then 700 MB the song will fit on an 80 minute CD.
(Make it less than 650 MB if using 74-minute CDs.)

Figure 6.7 To create MP3 CDs, you want a playlist that contains only MP3 songs.

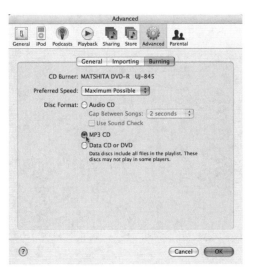

Figure 6.8 MP3 CD must be selected on the Burning tab of the Preferences window if you want to create an MP3 CD.

A Smart Playlist for Creating an MP3 CD

To create a Smart Playlist with enough music for an MP3 CD, make choices in the Smart Playlist window. Start with "Kind contains MPEG audio file," and "Limit to 700 MB selected by random" or selected in whatever way you prefer. (Limit it to 650 MB if you are using 74-minute discs.)

This playlist, however, may contain other forms of MPEG audio, if you happen to have them in your library; this might be the case if you've added old audio files that are on your computer hard disk. (See the next page if you want to confirm that these are MP3 files.)

2. Make sure all the songs in the playlist are checked.

3. Open the Preferences window, and on the Advanced tab, click Burning.

4. Select MP3 CD (**Figure 6.8**).

5. Click OK to close the Preferences window.

✔ Tips

■ You'll need a CD for each 650 MB worth of songs (if you're using 74-minute media) or for each 700 MB (if you are using 80-minute media).

■ You can't include items purchased from the iTunes Music Store on an MP3 CD. What you can do, however, is burn your purchased items to an audio CD, then import from the CD as MP3. (See Chapter 8 to learn how to change your importing format to MP3.) Once the songs are reimported this way, you can burn to MP3. (The downside is that the songs have been compressed once using AAC and then compressed again using MP3; this results in some quality loss.)

■ Files you purchase from Audible.com may be MP3 files, but they can't be burned to an MP3 CD.

Making Sure Songs Are MP3s

It's a good idea to make sure all the songs you want to burn to an MP3 CD are actually *in* the MP3 format before you start burning your CD. If you want to include a song that's not an MP3, you'll need to convert it first.

To see if a song is in an MP3 format:

◆ If a song is listed in the Kind column as "MPEG audio file" (refer to Figure 6.7), select it and from the File menu choose Get Info. On the right side of the window it lists the format (**Figure 6.9**). "MPEG-1, Layer 3" or "MPEG-2, Layer 3" is what you want to see.

If a song is listed in the Kind column as anything other than "MPEG audio file," it's not an MP3 file that can be burned to an MP3 CD. You want to convert it to MP3.

To convert songs to MP3 format:

1. On the Advanced tab of the Preferences window, under Importing, choose MP3 Encoder in the Import Using pop-up menu (**Figure 6.10**), and then click OK to close the Preferences window.

2. In the song list, select the songs you want to convert to MP3.

Shows format. MPEG-1, Layer 3 means that it's an MP3 file. (So does MPEG-2, Layer 3.)

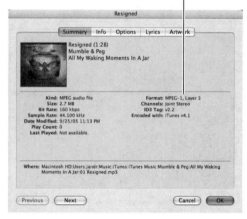

Figure 6.9 The only way to be sure that a song is MP3 is to get information on the song (File > Get Info).

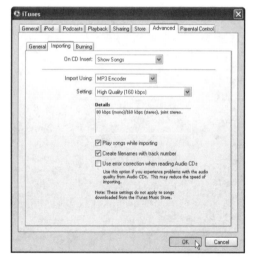

Figure 6.10 If you want to convert songs to MP3, you'll need to change your Importing preferences. (Yes, even though you're not importing.) Go to the Advanced tab of the Preferences window, click Importing, select MP3 Encoder, and pick a setting: 160 usually provides a good compromise between quality and amount of music you can fit on a CD. (**See Table 6.1.**)

Figure 6.11
Choose Convert Selection to MP3 to convert all selected songs to MP3. (You won't find this menu item unless you've first changed your importing settings.)

Table 6.1

How much audio fits on an MP3 CD

BIT RATE	NUMBER OF HOURS ON 74-MINUTE CD	NUMBER OF HOURS ON 80-MINUTE CD
128 kbps	11.5	12.4
160 kbps	9.2	9.9
192 kbps	7.7	8.3

3. From the Advanced menu, choose Convert Selection to MP3 (**Figure 6.11**). iTunes converts the selected songs.

4. Delete the non-MP3 versions from the playlist, unless you have a reason to keep them around.

✔ Tips

- MP3 *streams* (which can't be burned to an MP3 CD) are listed in the Kind column as "MPEG audio stream"; make sure the Kind column is wide enough so you can see if the last word is *file* or *stream*. (We cover how to adjust the width of your columns in Chapter 9.)

- When you select MP3 as your encoder, you can also select from the Setting pop-up menu (refer to Figure 6.10). See "Changing How Songs Are Encoded on Import" in Chapter 8 if you want to better understand what your Setting options are. Refer to Table 6.1 if you want to know how your bit-rate setting (the *kbps* figure) affects the number of hours of audio you can fit on the CD.

MAKING SURE SONGS ARE MP3S

Burning MP3 CDs

Finally, you're ready to burn an MP3 CD. The process is almost identical to burning an audio CD.

To burn an MP3 CD:

1. Follow the steps for preparing to burn an MP3 CD as described previously in this chapter.

2. Follow the steps for burning an audio CD: select the playlist, click Burn Disc (**Figure 6.12**), and insert a blank disc if directed to do so.

   As with an audio CD, iTunes will prompt you if you'll need more than one disc; click MP3 CD (**Figure 6.13**). It will warn you if any songs won't be burned (**Figure 6.14**).

3. Take out the CD when it's done and test it by playing it in an MP3-enabled audio CD player.

   If it doesn't play correctly, read "Tips for Successful Burning" at the end of this chapter and try again.

Figure 6.12 To create an MP3 CD from a playlist full of MP3-encoded songs, click Burn Disc.

Figure 6.13 If you have too much data to burn onto a single CD, iTunes shows this message.

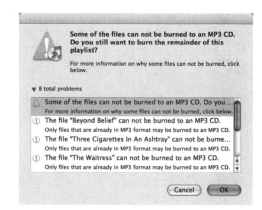

Figure 6.14 iTunes lets you know if there's a problem with any of the items in the playlist. (The most common error is that the songs aren't MP3s.)

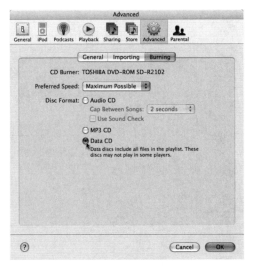

Figure 6.15 When you want to copy all your song files to a CD or a DVD for archiving purposes, select Data CD (or "Data CD or DVD") on the Burning tab of the Advanced tab of the Preferences window.

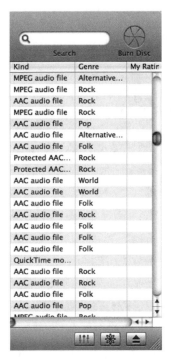

Figure 6.16 For a data disc, the playlist you intend to burn can contain all types of audio files.

Creating a Data CD or DVD for Archiving Purposes

We recommend creating a data disc (CD or DVD) so that you'll have a backup copy of some or all of your songs. This way, if something disastrous happens to your hard drive or you get a new computer, you won't have to re-rip all your audio CDs. Perhaps even more important, you'll have a backup of all your purchased music (as Apple won't replace purchased music).

To archive songs in a playlist to a CD-ROM or DVD-ROM:

1. Open the Preferences window, select the Advanced tab, and then click the Burning tab.

2. Select Data CD as the disc format (**Figure 6.15**).

   The choice will read "Data CD or DVD" if your system includes a DVD burner.

3. Click OK to close the Preferences window.

4. Make sure the playlist you want to archive is selected in the Source pane.

   This playlist can contain all types of song files (**Figure 6.16**). It can even point to all the songs in your library. (See the sidebar "A System for Backing Up Your Whole Library" for more info on creating a playlist for your entire library.)

5. Click Burn Disc.

6. If directed in the Status display to insert a blank disc, insert your blank CD or DVD.

   In the case of a DVD, iTunes asks if you're sure that you want to create a data DVD. Click Data DVD to continue.

continues on next page

CREATING A DATA CD OR DVD

7. If you have more data than can fit on the CD or DVD you've inserted, iTunes asks if you want to create multiple data discs with the playlist split across them (**Figure 6.17**). Click Data Discs to continue.

8. Sit back and watch the disc burn (or go about doing something else).

The Status display provides information about the burning process, including an estimate of how much longer the burn will take.

If the playlist requires more than one disc, it will prompt you to insert another when it's ready for it and will then prompt you to click Burn Disc again.

You end up with one or more CDs or DVDs, each with a name matching the name of the playlist. Each disc contains copies of all the audio files represented in the playlist, as well as an XML file with information about the songs on that disc.

To copy files from a data disc back into an iTunes library:

1. Insert the data disc.

The data disc appears in the iTunes Source pane.

2. *Do one of the following:*

▲ Drag the entry for the data disc in the Source pane to the library or to a playlist (**Figure 6.18**).

▲ Click the entry for the data disc, and drag selected songs from the song list to the library or to a playlist.

iTunes adds the songs to your library (and to the playlist to which you dragged, if any).

Figure 6.17 If you have more data than will fit on a single disc, you'll see this message.

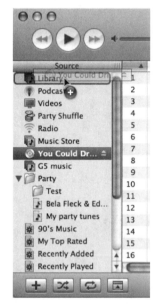

Figure 6.18 If you need to put files from a data disc back into your iTunes library, you can just drag the icon for the data disc to your library (or to any playlist).

Sidebar: CREATING A DATA CD OR DVD

A System for Backing Up Your Whole Library

If you want to make sure you always have a backup of all the items in your iTunes library, try this system.

First, back up your whole library in its current state. To do this, you'll need to create a playlist that contains all the songs in your library. One way to create such a playlist is to select your library in the Source pane, select all the items in it, and then choose File > New Playlist from Selection. Give the resulting playlist a name like "Full Library" and burn that playlist. (Figure that this burning process will take roughly 5 minutes per CD with a 24x CD burner. Remember that iTunes reports the amount of data in a playlist at the bottom of the window, and that a CD can hold 650 MB or 700 MB.)

Once you've got your full library burned, you can do incremental backups on a regular basis, burning a CD that contains only those songs you've added since your last backup. One way to do this is to create a Smart Playlist that has the condition "Date Added is after," with a value matching the date of your last backup (**Figure 6.19**). You'll need to edit this playlist after each full backup to change the date value to that of the latest backup.

Change this date to the date of your last backup.

Figure 6.19 This Smart Playlist keeps track of all songs added since a particular date.

✔ Tip

- To copy files from a data disc back into iTunes, you could also drag song files from Windows Explorer or the Finder into the iTunes window—but not all song information will necessarily come with the songs. (It's only when you do the copying entirely from within iTunes that it reads an XML file containing song information; this is especially important for files other than AAC and MP3 files.)

Tips for Successful Burning

If you've spent any time burning CDs, you know that the process isn't always foolproof. It's not uncommon to wind up with a few CD "drink coasters" after some failed burning attempts. But worry not. You can try several things if you don't successfully burn a CD the first time.

To improve your chances of a successful burn:

◆ Change the speed at which iTunes burns. It normally tries to burn at the maximum speed of the drive and/or blank disc. Sometimes this is just too fast to do a good job, and you'll need to tell the system to slow down. To do so, on the Advanced tab of the Preferences window, click the Burning tab, and from the Preferred Speed pop-up menu (**Figure 6.20**), select a lower burn speed. (We recommend first trying 2x, which is slower than the majority of drives out there today; if that works, try higher speeds on subsequent burns, until you reach a point where burning doesn't work again. If even 2x doesn't work, try 1x.)

◆ If you're using CD-RW blank discs, try switching to CD-R blanks.

◆ Change your computer's sleep timing preferences so that your computer won't go to sleep during the burn.

◆ Turn off programs that may interrupt the burning process; such as screensavers and antivirus programs.

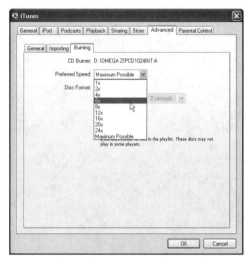

Figure 6.20 Some drives don't burn well at their maximum possible speed, so you should try lowering the preferred speed.

◆ Defragment your hard disk. A fragmented hard disk is one that has files and parts of files dispersed all over the disc, which means that during a burn the system may not find the pieces it needs when it needs them.

◆ Determine whether there's a problem with your CD burner that needs repairing. (For example, try to burn a CD with the software that came with the burner to make sure you are not having a problem with the burner rather than with iTunes.)

◆ Check with the manufacturer of your burner to make sure the burner has the latest firmware. (Most manufacturers will provide information about firmware updates on their Web site, in a support area.)

◆ If you're burning an MP3 CD and you find it doesn't work in an older MP3 CD player, it may be because that player can't handle the newer version of the ID3 tags in the files. Choose Advanced > Convert ID3 Tags, and in the window that appears, choose v1.0 or v1.1; then burn again. (If you're curious about ID3 tags, read Chapter 9.)

◆ (Windows Only) Run CD Diagnostics is a command in the Help menu. Try this command if you're having problems successfully burning a CD.

General Care of Discs

CD and DVD discs are somewhat fragile, so you should handle them with care, both before and after burning. Most of the following tips are common sense, but it can't hurt to be reminded, right?

◆ Do your best to keep your hands (and the hands of small, messy children) off the disc, especially the underside (meaning the side that has no manufacturer's imprint).

◆ Keep your discs dust-free. Before you burn, make sure your blank disc has no dust on it. (The best thing to do is blow off any dust with compressed air.)

◆ Don't write on a disc with anything but a felt-tip pen; and write only on the top side.

◆ Keep discs out of direct sunlight.

TIPS FOR SUCCESSFUL BURNING

Printing a CD Case Insert

There's a Print choice in the File menu, and it does a great job of printing song lists for CDs.

You have various "themes" to choose from. You can not only print a list of songs (with times) but also get a nice collage of the album artwork associated with the songs in the playlist you're burning from. (If you don't have artwork associated with your song, you may want to add it; see Chapter 8 "Adding Song Artwork," in Chapter 8.)

To print a CD case insert:

1. In the Source pane, select the playlist from which you burned a CD.

2. From the File menu, choose Print.

   A window opens (**Figure 6.21**), with a title of "Print" followed by the name of your playlist.

3. Make sure "CD jewel case insert" is selected, and choose a theme from the Theme pop-up menu (**Figure 6.22**).

   You have a variety of choices—a description appears for each choice, and you can see a preview on the right side of the window. One example is in **Figure 6.23**.

4. Click Print.

   The file prints.

Figure 6.21 This window appears. You want "CD jewel case insert."

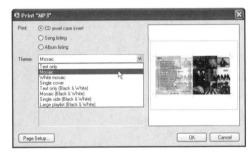

Figure 6.22 Pick your theme. (The default theme is "Text only".)

Figure 6.23 Here's the Mosaic theme (our favorite).

PRINTING A CD CASE INSERT

Part 2:

Getting Into It: Beyond the Basics

FINE-TUNING YOUR MUSIC STORE EXPERIENCE

7

In Chapter 2 we walked you straight through the basic steps for purchasing content in the iTunes Music Store. It's not hard to do.

Our goal in this chapter is to go a bit more slowly through the store, taking you into the interesting nooks and crannies, so to speak. We provide details about methods for finding and previewing content. Next we make sure your money-spending occurs in the way you want, covering how to sign in and out of that account, how to set purchasing preferences, and how to use the Shopping Cart. Then we get into how you can give the gift of music to others and end with some account management issues.

Before we get started, here's a little tip: You can open the iTunes Music Store in its own window by double-clicking Music Store in the Source pane.

Searching the Store

Do you know the exact name of an artist, album, or song? Can you remember just a fragment of a name? Or are you looking for all songs that have anything to do with a specific topic, such as "war"? In Chapter 2, we mentioned that you could use the Search field. Here we provide some details.

To perform a general search in the store:

1. In the Search Music Store field (located in the top right of the iTunes window), type the text you want iTunes to locate.

   Notice that iTunes doesn't start searching as you type (as occurs when searching your own library).

Just How Big Is This Store?

Apple has received cooperation from the five major music labels (BMG, EMI, Sony Music Entertainment, Universal, and Warner), as well as from more than 1000 independent artists and labels.

By September 2005, Apple claimed to have over 2,000,000 songs and was adding hundreds of new ones every week. (Take a look at the Just Added section of the store.)

The store also features more than 11,000 spoken-word items, including audiobooks and radio shows from Audible.com. Plus there's an ever-growing collection of podcasts, music videos, and TV shows, numbering easily in the thousands.

These figures do vary based on the country the Apple Music Store is in. For example, Sony Music Entertainment is not part of the Japanese iTunes Music Store.

2. Press Return (Mac) or Enter (Windows).

The Search Results page appears. The song list area shows the results of the search: songs that contain the search term(s) in the Artist, Album, or Name columns (**Figure 7.1**).

Often, above the song list you'll find albums, artists, or audiobooks featured (as in Figure 7.1).

Shows some of the artists, albums, audiobooks, or videos that match your search　　Search field

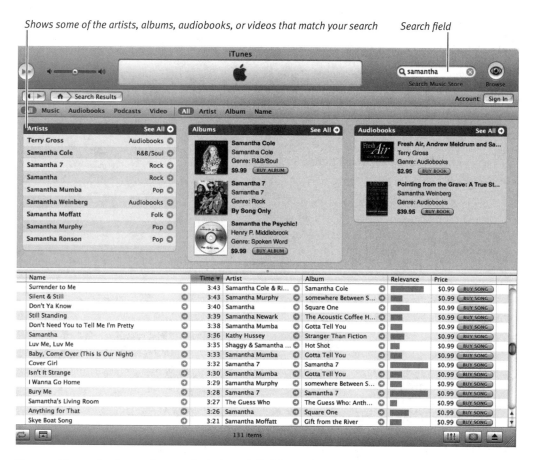

Figure 7.1 The results of a search appear in the lower half of the window.

To limit a search to a particular type of media:

◆ Click the Music, Audiobooks, Podcasts, or Video button in the Search bar (**Figure 7.2**).

iTunes reduces the items showing to those that fall into that category of media.

✔ Tips

■ As of this writing, the Search function wasn't finding any TV shows. (For example, a search for "Desperate Housewives" didn't find any video items.) We expect Apple will fix this in the near future.

■ If you type more than one word in the Search field, iTunes searches for items that have all the words in it, not necessarily in the same order. Thus, a search for *rooster red* will return items containing *red rooster.*

■ iTunes ignores certain words and characters in the search field. These include *and, or, not, &, +, -,* and quotation marks. In other words, it's smart enough to recognize these as something to ignore but not smart enough to use them to aid in a search, as a more sophisticated search engine would.

■ Clicking Artist or Album in the Search bar switches to an artist or album-oriented view and away from a song listing (**Figure 7.3**). There is currently no way to limit your search to items that contain the search term only in specific columns (as you could do in earlier versions of iTunes); you'll want to use Power Search (see next section) instead.

Figure 7.2 You can have iTunes show only a particular type of media.

Figure 7.3 Click Artist in the Search bar to switch to an artist-oriented graphical view of your search results. (If you click Album, you'll see a graphical view of the albums without the artist-oriented organization.)

■ If you perform a search and iTunes doesn't find your search term, it gives you the option of filling out a form to request that Apple add to the store a particular song, album, artist, composer, genre, or anything else you can think of. (We'd like to believe that part of the reason music by the Waifs can now be found in the store is because we made a request just like this two years ago!)

Figure 7.4 Click Power Search on the home page or any genre page...

Figure 7.5 ...to show the Power Search pane.

Figure 7.6 Enter search terms and pick a genre (or leave it as All Genres), and then click Search. Here, a search for *war* and *Bruce* brought up songs by Bruce Springsteen, Bruce Cockburn, and Bruce Dickinson.

Power Searching the Store

Since the store carries so many items, it provides a Power Search function to help you locate items more precisely. You can specify multiple search terms, each in a different field.

To perform a Power Search:

1. Click the Power Search link on the store's home page or any genre page (**Figure 7.4**).

   The Power Search pane appears (**Figure 7.5**).

2. Type in any of the fields.

3. Select a genre if you want to limit your search to a particular genre.

4. Click Search.

   The results are displayed in the song list (**Figure 7.6**).

Navigating with the Browser

The iTunes Music Store Browser provides a text-based, hierarchical way to navigate the store. It's probably best for left-brainers (who needs pictures, anyway?) or for those who know fairly specifically what they're looking for. It's also faster for those on a slow Internet connection, since you don't have to wait for graphics to download.

To navigate with the Browser:

1. If the Browser is not showing, *do one of the following:*

   ▲ Click the Browse button in the upper-right corner of the iTunes window (**Figure 7.7**).

   ▲ Click the Browse link on the left side of the Music Store pane (refer to Figure 7.4).

   ▲ From the Edit menu, choose Show Browser. (Or type a keyboard equivalent: Command-B on a Mac or Ctrl-B in Windows.)

   The Browse pane appears.

2. Select, in the leftmost column, the genre you want (**Figure 7.8**).

3. Select from the columns to the right of the Genre column. (For many music genres, this is Artist and then Album. For others, it will be a Subgenre column next. And you'll find other variations on column names for non-music genres.)

   The list of items that match your selections appears.

Browse link

Browse button

Figure 7.7 Click the Browse button or the Browse Music link to switch to the Browser.

Figure 7.8 First select a genre, then subgenre, then an artist, and then an album to see a list of songs.

✔ Tips

■ Once you've navigated to a specific album using the Browser, you can purchase individual songs by clicking the Buy Song (or Add Song) button; but there's no button to buy the entire album. If you want to buy the entire album, click an arrow next to the album name in the song list; the page for the album shows with its Buy Album button (or Add Album button, depending on your preference settings).

■ You can double-click an artist's name in the Browser to bring up the corresponding graphical page for that artist and switch out of Browse mode.

■ You can also double-click a genre name to bring up the corresponding graphical genre page. (For the few genres that have no genre page—Anime and Comedy were two last we checked—nothing happens.)

■ When browsing the iTunes Music Store, you may need to make a selection in each column to get a display of songs. (This contrasts with the Browser's operation when you are viewing your own collection: iTunes chooses "All" by default, so there are always songs showing.)

File Formats of Media Purchased at the iTunes Music Store

Audio files from the iTunes Music Store aren't the same as the audio files you create when you import songs from a CD. While both are AAC-compressed MPEG-4 files, the audio files you purchase from the store carry a file extension of .m4p or .m4b (the former is for music, the latter is for books). Both are restricted, as we describe in the sidebar "What Can You Do with Purchased Stuff?" in this chapter. The songs that you import from your own CDs carry a file extension of .m4a and are free of any kind of copy protection.

Video files you purchase from the store are also MPEG-4 files that are H.264-compressed. They are protected, and have a file extension of .m4v. (This extension, however, is the same as that for unprotected video files you can create using QuickTime Player Pro.)

Podcasts don't come in a standard flavor. They are most frequently mp3s, but can also be any number of MPEG-4 formats, such as .m4v, .m4a, and can even be .mov.

Previewing Songs

Once you get to a page that lists audio items, you'll usually want to listen before you buy or download. Previewing at the iTunes Music Store is half the fun, and you can pick your favorite method. Previews for songs are usually 30 seconds, while those for videos are 20 seconds, and audiobooks are often 90 seconds. For audiobooks and videos, you'll often find a round Preview button (**Figure 7.9**); when items are listed in a song list, however, it's a little less obvious.

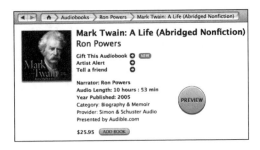

Figure 7.9 Long items that aren't composed of parts you can buy individually have a Preview button.

Slow Connection?

If you're connected to the Music Store over a dial-up modem, you may find that your previewed songs sputter and stop as you listen to them. Here's how you can change your Music Store preferences so that iTunes downloads the song sample before playing it, making for an improved—and less spotty—listening experience:

1. From the Edit menu (Windows) or iTunes menu (Mac), select Preferences.

2. Click the Store tab.

3. Check "Load complete preview before playing" (**Figure 7.10**), and then click OK.

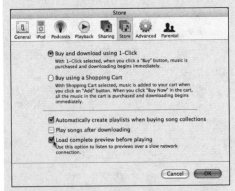

Figure 7.10 You can tell iTunes to download the full preview before playing—a good idea if you're experiencing stuttering.

About Explicit and Clean Lyrics

As you navigate through the iTunes Music Store, you may come across songs or albums labeled "Explicit" or "Clean." The former is a warning that the content may be objectionable; the latter means it is a version of a song or album with explicit lyrics edited out. If you double-click the word *Explicit* or *Clean* on an artist or album page, you'll see a Parental Advisory screen that explains in detail the system for parental advisory labeling.

If you don't want your kids to be able to preview or download content with the Explicit label, open your Preferences window, click the Parental or Parental Controls tab, and check "Restrict explicit content."

Ways to preview items in a song list:

◆ Double-click any line in the song list.

◆ Press the Play button or press the space bar on your keyboard.

The preview that plays is the one for the current song (the one with a speaker icon next to it), or whatever song is selected if there is no current song, or the first song in the list if there is no current song and nothing is selected. See **Figure 7.11**.

◆ Click a song's line in the song list to select it, and then press the Return key (Mac) or Enter key (Windows) on your keyboard.

✔ Tips

■ To preview the previous or next song in a list while a preview is playing, press the left or right arrow key.

■ If you're shopping for audiobooks, we highly recommend that you use that Preview button before you buy. You want to be quite sure that the vocal quality of the reader doesn't get on your nerves.

Current song: Press the space bar (or click the Play button or choose Controls > Play) to play this song.

Double-click to play any song that's not selected and isn't current, such as this one.

Selected song: Press Return (Mac) or Enter (Windows) to play. (If there's no current song, you can also play the selected song by clicking the Play button, pressing the space bar, or choosing Controls > Play.)

Figure 7.11 There's no Preview button for items in a song list, but you preview in the same ways you play music in your own library.

Saving Links

As you navigate through the store, you'll encounter all sorts of interesting pages and songs that you might want to revisit later. Or you may want a friend to hear a new single from an artist you've recently discovered. iTunes provides three simple methods for saving links to most anything in the store: via a preview in your own library, via a shortcut (or alias) on your desktop, and by copying a URL.

To save a preview to your library:

◆ Drag from the song list in the Music Store to one of your playlists to add the preview to your own collection. Or you can drag to the area below your playlists to make a new playlist containing the song or songs you dragged.

When you look at the playlist, you'll see these previews listed (**Figure 7.12**) with a Buy or Add button next to a price in a newly added Price column. (The Price column appears as long as you have any store previews.) There's also a Link arrow button to get you back to the store.

To save a shortcut or alias to your desktop:

◆ Click any clickable element in the store (a link to a page in the store or a song in a song list), and drag it to your desktop (**Figure 7.13**).

When you release the mouse button, a pointer file—called an *alias* on the Mac and a *shortcut* in Windows—is created on your desktop (**Figure 7.14**). You can click this at any time to return to a page for that item in the store.

Figure 7.12 You can have Music Store previews in your own library or its playlists. (Just drag from the store to your own library or playlist.)

Figure 7.13 Drag any link or song from the store to your desktop...

Figure 7.14 ...to create a shortcut (Windows) or alias (Mac). Clicking the shortcut or alias will get you back to that page or song.

Figure 7.15 Right-click (Windows) or Control-click (Mac) almost any link or song, and you'll see Copy iTunes Music Store URL. Select this, and then you'll be able to paste it in an e-mail message or document.

Web Page Authoring with iTunes Music Store Links

Do you want to create a Web page with links to your favorite items in the iTunes Music Store?

Apple's iTunes Link Maker, (http://www .apple.com/itunes/linkmaker) is a Web page from which you can search the store. You select from the results of this search, and the Link Maker then generates the necessary HTML code for embedding the link to the selected item (be it a song, an album, or an artist).

If viewers of your Web page have iTunes and click a link on the page, they will be taken directly to the right place in the store. iTunes Link Maker also provides the code for putting a Download iTunes button on your page, so those viewers who don't have iTunes can get it easily.

To copy the URL of an item:

1. Right-click (Windows) or Control-click (Mac) a graphic or text link, or a song in a song list.

2. Select Copy iTunes Music Store URL (**Figure 7.15**).

   The address is copied to the Clipboard so you can paste it into most any other application that will let you paste in text. For example, you can paste it into an e-mail message or an instant message session to share it with a friend. ("Listen to this song, dude!")

✔ Tips

- The ability to drag previews to your own library allows you to create something of a shopping cart without switching your store purchasing preferences to Shopping Cart (see "Setting Purchasing Preferences" later in this chapter). Simply create a playlist called something like "Might want to buy," and drag your previews there.

- The URL that's copied begins with http://. This means that when you click this URL, your operating system opens a Web browser, which in turn opens iTunes. However, if you replace the http:// with itms://, iTunes opens directly. This is a bit faster and doesn't open a Web browser if one isn't already open.

- If you link to a song, you'll find that the page opens with the song selected, so you just need to press Return (Mac) or Enter (Windows) to play it. Other methods, such as pressing the space bar, will also usually work.

Signing In and Out of the Store

It's probably obvious by now, but here's how to sign in to the store. You'll also want to know how to sign out, to be sure that nobody else downloads songs on your computer, running up hefty charges on your credit card.

Figure 7.16 Click the Sign In button.

To sign in:

1. Click the Account Sign In button (**Figure 7.16**).

2. If you are signing in with an AOL screen name, click the AOL radio button; otherwise, make sure the radio button with the Apple icon next to it is selected (**Figure 7.17**).

3. Enter your Apple ID or AOL screen name and password.

4. Click Sign In.

   Your Apple ID or AOL screen name appears as the label of the button that was the Sign In button.

Figure 7.17 Enter your Apple ID or AOL screen name and password, and click Sign In.

To sign out:

1. Click your account name in the location you clicked to sign in (**Figure 7.18**).

   A window appears, giving you the options of viewing your account or signing out.

2. Click Sign Out (**Figure 7.19**).

✔ Tips

- Quitting or exiting iTunes also signs you out.

- Remember that your password is case sensitive. If your Caps Lock key is on, you'll see a warning in the window in which you enter your password.

Figure 7.18 To sign out of the store, first click your account name.

Figure 7.19 Click Sign Out to disable purchasing. Once you're signed out, you can still browse the store, but you'll need to sign in again to make additional purchases.

This will make a playlist if you purchase collections, such as iMixes or iTunes Essentials.

Select if you prefer to pay for multiple songs at the end of your shopping session.

Select if you want to download songs instantly.

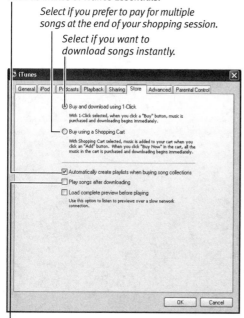

Check this if you want a song to play immediately after it's been downloaded.

Figure 7.20 The Store tab of the iTunes Preferences window.

✔ Tips

■ We explain the "Load complete preview before playing" option you see in Figure 7.20 in the section "Previewing Songs" earlier in this chapter.

■ In version 4 of iTunes there was an option on this tab to not show the Music Store in your list of sources; this option is now in the Parental or Parental Controls tab of the Preferences window.

Setting Purchasing Preferences

Before you start spending lots of money at the iTunes Music Store, take the time to specify the settings in the Preferences window that will shape your shopping experience.

To set purchasing preferences:

1. From the Edit menu (Windows) or iTunes menu (Mac), select Preferences.

2. Click the Store tab.

3. Make choices (**Figure 7.20**):

   The most important of these is whether you want to use 1-Click shopping or a Shopping Cart. Leave "Buy and download using 1-Click" selected if you like the idea of immediate gratification—it lets you buy songs with a single click of your mouse. Choose "Buy using a Shopping Cart" if you want to gather up a number of items before making a purchase; this option is better if you're trying to control impulse buying or if you have a slow Internet connection. Your choice of 1-Click or Shopping Cart impacts whether you will see Buy buttons or Add buttons throughout the store.

   For those who buy groups of songs in the store that aren't necessarily albums and want to be able to locate that precise collection of songs, you'll want to leave "Automatically create playlists when buying song collections" checked. You might want to uncheck this if you don't like having lots of playlists in your Source pane.

   You can also opt to have songs play automatically after downloading (another feature for those who demand instant gratification).

Shopping Cart Purchasing

If you switched to Shopping Cart purchasing, here's the process you'll use.

To buy songs if using the Shopping Cart:

1. Click the Add button (**Figure 7.21**) for each item you want to add.

   The first time you click an Add button in a session, you may see a sign-in screen, similar to that in Figure 7.17. Fill in your info, and click Add to Cart.

2. When you're done adding all the items you want to purchase, click Shopping Cart in the Source pane (**Figure 7.22**).

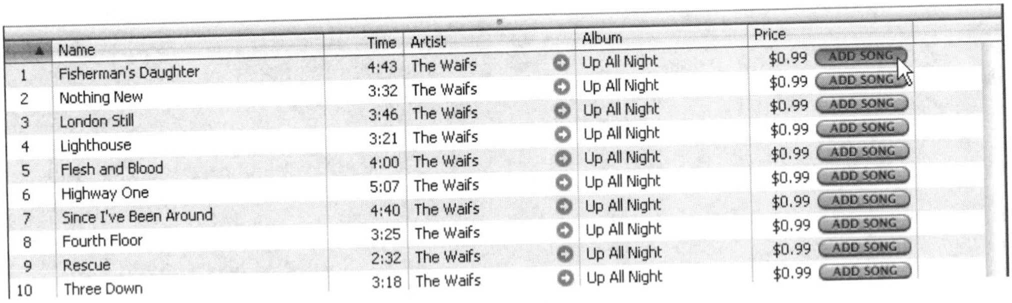

	Name	Time	Artist		Album	Price	
1	Fisherman's Daughter	4:43	The Waifs	○	Up All Night	$0.99	ADD SONG
2	Nothing New	3:32	The Waifs	○	Up All Night	$0.99	ADD SONG
3	London Still	3:46	The Waifs	○	Up All Night	$0.99	ADD SONG
4	Lighthouse	3:21	The Waifs	○	Up All Night	$0.99	ADD SONG
5	Flesh and Blood	4:00	The Waifs	○	Up All Night	$0.99	ADD SONG
6	Highway One	5:07	The Waifs	○	Up All Night	$0.99	ADD SONG
7	Since I've Been Around	4:40	The Waifs	○	Up All Night	$0.99	ADD SONG
8	Fourth Floor	3:25	The Waifs	○	Up All Night	$0.99	ADD SONG
9	Rescue	2:32	The Waifs	○	Up All Night	$0.99	ADD SONG
10	Three Down	3:18	The Waifs	○	Up All Night	$0.99	ADD SONG

Figure 7.21 Click an Add button to add an item to your shopping cart.

Figure 7.22 Click Shopping Cart in the Source pane...

3. If you've decided you definitely don't want an item, click the encircled x icon next to the Buy (Buy Song, Buy Video, and so on) button for that item (**Figure 7.23**) in the Price column.

4. When the list shows the items you want to buy, click Buy Now.

5. When asked if you're sure you want to buy and download the items in your shopping cart, click Buy.

All items in your shopping cart are downloaded to your library. You'll find them in your Purchased playlist (refer to Figure 7.22.)

Click to remove from Shopping Cart.

Click to buy just this item.

Click Buy Now when/if you're sure you want to buy everything in the list.

Figure 7.23 ...to see a list of items you've added to your cart.

✔ Tips

- You can buy items in your shopping cart individually by clicking the Buy button in the Price column (refer to Figure 7.23). You'll be asked to confirm that you want to buy. After you've purchased, the item will no longer be in your Shopping Cart.

- If you put something in your Shopping Cart on one computer and then sign in using the same account on another computer, your shopping cart will contain the items that you placed in it earlier.

- An alternative way to collect items before purchasing is to drag previews into your library or a playlist. See "Saving Links" earlier in this chapter.

What Can You Do With Purchased Stuff?

While the iTunes Music Store will let you download an almost unlimited number of items, Apple does place restrictions on how and where you listen to the files you've purchased. You can play your purchased music on only five different computers (Macs or PCs), as long as they're *authorized* (see "Authorizing Multiple Computers to Play Your Songs" later in this chapter). You can, however, transfer your purchased items to an unlimited number of iPods. And while you can burn an individual song to as many audio CDs as you want, you're prevented from burning the same playlist with a purchased song more than seven times, as we covered in Chapter 6.

These restrictions are enforced via FairPlay, a Digital Rights Management (DRM) technology that Apple uses.

Figure 7.24 Click the Gift Certificates link to start the process of buying a gift certificate.

Figure 7.25 Click the Email button, assuming you want to send an electronic gift certificate.

Figure 7.26 Click Continue when you're done filling in the form. (After this there will be another screen on which you can confirm or cancel.)

Giving Gift Certificates

Stuck for an idea for a birthday or holiday present? An iTunes Gift Certificate may be just what you're looking for: easy for you to buy, and flexible enough to fit just about anybody.

To give a gift certificate:

1. Click the Gift Certificates link on the home page or a genre page (**Figure 7.24**).

2. On the Gift Certificates page, click the Buy Now button.

3. Click the button for your preferred method of giving: Email, Print, or U.S. Mail (**Figure 7.25**).

4. The rest of the process will vary depending on the method you've chosen:

   For the e-mail and print options: A form appears in the iTunes Music Store after you sign in (**Figure 7.26**). Click Continue once you've filled it out. Then click Buy on the "Confirm Your Purchase" page. For e-mail, you'll see a screen with a message that the gift certificate was sent; your recipient will get the certificate in e-mail with a link to the iTunes Music Store for redeeming the gift certificate. For print, you'll see a screen with instructions for printing your gift certificate; what you print includes instructions for redeeming the gift certificate (including getting iTunes, if they don't already have it).

   For the U.S. Mail option: Your Web browser opens if not already open and a form appears in a Web page at the Apple Store; you'll complete the purchasing process in the Apple Store rather than in the iTunes Music Store. You'll have to use the Check out button to complete your purchase. Your recipient will receive the gift certificate in the mail.

continues on next page

GIVING GIFT CERTIFICATES

Once a user redeems her gift certificate, the amount credited to her account appears next to her account name in the upper right of the iTunes window (**Figure 7.27**) whenever they're logged in.

✔ Tips

- You don't have to start at iTunes to purchase an iTunes Music Store gift certificate. You can also go directly to the Apple Store, http://store.apple.com, to buy e-mail or paper gift certificates. This allows someone who doesn't have a system modern enough to run iTunes (your mother, perhaps) to buy someone (you, perhaps) an iTunes Music Store gift certificate. You should be able to find a link to buy an iTunes Music Store Gift Certificate on the Apple Store home page. Or search for iTunes at the store; your search results will show that you can also purchase $25 and $50 gift cards.

- Sending a gift certificate is like sending cash, so it's very important that you get the e-mail or postal address of your recipient right, if sending via e-mail or U.S. Mail. If you err, you may send a gift certificate to someone you don't even know.

- Regardless of the method you use to buy a gift certificate, you'll at some point come across a Terms and Conditions section. It's a good idea to read this, as it covers topics such as expiration dates.

Figure 7.27 Once your recipient successfully redeems the gift certificate, iTunes shows them the amount they have to spend.

Figure 7.28 Tell iTunes you want to give this to someone: Gift This Music.

Figure 7.29 Click a Gift button to say specifically what you want to give. (You won't see this screen if there was only one thing you could possibly give when you started the gifting process.)

Giving Specific Items

Gift certificate too impersonal? If you know someone (and their music collection) well enough, you may want to give them a specific song or album. (Yes, you can give an item as small as a 99 cent song!)

To give a specific item:

1. Locate, in the iTunes Music Store, the page on which you would buy the item you want to give.

2. Click the Gift This Music link (**Figure 7.28**).

   Or you may see Gift These Episodes (for TV shows), Gift This Video (for other video items), or Gift This Audiobook.

3. If you were on a page with multiple items that you could buy, you'll see that the Buy (or Add) buttons have turned to Gift buttons. Click the Gift button for the item you wish to give (**Figure 7.29**).

4. If you see a sign-in window, enter your Apple ID or AOL screen name (if it's not already there) and password, and then click Continue.

continues on next page

5. Fill out the form to provide the necessary information about your recipient, and click Continue (**Figure 7.30**).

6. On the page on which you can review your gift, click Buy Gift.

iTunes tells you that the gift has been sent. The person (or people) to whom you've sent the gift will receive an e-mail, with a link to redeem the gift; when they click the link, the item you've chosen for them will download immediately (as soon as they sign in or verify their account information).

Figure 7.30 Click Continue when you're done filling in the form.

✔ Tips

■ Don't forget that you can create a playlist and give the songs in that playlist to someone you love. See "Sharing a Playlist Through the Music Store" in Chapter 5.

■ Currently, the only option for giving a specific item is via e-mail. We hope it won't be long until you can print them, too. (Wouldn't it be fun to give them as party favors?)

■ Recipients of specific items will need to upgrade to iTunes 6 to get their gift. (The e-mail message they'll get may say that iTunes 5 is required, but they'll still be forced to go to iTunes 6.)

Figure 7.31 After you click Allowance on the home page or a genre page, you'll see this screen. Fill in the information requested and click Buy Now.

Figure 7.32 If the recipient of your iTunes allowance doesn't already have an Apple ID (that you know about), you'll have to fill out this form to create an account for him or her.

Giving a Music Allowance

Got kids? Allowances are a great feature of the Music Store, allowing your children (or others) to make purchases in the store without requiring access to your credit card. You can set up an account for your child that is automatically credited on the first of each month with an amount of your choosing—between $10 and $200.

To set up an iTunes allowance:

1. At the iTunes Music Store home or genre page, click Allowance (refer to Figure 7.24).

2. Fill in the form fields on the page that appears, and click Continue (**Figure 7.31**).

3. When a window appears asking you for your account name and password, provide them and then click Setup.

   If you had previously signed in, your account name will be automatically filled in.

4. If you selected "Create an Apple Account for recipient" (refer to Figure 7.31), you will be presented with a "Create an Apple Account" page. Fill in the information here, and click Create (**Figure 7.32**).

   Notice that you are not required to enter credit card information to create this account.

continues on next page

GIVING A MUSIC ALLOWANCE

5. On the Confirm Your Purchase page, assuming that you are sure about giving at least this first installment, click Buy (**Figure 7.33**).

A page appears saying that the allowance has been successfully set up and letting you know when installments will be made.

The recipient will receive an e-mail message telling them that they've been given an allowance. If they didn't previously have an account, the message includes the Apple ID and password you provided. When they sign in, they will have to agree to Terms and Conditions but they won't have to provide any credit card info. Their iTunes window will show the amount in their account that's available to spend just as it does for gift certificates (refer to Figure 7.27).

Figure 7.33 When you're ready to purchase the first allowance installment, click Buy. (See the last page of this chapter if you need to cancel the allowance.)

✔ Tip

- You can cancel an allowance; see "Managing Your Account" later in this chapter.

Figure 7.34 Enter the password for the account you want to authorize for this computer, and click Authorize.

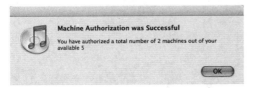

Figure 7.35 iTunes tells you that authorization is successful and lets you know how many computers have been authorized.

Authorizing Multiple Computers to Play Your Songs

Do you work on many computers and want to be able to play your music on all of them? You can listen to music purchased from your iTunes account on as many as five *authorized* computers.

The computer you use to first create your account is automatically authorized. After that you must explicitly authorize each additional computer that you will copy purchased music to or that will access purchased music via sharing.

Once you authorize a computer for an account, that computer is authorized to play *all* the music purchased with that account. (There is no per-song authorization.)

To authorize another computer to play songs you've purchased from the iTunes Music Store:

1. In iTunes, try to play any one of your purchased songs. (Double-clicking the song will work, although you can use any other method of playing.)

    A window appears, requesting a password for the account you purchased the song with (**Figure 7.34**).

2. Enter the password for the account you used to purchase the music.

3. Click Authorize.

    It will take a few seconds before a dialog appears telling you that authorization was successful (**Figure 7.35**) and the song begins playing.

4. Take note of how many computers you have authorized, and click OK to dismiss the dialog.

✔ Tip

■ It's a really bad idea to give your password to someone else so that they can enter it in the authorization window—unless you *really* trust that person. They'll have full access to your account and will be able to purchase songs, possibly running up quite a bill on your credit card.

Deauthorizing a Computer for Your Account

You may decide you no longer want a particular computer to be authorized to play your purchased music. This may be because you are selling the computer or simply because you need another computer to have one of your five authorizations.

To deauthorize a computer:

1. With iTunes open at the computer you want to deauthorize, from the Advanced menu, choose Deauthorize Computer (**Figure 7.36**).

   A window appears in which you can select Deauthorize Computer for Music Store Account or Deauthorize Computer for Audible Account (**Figure 7.37**).

2. Select Deauthorize Computer for Music Store Account, and click OK.

Figure 7.36 From the Advanced menu, choose Deauthorize Computer.

Figure 7.37 Select the type of account for which you want to deauthorize, and click OK.

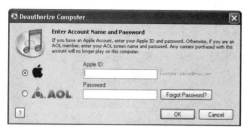

Figure 7.38 Enter the name and password for the account you want to deauthorize, and click OK.

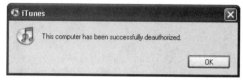

Figure 7.39 iTunes tells you that deauthorization was successful.

3. In the Deauthorize Computer window that appears, provide your iTunes Music Store account information (**Figure 7.38**) and click OK.

A window appears for a few seconds indicating that iTunes is accessing the Music Store, and then you'll see a window indicating that the computer has been successfully deauthorized (**Figure 7.39**).

4. Click OK.

You won't be able to use this computer to listen to songs purchased from your account unless you authorize it again.

✔ Tip

■ The instructions provided here explain how to deauthorize a computer as long as you still have access to that computer. If you have authorized five computers, however, you can deauthorize them all without access to the particular computers. See next section.

DEAUTHORIZING A COMPUTER FOR YOUR ACCOUNT

Managing Your Account

Let's say you've got a new credit card and you need to update your personal information so you can continue to buy music through iTunes. Or maybe you want to make sure your teenagers aren't downloading hundreds of dollars worth of Eminem songs on the family computer. Luckily, iTunes provides a page for you to manage various aspects of your account.

To view your account information:

1. Once you've signed in, click your account name in the button at the top right of the iTunes window (**Figure 7.40**).

2. In the window that appears, enter your password and click View Account (refer to Figure 7.19).

    You'll see your Account Information page (**Figure 7.41**).

3. *Click any of the following:*

    ▲ **Edit Account Info.** Use this to make changes to the basic information you entered when you originally set up your account.

    ▲ **Edit Credit Card.** Use to change your credit card info. (If you need to change the country of your billing address, you'll need to use the Change Country button on the main Account Information page.)

    ▲ **Change Country.** Use to tell iTunes the country from which you are buying. (There are actually different iTunes Music Stores for different countries. The one you buy from must match the billing address of your credit card.)

Figure 7.40 Click your account name when you want to manage your account.

Figure 7.41 The Apple Account Information is "command central" for managing your account.

Figure 7.42 The Purchase History page can offer a sobering dose of reality. Have you really downloaded that many songs?

▲ **Purchase History.** This lets you see your most recent purchase as well as any previous purchases (**Figure 7.42**). If you want to see more detailed information about any single purchase, click the arrow icon to the left of the entry. Click Done to return to the Purchase History page.

▲ **Deauthorize All.** This option will only appear if you have already authorized five computers to listen to music from your account. (See "Authorizing Multiple Computers to Play Your Songs" earlier in this chapter.) You'll need to use this in the case where you've authorized systems to which you no longer have access and now need to deauthorize. (If you do have access to a computer you want to deauthorize, you can do it individually; see "Deauthorizing a Computer for Your Account.") Warning: you can only deauthorize all computers once a year.

▲ **Edit Nickname.** If you write any customer reviews, they'll normally be listed as "anonymous," but you can use this option to provide a nickname to be used instead.

▲ **Manage iMixes.** You'll only see this if you've published any iMixes. Use it to remove any iMixes you no longer want to appear in the Music Store.

▲ **Manage Artist Alerts.** If you've added Artist Alerts (which you do by clicking an Artist Alert link, as in Figure 7.28), you can use this screen to opt out of getting future alerts. And, whether or not you've added any alerts, you'll find a checkbox to indicate that you want the store to send you alerts for *all* the artists of songs that you've purchased in the past.

continues on next page

MANAGING YOUR ACCOUNT

▲ **Manage Allowances** appears only if you've given at least one allowance and haven't cancelled it. You can suspend or cancel an allowance by clicking the Suspend or Remove button (**Figure 7.43**). The amount currently in the recipient's account remains there but no future installments will be made to their account. There's also a create New Allowance button, so you don't have to go back to the Home page to set up an allowance for another child.

▲ **Reset Warnings.** If you have previously told iTunes not to warn you before buying and you have now decided that you do want that warning, click this button.

Figure 7.43 Has your child been naughty? The Manage Allowances page lets you temporarily suspend or permanently cancel an allowance you've given.

✔ Tip

■ When looking at the main Purchase History page (refer to Figure 7.42), you won't always see all the purchases. If you made multiple purchases in one day, not all may be listed; you'll need to click that arrow icon to see the full list.

Music Store Customer Service

Have you run into problems with your account? From iTunes' Help menu, choose iTunes and Music Store Service and Support, which opens the iTunes support page in your browser. Then click iTunes Music Store Customer Service. (When we looked, we found this link on the right side of the page in the second box down; Apple could change the layout of this page at any time, of course.) If your question or topic of concern isn't addressed appropriately, click any question or topic and scroll to the bottom of the page where you can fill out a form to e-mail support.

TWEAKING YOUR PLAYBACK EXPERIENCE

8

You can do a handful of things to alter the playback experience you have in iTunes. We start this chapter by letting you know how you might change the way songs are encoded when imported from CD as well as how to change how songs already in your library are encoded. Then we move on to the use of the Equalizer, which allows you to alter the tonal quality of your music. You can make a few additional tweaks in the Playback pane of your Preferences window; we explain these. Next we cover those aspects of playback related to time: how to change start and stop times as well as how to get iTunes to remember where you last stopped playing a particular item. Visual accompaniment for your audio comes next: song artwork and using the Visualizer. And finally, we end by showing you some ways to customize the iTunes window.

Changing Import Preferences for CDs

When you import tracks from a CD, you have a few options to choose from. The defaults are usually fine, but you may find that you want to adjust your encoding settings or that you'd prefer to have iTunes start playing a CD's songs immediately upon importing, for example.

To change your importing preferences:

1. From the iTunes menu (Mac) or the Edit menu (Windows), choose Preferences (**Figure 8.1**).

2. Click the Advanced tab and then the Importing tab.

   The Importing tab (**Figure 8.2**) provides you several encoding and settings options:

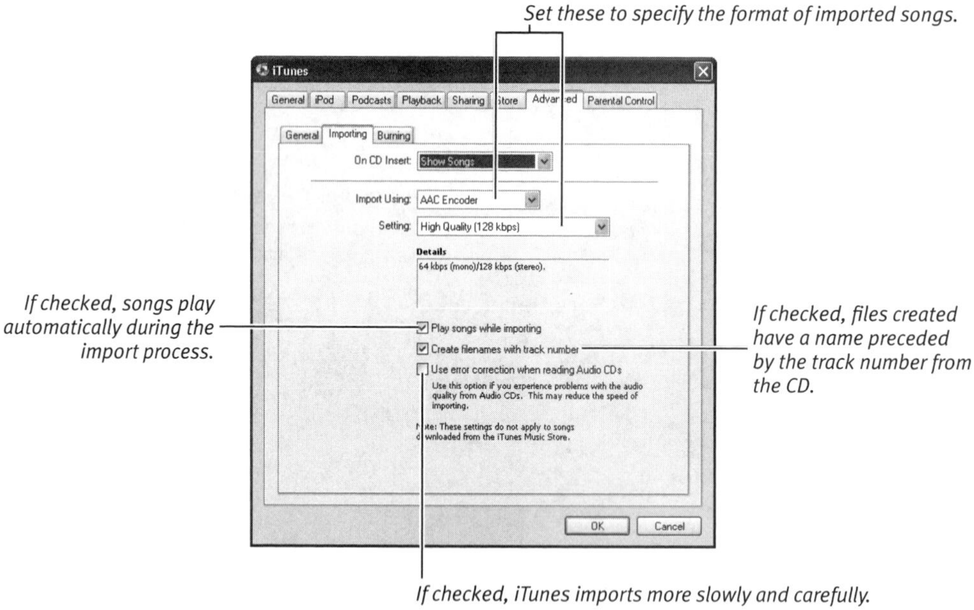

Figure 8.1 Open the Preferences window.

Set these to specify the format of imported songs.

If checked, songs play automatically during the import process.

If checked, files created have a name preceded by the track number from the CD.

If checked, iTunes imports more slowly and carefully.

Figure 8.2 The Importing tab of the Preferences window.

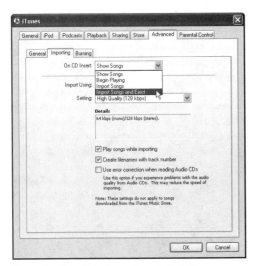

Figure 8.3 If you'll be importing a lot of CDs, you can save time by changing your On CD Insert option to Import Songs and Eject.

▲ **On CD Insert.** You can tell iTunes what to do whenever you insert an audio CD (**Figure 8.3**).

▲ **Import Using** and **Setting.** You can change your encoder and its settings. The section "Changing How Songs Are Encoded on Import" later in this chapter explains these two options.

▲ **Play songs while importing.** Leave this option checked to have your CD begin playing during the import process. If you are encoding songs as AAC, iTunes begins playing the first song only after it is fully imported. For other formats, iTunes can begin playing the song it is importing after only a few seconds. If you uncheck this option, your import happens slightly faster.

▲ **Create file names with track number.** If you leave this option checked, the file that's copied to your hard drive is given a name that begins with the track number. (For example, a file called "Harvest Moon.m4a" would be called "04 Harvest Moon.m4a" if this option were checked.) This is significant only if you will be manipulating your files in the Mac OS X Finder or in Windows Explorer, because if the filenames are preceded with numbers, you won't be able to list them alphabetically.

▲ **Use error correction when reading Audio CDs.** Check this if iTunes has problems importing from your CDs. Checking this option causes iTunes to import data more slowly and carefully than it would otherwise.

✔ Tip

■ If you import a lot of CDs in quick succession, you'll save time if you set iTunes to automatically import the songs from a CD: In the On CD Insert pop-up menu, select Import Songs and Eject (refer to Figure 8.3).

CHANGING IMPORT PREFERENCES FOR CDS

About iTunes Encoding Choices

In the world of digital media, there are a variety of *file formats* and a variety of *compressors*. You can think of the file format as specifying the packaging of the media. Not all media in these files is compressed, but when it is, there's always a specific compressor that has done the job. Sometimes a file format and a compressor have the same name; other times they don't.

When iTunes imports audio from a CD, it can change how the music is *encoded*, which can mean a change in file format, in the compressor, or both. iTunes provides five possible encoding choices: AAC, AIFF, Apple Lossless, MP3, and WAV. We'll go into the mechanics of selecting these a bit later in this chapter; but we'll briefly explain each of these options here.

AAC

AAC (Advanced Audio Coding) is an audio compressor developed as part of the MPEG-4 standard, which is relatively new. As such, files compressed with AAC can't yet play in as many applications or on as many devices as MP3s can, but it's more modern and more efficient: You get the same high quality using AAC as with MP3, but in an even smaller file (approximately 80 percent of the size). It's a perfect choice for playback in iTunes or on an iPod.

When AAC is selected as the encoder in iTunes (as it is by default), the files created are MPEG-4 files that are compressed using the AAC compressor. (The file extension is .m4a, one of several extensions for MPEG-4 files.)

Different MPEGs

Several file formats bear the MPEG label. (MPEG stands for *Moving Picture Experts Group* and is an organization that has developed all the specifications of the various MPEG standards.)

You'll find three versions of MPEG in use today: MPEG-1, MPEG-2, and MPEG-4.

MPEG-1 is more than 10 years old, but it's still used often because a wide range of media players play MPEG-1 files. In the audio world, in particular, many players play MPEG-1 Layer III, audio—more commonly referred to as MP3. (We hope this clears up a common misconception: MP3 is not MPEG-3; it's most often a form of MPEG-1.)

MPEG-2 is the format used for DVD; MPEG-2 audio files are not all that common, but iTunes can play back some of them. (MPEG-2 Layer III, an extension of MPEG-1 Layer III, is also called MP3, though it's far less common.)

MPEG-4, the new kid on the block, is based on the QuickTime file format. (Like QuickTime, it can contain much more than audio and video and is useful for the Web, CD-ROMs, and a variety of hardware devices, such as iPods). Not a lot of MPEG-4 audio players are available. iTunes and iPod take full advantage of this format. So, when Apple refers to AAC files, it is *actually* talking about MPEG-4 audio files in which the audio is compressed with the AAC compressor. MPEG-4, is also the format of all of the video sold in the iTunes Music Store and what plays on the iPod.

MP3

MP3 (which actually stands for MPEG Layer 3) refers to both the name of a file format and the compressor used within files of that format. It has been a very popular choice for encoding audio, due largely to the efficiency of MP3 compression; MP3 files are approximately one-tenth the size of uncompressed audio of equivalent quality. MP3 is not, however, as efficient as the newer AAC.

You'll want to encode as MP3 if you will be creating an MP3 CD (covered in Chapter 6) or putting the files on a portable MP3 player that's not an iPod.

Apple Lossless

This choice results in a file five to seven times larger than an equivalent AAC or MP3 but does not remove any of the sound information. (The term "lossless" means that no audio information is thrown away during compression; rather, the decrease in file size is a result of a more efficient way of storing the same data.) Highly discriminating listeners may want this version for burning back to audio CD (as we mentioned in Chapter 6); also see the sidebar "Ripping for the Future." This choice provides all the quality that you'd get from AIFF and WAV at about half the file size.

AIFF

AIFF (Audio Interchange File Format) files contain audio data that is virtually identical to what is stored on an audio CD. Although AIFF files *can* be compressed with a variety of compressors, iTunes applies no compression when you select AIFF as the encoder. (The audio on audio CDs is also uncompressed.)

The main reason for choosing AIFF as your iTunes encoder is if you absolutely need a version that's uncompressed (but larger than the Apple Lossless version, and much larger than MP3 or AAC).

ABOUT ITUNES ENCODING CHOICES

WAV

WAV is a long-used Windows audio file format. Just about any Windows tool can handle WAV files. WAV files *can* be compressed, but typically they're not. iTunes does not compress when encoding as WAV.

There's no reason to use WAV for importing CDs or for any other iTunes function (playback, burning CDs, or transfer to an MP3 player or iPod). But if you have a need for WAV files (for use with some other Windows program), iTunes will work as a converter. (See "Converting Songs to a Different Audio Format" later in this chapter.)

Ripping for the Future

By default, iTunes is set to compress your audio using what's currently the best and most efficient compressor, AAC. Will this remain the best? Almost certainly not. If you want to be prepared to create audio files using whatever emerges as the best option next, you may want to import as Apple Lossless. It'll take up more space—much more—but you'll always have an uncompressed version that you can convert to another format. (It's a bad idea to compress something that's already been compressed.)

You could do AIFF or WAV, too, but they're even larger than Apple Lossless (almost twice as large) and don't provide any additional quality.

Remember, however, that Apple Lossless files are about five to seven times larger than MP3s or AACs of near-equivalent sound quality. Thus, we recommend importing as Apple Lossless only if you have a lot of hard drive space or if you're not importing a lot of songs.

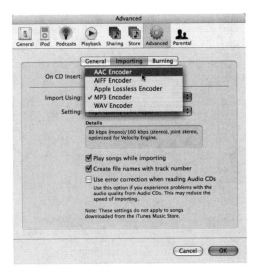

Figure 8.4 Change the encoding format by choosing an option from the Import Using pop-up menu.

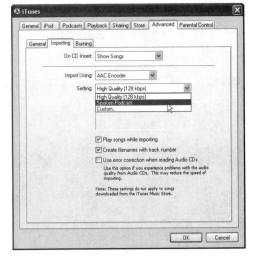

Figure 8.5 Change the settings for the selected encoder by choosing from the Setting pop-up menu.

✔ Tip

■ The changes you make here also apply to files you convert, and (on Windows) Windows Media Audio files added to your library. See "Converting Songs to a Different Audio Format" later in this chapter.

Changing How Songs Are Encoded on Import

By default, iTunes 6 is set to convert all imported songs to AAC. You can change the default encoding format. For example, you may want to import your songs as MP3 files if you plan to burn an MP3 CD (see Chapter 6). And for any format, you may decide that you want to change encoding settings to improve audio quality or create smaller files.

To change the encoding format and settings:

1. Click the Advanced and then the Importing tabs in the Preferences window (refer to Figure 8.2).

2. Change the encoding format by choosing from the Import Using pop-up menu (**Figure 8.4**).

3. If you've selected an encoder other than Apple Lossless, you can change the settings for the selected encoder by choosing from the Setting pop-up menu (**Figure 8.5**).

   You can either select a preset combination of settings or select Custom to pick your own combination.

   If you choose one of the presets, details about that preset appear in the Details field below the pop-up menu (refer to Figure 8.4).

4. If you've selected Custom, make choices in the window that appears (we cover these options in the following section, "About Custom Encoder Settings"); then click OK.

5. Click the OK button at the bottom of the Preferences window.

   The Preferences window closes. Your encoding settings are saved and will be used the next time you import an audio CD.

About Custom Encoder Settings

If you select Custom for your encoder setting (refer to Figure 8.5), a new window appears from which you'll pick a variety of settings. The options available differ depending on which encoder you selected. (See **Figures 8.6, 8.7, 8.8**.)

If you opt to pick custom settings, it's because you're not quite satisfied with the results you've achieved from the presets found in the Settings menu. To get results that sound better to your ears, you'll want to understand what each of the options means.

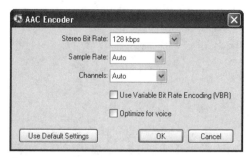

Figure 8.6 The window for setting custom MP3 encoding settings.

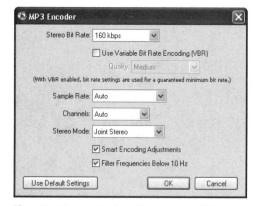

Figure 8.7 The window for setting custom AAC encoding settings.

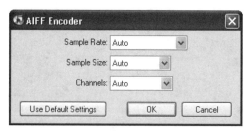

Figure 8.8 The window for setting custom AIFF encoding settings. (These options are identical for WAV custom encoding.)

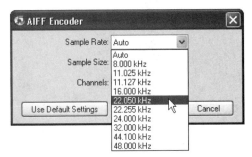

Figure 8.9 You can select a sample rate for all encoders.

Settings for all formats (except Apple Lossless)

◆ **Sample Rate.** Digitized sound is actually composed of a sequence of individual sound samples. The number of samples per second is the sample rate. The more sound samples per second, the higher the quality of the resulting sound but the larger the file.

For AAC, you have a choice only of 44.100 and 48.000 kHz (kilohertz); for the other encoders you have choices ranging from 8.000 kHz to 48.000 kHz (**Figure 8.9**). If you choose Auto (the default), it uses the same sample rate as the original, which is generally what you want for audio CD import. (Audio CDs, in case you care, are recorded at 44.1 kHz.)

◆ **Channels.** You'll have a choice of Stereo (two channels), Mono (one channel), or Auto (the same number of channels as the original). Most music from CDs has two channels of audio, so you'll want to set this option to Stereo or Auto for importing audio CDs. On the other hand, if you're converting existing audio files on your computer (as we describe later in this chapter), you may be better off with this set to Mono, since odds are that those files were recorded in mono.

ABOUT CUSTOM ENCODER SETTINGS

Settings for MP3 and AAC only

◆ **Stereo Bit Rate.** Possible bit rates range from 16 to 320 kbps (**Figure 8.10**). This setting specifies the average amount of data per second that is contained in the file (in kilobits per second), assuming that it's encoded in stereo. (If you choose Mono rather than Stereo as your Channels setting, the actual resulting bit rate is half of what you select for Stereo Bit Rate.) Higher bit rates mean higher quality but larger file sizes. A setting of 128 kbps is usually about right for music encoded with AAC, and 160 is good for MP3; these are the defaults.

◆ **Use Variable Bit Rate Encoding (VBR).** The idea behind variable bit rate encoding is that some parts of an audio recording (for example, where there's a higher range of frequencies) require more bits than others for optimal quality. Checking this box (refer to Figures 8.6 and 8.7) allows the encoder to "rob Peter to pay Paul"—in other words, to devote more bits to the parts that need it and less to the parts that don't, resulting in better overall quality—often without an increase in file size.

Settings for AAC only

◆ **Optimize for voice.** This one's pretty obvious; it's good for spoken word audio, such as podcasts. Don't use this for music.

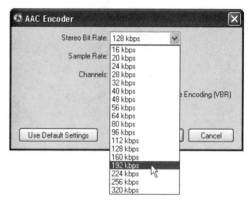

Figure 8.10 For MP3 and AAC, you can also specify a stereo bit rate.

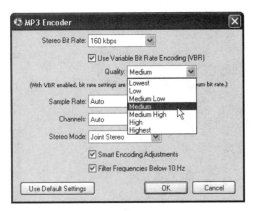

Figure 8.11 For MP3 encoding, you can request variable bit rate encoding at a specified quality level.

Settings for MP3 only

◆ **Quality.** If you check Use Variable Bit Rate Encoding, you can pick a Quality setting (**Figure 8.11**) that tells iTunes how flexible it can be in devoting extra bits to the "hard parts." The higher the quality setting, the better the resulting sound, but the price you pay is a larger file size.

◆ **Stereo Mode.** You can choose Joint Stereo or Normal. With Normal chosen, the MP3 file stores a "track" each for the right and the left channels, which can be redundant. Joint Stereo puts similar information in one track and the unique information in the other, producing smaller files; this can give you a better-sounding file when you encode at low bit rates (under 128 kbps).

◆ **Smart Encoding Adjustments.** If you select this, iTunes may adjust other settings (such as bit rate, number of channels, and sample rate) if it decides such changes will produce better-sounding audio. It makes adjustments only to settings that you haven't explicitly set.

◆ **Filter Frequencies Below 10 Hz.** Since frequencies below 10 Hz are essentially inaudible, this removes those frequencies, resulting in a smaller file.

Settings for WAV and AIFF only

◆ **Sample Size.** The size of the audio samples can be either 16 bit or 8 bit. A 16-bit sound sample represents audio more accurately but is twice as large as an 8-bit sound sample; for music you typically want a 16-bit sample size for best quality, but you pay with a file that's twice as large. If you choose Auto (iTunes' default), it uses the same sample rate as the original.

Converting Songs to a Different Audio Format

iTunes works as a nice little audio-conversion tool. This is useful, since the individual audio files you add from your hard drive (with the exception of Windows Media Audio files on Windows computers; chapter 2) don't get automatically converted to AAC or MP3 files, as do imported audio CD files.

To convert songs to a different audio format:

1. Set your encoding options in the Importing tab to indicate the format to which you want to convert. (See "Changing How Songs Are Encoded on Import" earlier in this chapter.)

2. Select the song or songs you want to convert.

3. From the Advanced menu, choose Convert Selection to AAC, Convert Selection to MP3, Convert Selection to Apple Lossless, Convert Selection to AIFF, or Convert Selection to WAV (**Figure 8.12**); only one of these appears depending on which format is selected in the Importing tab.

   iTunes converts the song, informing you of its progress in the status area (**Figure 8.13**). It typically begins playing the converted version of the song a few seconds after starting the conversion process.

   You'll find two versions of the song in your library when done (**Figure 8.14**).

Figure 8.12 From the Advanced menu, you can choose to convert to whatever encoding format is selected in the Importing tab of the Preferences window.

Figure 8.13 The status area shows you the progress of the conversion.

Figure 8.14 Both the original and the converted version are in your library.

✔ Tips

- You can also control-click (Mac) or right-click (Windows) on the item(s) in the Detail pane and choose Convert Selection to AAC (or other format) from the contextual menu that appears.

- Depending on your needs, you may want to delete the original song once you have the converted version.

- You can even use iTunes to convert files that aren't already in your library. Hold down the Option key (Mac) or Shift key (Windows) when clicking the Advanced menu, and your Convert choice is different. Instead of "Convert Selection to AAC," for example, the choice is "Convert to AAC." If you select this, a standard window for choosing a file appears. Locate and select the file(s) or folder(s) you want to convert, and click Choose. iTunes performs the conversion, putting the converted version in your library, and leaving the original as it was.

- This conversion ability means that iTunes is a free MP3 encoding utility. This is particularly useful if you're dealing with QuickTime files, since MP3 is not one of QuickTime's built-in export options.

- It's a bad idea to recompress something that's already been compressed. If you convert an MP3 file to AAC, for example, you'll suffer quality loss. It's always best to locate an uncompressed version, often an AIFF or WAV file. In the case of music from an audio CD, you should reimport the file if you don't already have an uncompressed version in your library. (See the sidebar "Ripping for the Future" earlier in this chapter.)

CONVERTING SONGS TO A DIFFERENT AUDIO FORMAT

Using the Equalizer

iTunes comes with a standard equalizer that allows you to optimize the tonal quality of your music. Do you prefer a heavier bass sound with your AC/DC? Looking for a clearer treble sound for your Gershwin tracks? The iTunes equalizer lets you tinker to your heart's content.

You can think of the equalizer as functioning somewhat like the bass and treble controls on your stereo, but with more precision and control over different frequencies.

To open the Equalizer window:

◆ Click the Equalizer button, located in the lower right corner of the iTunes window (**Figure 8.15**).

 Or

◆ (Mac only) From the Window menu, choose Equalizer.

The Equalizer window appears (**Figure 8.16**).

To choose an equalizer preset:

◆ Select from the pop-up menu at the top of the Equalizer window (**Figure 8.17**). You should choose an option that seems to describe the song you're listening to (for example, Jazz) or the change you'd like to make (for example, Treble Booster) or the environment in which you're listening (say, Small Speakers).

Figure 8.15 Click the Equalizer button to...

Figure 8.16 ...open the Equalizer window.

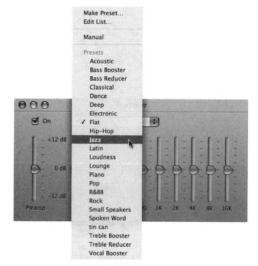

Figure 8.17 To enhance the sound of a song or audio file, you can choose a preset.

To manually adjust frequencies:

◆ Move any of the sliders up or down (refer to Figure 8.16).

   If you want more or less bass in your music, adjust the three leftmost frequency sliders. If you want more or less high-end frequencies (treble), adjust the rightmost three. If you want more mid-range tones (which tends to be the range for voice), adjust the middle four sliders. If you want all frequencies increased or decreased (because the music is too quiet or too loud), adjust the preamp slider.

✔ Tips

■ As you adjust the equalizer settings, it helps to keep the markers in a curve; otherwise, the audio will probably sound odd.

■ If you've adjusted equalizer settings but then decide the settings don't apply to what you're currently listening to, you should turn the equalizer off. To do this, uncheck the "On" box in the upper left of the Equalizer window (refer to Figure 8.16).

■ To get any one frequency to 0 dB, click its label at the bottom of the slider.

■ To return all sliders to 0 dB, click 0 dB or choose Flat from the pop-up menu.

■ To shrink the Equalizer window so it shows only the On check box and the pop-up menu for choosing presets, click the Zoom (Mac) or Maximize (Windows) button. Click the same button again to expand the window back to its full size.

What Do Those Sliders Really Mean?

Each of the 10 sliders represents a portion of the sound spectrum (a frequency); 32 Hz is the lowest (bass) and 16 kHz (16,000 Hz) is the highest (treble). The vertical axis is labeled in dB (decibels); this is a measurement of the intensity of the sound for that frequency. When you move a slider up, you're strengthening that frequency; when you move it down, you're decreasing its intensity.

USING THE EQUALIZER

Saving Equalizer Adjustments as Presets

If you've gone to the trouble of creating manual equalizer adjustments, you may want to save those adjustments as *presets*. You can call them up in the future, or you can assign them to specific songs or streams, as we describe in the next section.

To save your manually adjusted equalizer settings as a preset:

1. From the pop-up menu in the Equalizer window, choose Make Preset (**Figure 8.18**).

2. Type a name, and click OK (**Figure 8.19**). Your equalizer settings are saved as a preset and now appear in the pop-up menu in the Equalizer window.

To delete a preset:

1. From the pop-up menu in the Equalizer window, choose Edit List (refer to Figure 8.18).

2. In the Edit Presets window (**Figure 8.20**), select the preset you want to delete and click Delete.

3. If you are asked if you're sure you want to delete the preset, click Yes.

4. When you are asked if you want to delete the preset from songs that use it, click Yes.

5. Click Done.

   The preset is removed from the pop-up menu and any songs that use it.

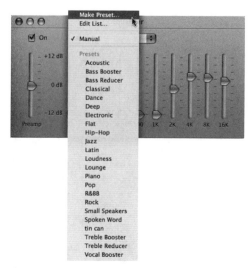

Figure 8.18 If you want to save your current settings as a preset, start by choosing Make Preset.

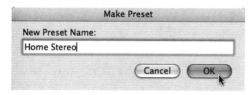

Figure 8.19 Provide a name for your current settings and click OK.

Figure 8.20 If you choose Edit List (refer to Figure 8.18), you can select and delete any preset.

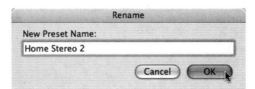

Figure 8.21 You can also choose Rename (refer to Figure 8.20) and then provide a new name in this window.

To rename a preset:

1. From the pop-up menu in the Equalizer window, choose Edit List (refer to Figure 8.18).

2. In the Edit Presets window, select the preset you want to rename (refer to Figure 8.20).

3. Click Rename.

4. In the Rename window, type a new name and click OK (**Figure 8.21**).

5. When you are asked if you want all songs that use the setting with the old name to use the setting with the new name, click Yes.

6. Click Done.
   The preset is renamed.

✔ Tips

- In the window that asks if you're sure you want to delete the preset, you can check "Do not warn me again" to avoid seeing this window in the future.

- If you click No in the window that asks if you want to delete the preset from songs that use it, you'll find that the preset remains assigned to the song, but since it's no longer in the presets pop-up menu, you can no longer apply it to other songs.

SAVING EQUALIZER ADJUSTMENTS AS PRESETS

Assigning Equalizer Presets to Streams or Songs

Although it's fine to make equalizer adjustments while you're playing music (just as you make adjustments on your stereo as you're listening), you may want to set equalizer adjustments for particular songs or radio streams.

To assign a preset to an individual song or stream:

1. Select the song or stream to which you want to assign a particular preset.

2. From the File menu, choose Get Info.

3. Click the Options tab.

4. Choose from the Equalizer Preset pop-up menu (**Figure 8.22**).

    The preset you've chosen is applied to the selected song or stream.

Figure 8.22 You can also assign an equalizer preset in the Info window for the song. (Select the song, choose File > Get Info, and click the Options tab to get this screen.)

Presets That Have Worked Well for Us

Our taste in music is bound to be different than yours, but these are the presets we've used most often.

◆ **Small Speakers.** We use this when we're using iTunes on computers with inexpensive speakers. (These don't generally produce enough bass; this preset boosts the low-end frequencies.)

◆ **Spoken Word.** We've used this for news radio streams and podcasts. This helps because these are often quite compressed and benefit from a boost in the middle frequencies.

◆ **Acoustic.** We like this for a lot of the folk music we like to listen to.

Figure 8.23 You can also assign a preset to a group of songs. (Select the songs and choose File > Get Info to see this screen.)

Figure 8.24 You can pick any equalizer preset just by clicking the pop-up icon for the song in the Equalizer column.

To assign a preset to multiple songs or streams:

1. Select multiple songs in the song list or one or more albums, artists, or genres in the Browser.

2. From the File menu, choose Get Info.

3. If asked if you're sure you want to edit multiple songs, click Yes.

4. Choose from the Equalizer Preset pop-up menu in the lower right of the window (**Figure 8.23**).

5. Click OK.

✔ Tips

■ If the Equalizer column is visible in your song list, you can click the pop-up button in the Equalizer column for the song to which you want to assign a preset and select a preset (**Figure 8.24**). (See "Hiding and Showing Columns" in the next chapter to see how to make the Equalizer column visible.)

■ One word of caution for those who will transfer their songs to the iPod: Equalizer settings are transferred with your songs and cause the iPod to process the song at playback; this processing takes extra battery power. This won't matter for one song, but if you do it for a lot you may find yourself recharging more often.

Adjusting Sound Settings

Besides the equalizer, iTunes provides a few other controls for enhancing your auditory experience. You'll find these on the Playback tab of the Preferences window.

To change sound settings:

1. From the iTunes menu (Mac) or the Edit menu (Windows), choose Preferences.

   The Preferences window appears.

2. Click the Playback tab (**Figure 8.25**), and then choose from the following options:

   ▲ **Crossfade playback.** This option affects what happens as one song ends and another starts. If it's checked (as it is by default), it causes the first song to fade out while the second song fades in, without any silence between them. The slider determines how long the overlap lasts.

   ▲ **Sound Enhancer.** When you check this, iTunes dynamically adjusts the loudness of various frequencies, as it sees fit. (This is similar to the loudness control on your stereo.) Some people have complained that it has made their MP3-encoded files actually sound worse; you should experiment with this on your own system.

   ▲ **Sound Check.** If you check this, iTunes looks at the volume of each song, compares it to the rest of the songs in your library, and makes adjustments so that all songs are equally loud. (This way, you won't have a situation where one song is relatively quiet and the next is so loud it blasts you out of your seat.)

3. Click OK to close the Preferences window and apply the settings you've chosen.

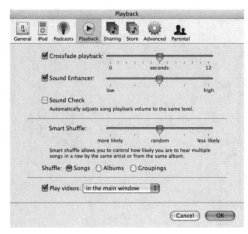

Figure 8.25 The Playback tab of the Preferences window lets you enhance your listening experience.

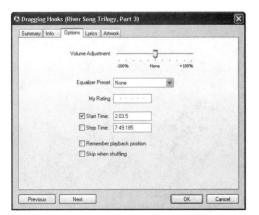

Figure 8.26 Type a start or stop time if you only want to listen to a specific portion of a song every time it's played.

Specifying Start and Stop Times

Occasionally, you'll find a song you'd rather not listen to from beginning to end. While you can skip over the beginning of a song (because of that boring introduction, for example) or stop playing it before it ends, iTunes also lets you assign a start and stop time so that every time you play the song it plays only the portion you like.

To specify start and stop times:

1. Select the song.

2. From the File menu, choose Get Info. The Info window for the song appears.

3. Click the Options tab.

4. Enter a new time in the Start Time and/or Stop Time fields (**Figure 8.26**).

   You can enter times as seconds or as minutes:seconds:thousandths of a second. For example, if you want 2 minutes and 3.5 seconds, you can enter 123.5 or 2:03:500.

5. Click OK to close the Info window.

Note that the value in the Time column (if it's showing) does not change, since the song itself has not been altered. You have merely told iTunes that, when it plays this song, you only want to hear a portion of it.

Your new start and stop times are respected when the song is played on your iPod, too.

Setting a Song to Remember Playback Position

You may have noticed that, when you play a podcast or audiobook or TV show, iTunes and the iPod remember where you stop listening so that the next time you play (no matter what you've played in between), it starts at the point you stopped. This is an option you can set for any item. Go to the Options tab in the Info window for the item in question (refer to figure 8.26), and check "Remember playback position." (This works only on iPods made after January 2004.)

Using the Visualizer

iTunes has one very cool feature for adding a visual component to your listening experience. This, of course, is the *visualizer,* which dynamically creates animated, abstract imagery that accompanies your music as it plays. (*Groovy, trippy,* and *far-out* are words that come to mind.) This is something you absolutely *have* to experience yourself; words are inadequate to describe it.

Ways to turn the visualizer on or off:

◆ Click the Visualizer button, located in the lower-right corner of the iTunes window (**Figure 8.27**).

◆ From the Visualizer menu, choose Turn Visualizer On or Turn Visualizer Off (**Figure 8.28**).

To choose the size of the visualization:

◆ From the Visualizer menu, choose Small, Medium, or Large (refer to Figure 8.28).

To turn full-screen mode on or off:

◆ From the Visualizer menu, choose Full Screen to check or uncheck this option (refer to Figure 8.28).

If you turn on full-screen mode, the visualizer takes over your whole screen; if you've selected Small or Medium, the actual visualization graphics show in a portion of the screen with a black background (**Figure 8.29**). When full-screen mode is off, the visualization occurs only within the confines of the iTunes window.

Figure 8.27 Click the Visualizer button to turn on the visualizer. Click it again to turn it off.

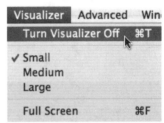

Figure 8.28 You can also turn the visualizer on or off from the Visualizer menu.

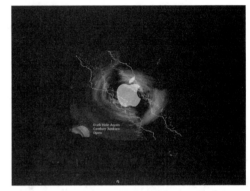

Figure 8.29 This is a result of selecting Small for the size of the visualization, and choosing Full Screen.

✔ Tips

■ To turn off the visualizer when it's in full-screen mode, simply click anywhere or press the Esc key.

■ You can temporarily turn on full-screen mode. You can do so when you turn the visualizer on: hold down the Option (Mac) or Shift (Windows) key when you click the Visualizer button. Or you can do so when the visualization is already playing in the iTunes window: click the Full Screen button in the lower left of the iTunes window.

Figure 8.30 Click the Options button in the top right corner of the iTunes window...

To specify basic visualizer options:

◆ With the visualizer running, click the Options button, located in the upper right corner of the iTunes window (**Figure 8.30**).

The Visualizer Options window opens and provides a handful of check boxes. (See **Figure 8.31** for a description of these check boxes.)

Puts a numeric value in the upper-left corner of the visualizer display. Represents how often the screen is changing, in frames per second.

Won't let the visualizer go beyond 30 frames per second. (This is an issue only on very fast computers.)

(Mac only) Uses the special 3-D graphics drawing engine of Mac OS X. Use if you have a fast graphics card.

Visualizer Options

- ☐ Display frame rate
- ☑ Cap frame rate at 30 fps
- ☐ Always display song info
- ☑ Use OpenGL
- ☐ Faster but rougher display

Cancel   OK

Puts song name, artist, album, and artwork (if there is any) in the lower-left corner (refer to Figure 8.29).

Draws fewer pixels on the screen, so images can draw faster.
Figure 8.31 ...to open the Visualizer Options window.

More Control Over Visualizations

If you watch the visualizer, you may become curious about what it's doing. There is actually something systematic going on: the visualizer starts with the basic waveform that represents the currently playing audio (which is constantly changing), and applies various graphical manipulations to that form.

Getting a little more specific, three properties change as a song plays: waveform representation, effects, and color scheme. The visualizer offers more than 75 possible waveform representations, 150 possible effects, and 60 possible color schemes. iTunes randomly changes each of these as the music plays. At any time, you can see the current value of each of these three properties, change any one of them, save the current configuration, and reload a configuration—all using keys on your keyboard. For a little experiment, with the visualizer running, try pressing Q, W, A, S, Z, X and notice how you affect the text display in the upper right of the window. Press the ? key to get more information.

Much more is documented in detail for iTunes 4 (but you'll still find it useful) at Susanne Z. Riehemann's iTunes Cheat Sheet, http://doors.stanford.edu/~sr/itunes/

USING THE VISUALIZER

Adding Song Artwork

If you've purchased songs at the iTunes Music Store, you've surely noticed that they came with album artwork; we also covered methods for viewing artwork in Chapter 2. You can add one or more graphics to songs yourself, regardless of the songs' origins.

The graphics you add can be in any number of formats, such as JPEG, TIFF, PNG, or GIF.

You can add artwork by dragging directly to the Artwork pane or by using the iTunes Info window; the former is easier but the latter provides a way to view multiple graphics, reorder them, and delete them.

To add Artwork to song(s) by dragging and dropping:

◆ Make sure the Artwork pane is showing, select the song(s) in the Detail pane, and drag a graphics file from the Finder (Mac) or Explorer (Windows), to the Artwork pane (**Figure 8.32**).

You can repeat this step to add additional graphics.

Click here to hide or show the Artwork pane

Figure 8.32 Drag files right into the Artwork pane.

Places to Find Album Artwork

If you're looking for album artwork on the Web to copy, your best bet is to look for sites that sell the albums. Amazon.com has the largest collection, but Walmart.com has higher resolution images. (At both of these sites, make sure to click to see the larger image and copy that one.) If you're looking for an independent artist, try allmusic.com. You may also want to try the Web site of the artist in question or try performing image searches at Google (www.google.com) or alltheweb (www.alltheweb.com).

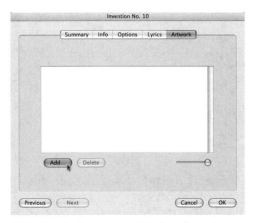

Figure 8.33 On the Artwork tab in the Info window, click the Add button (or you can copy and paste a graphic into the field on this tab).

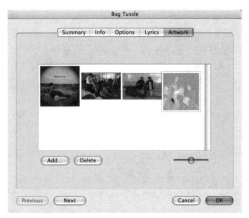

Figure 8.34 You can reorder graphics by dragging them right or left.

To add artwork to a song using the Info window:

1. Select the song in the Detail pane, and from the File menu, choose Get Info to bring up the iTunes Info window.

2. Click the Artwork tab, and *do one of the following:*

   ▲ Click the Add button (**Figure 8.33**), and in the window for choosing a file, navigate to a graphic file and click Open (Windows) or Choose (Mac).

   ▲ Select and copy the graphic from another application window, click in the Info window, and paste.

   ▲ Drag from another application or the Finder or Explorer to the field in the Artwork tab of the Info window.

   The graphic appears in the window.

3. If you want to add additional graphics for this song, repeat step 4. You can reorder these graphics: Click a graphic, and drag it to a new position (**Figure 8.34**).

4. Click OK to close the Info window.

   The artwork is added to the song and appears in the Artwork pane.

✔ Tips

■ If you have added multiple graphics, you view them by clicking the right-pointing and left-pointing arrow buttons that appear above the artwork pane. (These are not graphics that appear automatically at specified times when the song is playing.)

■ You can also drag a graphic from an application window or even a Web page to the artwork pane. (This needs to be an application that lets you drag from it. Most Mac applications let you do this; only some Windows applications do.)

continues on next page

ADDING SONG ARTWORK

- Mac users can drag file icons directly from iPhoto; the full-resolution image is added to the iTunes song.

- To paste into the Info window, Windows users can press Ctrl-V or right-click and choose Paste; Mac users can press Command-V or choose Paste from the Edit menu.

- Be forewarned that when you add art to an iTunes song, graphic information *also* gets added to the actual song file, thereby increasing its size. (The higher-res graphics you find at Amazon.com, for example, are typically around 25 kilobytes.) This makes a difference if you're planning to copy a lot of songs to any limited-space device, such as a small hard drive or one of the smaller capacity iPods such as the shuffle or nano.

- You can also drag a graphic directly from a Web page to the Artwork pane.

- To delete a graphic—regardless of the method you have used to add it—select it in the Artwork tab of the Info window (refer to Figure 8.33) and click the Delete button or press the Delete key on your keyboard.

- If you select multiple songs and then choose File > Get Info, you access the Multiple Song Information window (**Figure 8.35**), which has a small Artwork field. Double-click this field to open a window in which you can browse your computer for a graphic file; you can also paste a copied graphic or drag a graphic to this field. When you close the window the graphic is added to all selected songs.

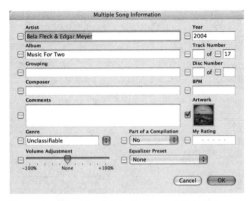

Figure 8.35 Double-click in the artwork field to be able to select a graphic file to be used as artwork for multiple songs. (Or click and paste into this field).

Tools to Help Get Artwork

You can find third-party software that helps you find and retrieve artwork for iTunes. Here are some that we've tried and liked:

◆ **iTunes Art Importer for Windows** (www.yvg.com/itunesartimporter.shtml) automatically "fetches" art from Amazon.com for the selected songs in iTunes (so you don't have to) and lets you add the artwork to iTunes.

◆ **Clutter for Mac OS** (www.sprote.com/ clutter) automatically retrieves artwork from Amazon.com when a song is playing in iTunes. You can tell Clutter to add the artwork to iTunes, or if you like, you can drag the artwork to your desktop, which creates an icon (cluttering your desktop in the process); when clicked, all the songs in your iTunes library from that album play.

◆ **Find Album Artwork with Google** (for Mac OS) is an AppleScript that you'll find at Doug's AppleScripts for iTunes (http://www.dougscripts.com/ itunes/index.php). Using the album name, it employs Google's image search to look for the artwork.

Figure 8.36 You can widen or narrow the Source and Artwork pane. This is especially helpful if you've having trouble viewing the full names of your playlists or audio CDs or if you're viewing videos in the Artwork pane.

Click the bar and drag up or down.

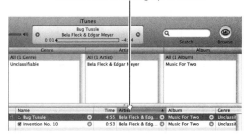

Figure 8.37 If you want to view more (or fewer) songs at one time, you can adjust the Browser area to make it taller or shorter.

Customizing the iTunes Window

As you become more familiar with iTunes, you may decide that your main iTunes window isn't precisely as you'd like it. You can make small tweaks to change the size of its elements or completely shrink the window down to a small window with only basic playback controls.

To change the width of the Source and Artwork pane:

1. Position your cursor anywhere on the narrow line to the right of the Source or Artwork pane.

   The cursor changes to a double-headed arrow.

2. Press your mouse button and drag to the right or left (**Figure 8.36**).

   As you drag right, the Source pane widens. As you drag left, it narrows.

To change the height of the Browser pane:

1. Position your cursor anywhere on the bar below the Browser pane.

   The cursor turns into a hand.

2. Press your mouse button and drag up or down to make the Browser pane shorter or taller (**Figure 8.37**).

   The cursor changes to a clenched hand when the mouse button is down.

To change the size of the text:

1. Open the General pane of the Preferences window.

2. Choose either Large or Small in the Source Text pop-up menu and the Song Text pop-up menu (**Figure 8.38**).

   Source Text refers to the items in your Source pane. Song Text refers to both the listing of songs and the items in the Browser.

3. Click OK to close the Preferences window.

   The size of the text appears slightly larger or slightly smaller, depending on which option you selected.

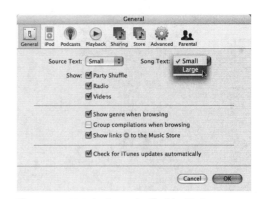

Figure 8.38 Use the General tab of the Preferences window to change the size of the text in the Source and Detail panes.

Figure 8.39 Mac users can click the Zoom button to switch to a mini player.

Figure 8.40 Windows users can choose Advanced > Switch to Mini Player.

Figure 8.41 The mini player—we show both Windows and Mac versions here—includes the basic playback controls and Status display. Click the Zoom button (Mac) or Maximize button (Windows) to return to the full iTunes window.

To switch between the full iTunes window and a mini player:

◆ Click the green Zoom button (Mac; **Figure 8.39**), or from the Advanced menu choose Switch to Mini Player (Windows; **Figure 8.40**).

The iTunes window shrinks to a mini player window (**Figure 8.41**).

Clicking the Zoom or Maximize button on the small window expands the window back to the full iTunes window.

✔ Tips

■ In the next chapter, we show you how to customize what you see in the Detail pane (hiding and showing columns, resizing them, and moving them).

■ If you drag the bar below the Browser (refer to Figure 8.37) up all the way, you'll hide the Browser. To reopen it, click the Browse button or choose Edit > Show Browser.

■ You can resize the entire iTunes window by dragging on the bottom-right corner, as you can windows in most Mac or Windows applications.

■ You can make the mini player even smaller by dragging the bottom right corner to the left; this removes the Status display.

■ If you want to make sure that mini player doesn't get lost behind any other windows, open the Preferences window, click the Advanced tab, and then click General. Check "Keep Mini Player on top of all other windows."

■ Windows users can use the minimize button in the iTunes window to put a mini player in the Windows task bar, if they change the default minimizing behavior: right-click in the task bar and choose Toolbars > iTunes (**Figure 8.42**). Once you set this, when you click the minimize button (in either the full iTunes window or the mini player window) the window collapses to a mini player in the task bar (**Figure 8.43**).

Figure 8.42 Windows users can right-click and choose Toolbars > iTunes.

Figure 8.43 ...so that a mini player shows in the task bar.

MANAGING YOUR LIBRARY

In the last chapter, we covered concepts and tasks that enhance your listening and viewing experience. In this chapter, we move to those topics that impact what happens in iTunes when you're not *playing* anything but, rather, when you're organizing, searching, updating, or otherwise managing your library.

A song is not just music (and podcasts and audiobooks are not just spoken words); each item in your library has information associated with it. This information affects how things look, how you can find specific content, and how files are stored on your hard drive.

Thus, in this chapter we cover the ins and outs of how your library "works": the important role of song information, how you can edit that information, and how you can show different categories of information. We'll then take you outside of iTunes, to the location on your hard disk where the actual song files reside and show you how to deal with them if you need to move them. At the end of the chapter we'll cover managing podcasts.

About Song Information

Many of the songs in your library already have information associated with them, such as the song title, artist, album, and file size. You've seen this information populating the columns in the song list.

How does this information get there? When you import songs from an audio CD, information for that specific CD is automatically downloaded from the Gracenote CDDB (Compact Disc Database), the online music database, as long as you're connected to the Internet. When you purchase music from the iTunes Music Store, the songs you download to your computer arrive complete with information and album artwork. And most MP3 files that you obtain from other sources have special tags that contain information about the songs (see the sidebar "About ID3 Tags").

The basic information that comes with just about all files includes name, artist, album, and genre. Year, track number, and disc number are often included as well, especially for music. Also for music, occasionally you'll see a composer or grouping listing provided. (The latter is used most often to indicate that a track is part of a larger piece and is most commonly included with classical music.) TV Shows have some specialized types of information associated with them, such as season.

✔ Tip

■ If basic information about a song is missing (or if you accidentally edit information), you can tell iTunes to try to get the data from the CDDB. To do this, select the song, and from the Advanced menu choose Get CD Track Names.

About ID3 Tags

ID3 tags, which contain song information, are found only in MP3 files. When you insert an audio CD into your CD drive, iTunes accesses CDDB, the online database that contains song information; if iTunes imports the song as an MP3, this data is placed in the file as an ID3 tag. (iTunes also places the CDDB data in AAC files, which can contain information much like ID3 tags, although what's in an AAC file is technically not an ID3 tag.)

Early versions of ID3 stored limited types of information (only artist, song name, album, year, genre, comments, and track number) and also restricted the maximum number of characters for each type of information to 30. The current implementation is much more flexible and supports all the information types that iTunes does. However, iTunes can read any version of ID3 tags through the current version (ID3 2.4.0).

You may find that you need to change the version of the ID3 tags in your MP3 file—for instance, if you have an older MP3 CD player that can't handle newer (version 2) ID3 tags. In this case, select the MP3 song, and from the Advanced menu, choose Convert ID3 Tags. A window appears in which you can change the version of the ID3 tags in your MP3 file. In this window, you can also select Reverse Unicode, something you may want to try if your song information contains odd or illegible characters. For Mac users, this window also offers options to switch between the ASCII (American Standard Code for Information Interchange) and ISO (International Organization for Standardization) Latin-1—use one of these options if you know you need one or the other of these character sets.

Figure 9.1 From the File menu, choose Get Info if you want to edit the information for one or more selected songs.

Editing Song Information

You can edit much of the information associated with your songs. Take advantage of this fact to correct data or fill in missing info. In particular, you can populate the Comments field with all sorts of keywords that will help you or iTunes locate or organize songs.

Ways to edit song information:

◆ Select the song(s) in the song list (see the sidebar "Selecting Songs" in Chapter 5 if you want to know methods for selecting). Then, from the File menu, choose Get Info (**Figure 9.1**); or right-click (Windows) or Control-click (Mac) and choose Get Info from the contextual menu.

continues on next page

Adding Lyrics to Your Songs

If you can find lyrics for a song (try www.searchlyrics.org or the Web site for the artist), or feel like typing them yourself, you can store them in your library. You can even show lyrics on an iPod.

To add lyrics to a song, select the song, choose File > Get Info, and click the Lyrics tab. Then click in the field and paste the lyrics.

If you've selected a single song, edit the information on the Info tab (**Figure 9.2**) of the Info window for that song. If you've selected multiple songs, the Multiple Song Information window (**Figure 9.3**) has fields in which you can edit or enter information that's common to all the songs.

◆ Click to select a song in the song list. Then click *once* in the column you'd like to edit for that song and type (**Figure 9.4**).

Typing directly in the song list like this works only for some columns: Name, Album, Artist, Comment, Composer, Genre, and Grouping.

✔ Tips

■ In the information window for a single song, click the Next or Previous button (refer to Figure 9.2) to edit the information about the next or previous song in the song list.

■ When you edit the text for Album, Artist, Composer, Grouping, or Genre directly in the song list (as in Figure 9.4), iTunes types ahead to match the first name (alphabetically) in your library that matches what you've typed thus far. Press Return (Mac) or Enter (Windows) to accept what iTunes has matched for you. Or just keep typing if it hasn't matched the right thing.

■ When you edit song information, iTunes may, depending on the preferences you've set, make changes to the files and folders on your hard drive that contain the songs. To understand more about what happens on your hard drive, see "How iTunes Organizes Files on Your Hard Drive," later in this chapter.

■ Don't expect to be able to edit everything in the Info windows that you can in the columns, and vice-versa.

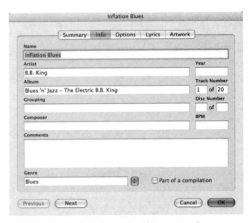

Figure 9.2 If you're editing the information for a single song, the information window for the song appears. You edit on the Info tab.

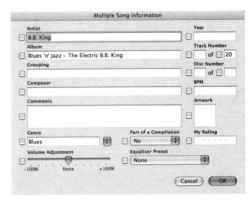

Figure 9.3 If you're editing information about multiple songs at one time, the Multiple Song Information window appears. Changes you make here apply to all the songs you selected.

Figure 9.4 You can also click and edit information directly in the song list. This text has been clicked and is now editable.

Figure 9.5 Link arrows like this appear in the Name, Artist, and Album columns.

Figure 9.6 After clicking the B.B. King Link arrow, you're at the B.B. King page inside the Music Store.

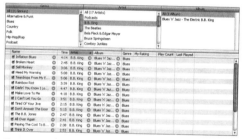

Figure 9.7 After Option-clicking (Mac) or Ctrl-clicking (Windows) the B.B. King Link arrow, you'll be in your music library, looking at all your B.B. King songs.

✔ **Tip**

■ Don't like the arrows? Open the General tab of the Preferences window and uncheck the "Show links to the Music Store" checkbox.

Locating Similar Songs

Like the song in your library that you just listened to? Want to hear more like it? iTunes provides a quick way to locate other songs by an artist or on an album, in the Music Store or in your own library, using the Link arrows that appear in the Name, Artist, and Album columns (**Figure 9.5**).

To locate an artist or album in the Music Store:

◆ Click the Link arrow for the artist, album, or song.

For a song you'll go to the album page with the song selected; for an artist or album you'll go to the corresponding artist or album page (**Figure 9.6**).

If you click the Link arrow for a song or album which isn't represented in the store, you'll end up on the page for the artist.

If the artist isn't represented in the iTunes Music Store at all—as of this writing there was no Led Zeppelin, for example—the Music Store Power Search page opens with song, album, artist, composer filled in, so that presumably you can change your search.

To locate an artist or album in your library:

◆ Hold down the Option key (Mac) or Ctrl key (Windows) and click a Link arrow in the Artist or Album column.

iTunes opens the Browser (see Chapter 3 if you're not familiar with the Browser) and automatically selects that artist (**Figure 9.7**) or album, resulting in a display of all songs in your library that have the artist name or album name that was next to the Link arrow you clicked.

Grouping Compilations for Better Browsing

If you've got a bunch of compilation albums (containing songs by a number of different artists) that you've imported from CD or purchased, it's usually a good idea to group them. This not only lets you browse your compilations separately from the rest of your albums but also removes from the Artists column of the Browser any artists that are only represented in compilations. (When we group our compilations, the number of artists showing in the Artist column of the browser goes from 560 to 228.) Here's how you can do it.

To group compilations:

1. Open the General tab of the Preferences window.

2. Check "Group compilations when browsing" (**Figure 9.8**).

The Artist column in the Browser includes an entry of Compilations, which when clicked displays all songs that have been marked as "part of a compilation" in the song's information window (refer to Figure 9.2). Additionally, if a particular artist represented in your library only has songs that are parts of compilations, their name won't show up in the Artist column of the Browser at all (**Figure 9.9**). You can click in the Album column of the Browser to display songs from a particular compilation album.

✔ Tip

■ If you group compilations, the Browser only lists artists that have their own albums. So, even if your library contains lots of songs by a particular artist, if they're spread out over compilation albums, that artist won't be listed. If you're in this situation, you may prefer not to group compilations.

Figure 9.8 Choose "Group compilations when browsing" in the Preferences window.

Figure 9.9 You now see Compilations in the Artists column and fewer total artists listed (assuming you had songs by artists only represented on compilation albums).

Figure 9.10 Control-click (Mac) or right-click (Windows) any column head to make this pop-up menu appear. Check or uncheck items to show or hide the column of that name.

Figure 9.11 From the Edit menu, choose View Options...

Figure 9.12 ...to open the View Options window. Add checkmarks to indicate which columns you want to have appear.

Hiding and Showing Columns

You can specify the song information you want to display by showing and hiding different columns.

To add or remove columns (I):

1. Control-click (Mac) or right-click (Windows) any column head.

   A pop-up menu appears (**Figure 9.10**).

2. Select any item that has no checkmark to add a column with that name; select an item with a checkmark to remove the column with that name.

   Since you can change only one item at a time, this method works best when you have only one or a few columns to show or hide.

To add or remove columns (II):

1. From the Edit menu, choose View Options (**Figure 9.11**).

   The View Options window appears (**Figure 9.12**).

2. Click items that have no checkmarks to add columns with those names; click items with checks to remove columns with those names.

3. Click OK.

✔ Tip

■ Option-click (Mac) or Ctrl-click (Windows) on any one check box in the View Options window to select or deselect all the check boxes at once.

Changing Order and Size of Columns

Once you've decided which columns you want to display, you can change their order and size. For example, you may want to widen the Name column so you can view your song titles in their entirety, or you might want to move the Size column to a more visible position, which is helpful when you're choosing songs to burn to a CD.

To change the order of the columns:

1. Click any column (other than Name), and drag it to the right or left.

   As you drag to the right or left of other columns, space opens up to show that you can drop the column there (**Figure 9.13**).

2. Release your mouse button when the column is located where you'd like it.

To change the width of a column:

1. Position your cursor over the dividing line between column heads, so that the cursor changes to a vertical bar with double arrows (**Figure 9.14**).

2. Click and drag right or left to widen or narrow the column to the left of the cursor.

   When a column is as small as iTunes will allow, the cursor changes to show a vertical bar with only a right-pointing arrow.

Figure 9.13 You can change the position of columns by dragging a column head. (The Name column, however, can't be moved from the far left.)

Figure 9.14 Change the width of columns by clicking the line between column heads and dragging right or left.

Figure 9.15 Control-click (Mac) or right-click (Windows) on a column head and choose Auto Size Column to make that column just wide enough to fit the longest item in it.

Figure 9.16 Control-click (Mac) or right-click (Windows) on a column head and choose Auto Size All Columns to make each column just wide enough to fit the longest item in that column.

How Many Versions of That Song?

Show Duplicate Songs is a command in the Edit menu. If you choose this, iTunes shows all the songs with duplicate titles. (Our warning: Be careful when deleting duplicates because iTunes doesn't look at any other columns when determining if a song is a duplicate. You wouldn't want to accidentally throw away your live version of a song just because you also have the studio version of that same song.) When you want to see all songs again, not just those for which you have duplicates, just click the Show All Songs button that's in the area below the song list.

To autosize columns:

◆ Control-click (Mac) or right-click (Windows) the column head and choose Auto Size Column (**Figure 9.15**) to make the column just wide enough to fit the longest item in the column.

◆ Control-click (Mac) or right-click (Windows) on any column head and choose Auto Size All Columns (refer to Figure 9.15) to make all columns just wide enough to fit the longest item in each of them (**Figure 9.16**).

✔ Tips

■ Some columns, such as Rating, can't be resized.

■ The Name column always needs to be at the far left. You can't move it right, and you can't move another column to its left.

■ If you want to move a column that's off-screen to a more visible position, it's sometimes quickest to remove the column and then add it back, using the first method covered in "Hiding and Showing Columns" earlier in this chapter.

How iTunes Organizes Files on Your Hard Drive

iTunes designates a special folder that it refers to as the *iTunes Music folder*. When you first install iTunes, this folder is named "iTunes Music." For Mac users, this special folder resides by default in the iTunes folder located in the Music folder of your home folder. In Windows, the default location of the iTunes Music folder is My Documents\ My Music\iTunes. You'll see the path to this folder listed on the Advanced tab of the Preferences window (**Figure 9.17**); you can, however, identify a different folder as your iTunes Music folder, as we'll discuss later in this chapter.

This is where iTunes stores music files.

If this is checked, everything in your iTunes Music folder will be structured and named according to song information.

If this is checked, iTunes copies all songs you move into your library from your hard drive to the folder listed above.

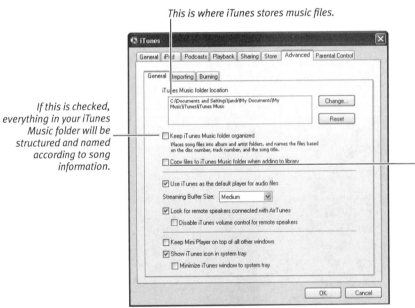

Figure 9.17 The Advanced tab of the Preferences window lists the location of the iTunes Music folder, which is where iTunes stores many, if not all, of the files for the music in your library.

Implications of Keeping Your Music Folder Organized

If you have selected the "Keep iTunes Music folder organized" check box, iTunes renames files and folders and moves song files around so that the songs are in folders that match what's listed for artist and album and so that the song files have names that match what's listed for song name. (This affects only files and folders that are in your iTunes Music folder.) Some examples:

◆ If you edit a song's artist info (for example, adding a middle initial or listing only last name) or album info (perhaps adding a subtitle), iTunes creates a new folder and moves the song file (and possibly other folders) around accordingly.

◆ If you add an MP3 or AAC file to your library, and you've checked "Copy files to iTunes Music folder when adding to library," iTunes renames the copied version of the file (if necessary) to match the song name embedded in the file. (The song name is stored in the ID3 tag for an MP3 file and in the equivalent of the ID3 tag for an AAC file.) iTunes may also create folders to match what's listed for album and artist.

◆ If you drag an entire folder of music into iTunes and you've checked "Copy files to iTunes Music folder when adding to library," the copied version of the folder may be completely restructured the way iTunes thinks it should be, which may not be the way it was. Note, however, that the original folder remains untouched (assuming that the original folder was not inside your iTunes Music folder).

What files are in your iTunes Music folder?

The files iTunes automatically places in the iTunes Music folder are those for songs that you import from CD or that you buy from the iTunes Music Store.

If you have "Copy files to iTunes Music folder when adding to library" checked (refer to Figure 9.17), any song files you add to your library from your hard drive are also added to this folder.

Additionally, if you are a Mac user and told iTunes to Find Music Files when you first launched (refer to Figure 1.18 in Chapter 1), your pre-iTunes music files were all copied there.

What's the folder structure?

Within your iTunes Music folder, iTunes organizes files in a simple artist-album-song hierarchy; that is, every song you import from CD or purchase from the iTunes Music Store goes into a folder named for an album (or "Unknown Album" if the album can't be determined), and almost every one of these album folders is located in a folder named for an artist (or "Unknown Artist" if the artist can't be determined). **Figure 9.18** shows how this looks in the file system.

Songs added from your hard drive are placed in the iTunes Music folder in the same way, assuming that you've checked "Copy files to iTunes Music folder when adding to library."

To achieve all this, iTunes depends primarily on the artist and album information you see and can edit (as described at the beginning of this chapter). iTunes also uses the song name information to determine the names of song files.

If you edit song name, album, or artist information in iTunes (as covered earlier in this chapter) and you've checked "Keep iTunes Music folder organized" (refer to Figure 9.17), you may change the names and/or the structure of what's stored on your hard drive. For examples, see the sidebar "Implications of Keeping Your Music Folder Organized."

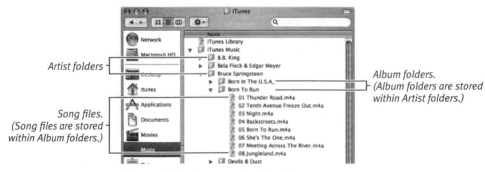

Figure 9.18 Here's an example of how iTunes structures the iTunes Music folder.

✔ Tips

- One exception to the artist-album-song hierarchy occurs in the case of a song that is checked as part of a compilation (refer to the bottom right of the window shown in Figure 9.2); in this case, the song is placed in its correct album folder, but that album folder is placed in a folder called Compilations that resides alongside the artist folders. (In other words, whatever is listed as artist is ignored for purposes of hard drive organization when a song is part of a compilation.)

- Another exception occurs with podcasts, which are all put in a Podcasts folder that resides alongside the various artist folders. Within the Podcasts folder, the podcasts are grouped in folders that match what's in the Album column (what you'd normally consider the name of the podcast). This, incidentally, matches the organization of the iTunes Music Store.

- If you've left "Keep iTunes Music folder organized" unchecked and then decide to check it, upon closing the Preferences window iTunes will create folders and move files as necessary within the iTunes Music folder so that everything resides in the preferred hierarchy. The program will not touch anything outside of the designated iTunes Music folder.

- If you're ever curious about where a particular song resides on your hard drive, you can select the song in iTunes and choose Get Info from the File menu; the location appears at the bottom of the Summary pane. Alternatively, you can select the song and choose Show Song File from the File menu.

Choosing a New iTunes Music Folder

If you want iTunes to start using a new folder to store all music files—perhaps because you've added a new, bigger hard drive to your computer that you want to start using to store your music—you can tell the program to change the iTunes Music folder.

To choose a new iTunes Music folder:

1. Open the Advanced tab of the Preferences window; make sure you are on the General sub-tab (rather than Importing or Burning).

   Notice the current location of your Music folder. By default, it's in Home/Music/ iTunes/iTunes Music (Mac) or My Documents\My Music\iTunes\iTunes Music folder (Windows).

2. Click the Change button (**Figure 9.19**).

3. Locate the new folder you want to use, and click Choose (Mac) or OK (Windows).

   The new location is listed as the iTunes Music Folder location (**Figure 9.20**).

Figure 9.19 Click Change if you want iTunes to store song files in a new folder.

Figure 9.20 Notice the new location for the iTunes music folder.

Moving Your Song Files to Another Location

As your library grows or as your computer system changes (or both), you may decide that you need to move your collection of song files from one physical location to another.

To move the files in your iTunes library to a different location (another hard disk, for example) on your current computer system, you should first change your iTunes Music folder location to the desired new location and then consolidate your library (as described on the next page). iTunes copies all the files in your library to the new iTunes Music folder and structures them in its preferred artist-album hierarchy.

If you need to move the files to a different computer, you should copy your iTunes Music folder (read the preceding pages if you have trouble finding this folder) to a temporary location on the new computer, perhaps transferring them via a portable hard disk. Then, with both "Copy files to iTunes Music folder when adding to library" and "Keep iTunes Music folder organized" checked in the General tab of the Advanced tab (refer to Figure 9.19), drag the copied iTunes Music folder to the Library icon in your Source pane. (Or use any other method for adding songs to your library; see "Adding Audio Files from Your Computer," in Chapter 2.) You'll want to delete the folder in the temporary location, so you don't take up all that space on your hard drive.

4. Cli... iTu... bar, and ... move... iTune... iTune... ence?' nizes a... to mat...

The file... ously in...

If you w... .... new loca-tion, read the next page.

The files for songs you import from CD or download from the iTunes Music Store in the future will be put in this new location. In addition, songs added from your hard drive in the future will be placed here, assuming you've checked "Copy files to iTunes Music folder when adding to library."

Consolidating Your Hard D...

It's possible ... iTunes lib... drive ...

...Songs on ...Drive

...hat the music files in your ...rary are scattered all over your hard ...perhaps even on multiple hard drives. ...is is most likely to happen if you have had "Copy files to iTunes Music folder when adding to library" unchecked in your iTunes preferences or if you've changed the location of your iTunes library. If you'd like to keep all your music in one place—especially handy if you want to back up your music—you can tell iTunes to gather everything up into your iTunes Music folder.

To move all your music files into your iTunes Music folder:

◆ From the Advanced menu, choose Consolidate Library (**Figure 9.21**).

iTunes shows a window giving you a chance to change your mind (**Figure 9.22**).

If you click Consolidate, any files not in your designated iTunes Music folder are moved there and placed in an artist-album hierarchical structure, based on the information iTunes stores about the songs.

Figure 9.23 shows the location of a song file as it is displayed in the information window before consolidation.

Figure 9.24 shows the location of the same song file after consolidation. Notice that the folder structure has changed considerably.

✔ Tip

■ If "Keep iTunes Music folder organized" is unchecked (refer to Figure 9.19) when you consolidate your library, iTunes moves song files into album and artist folders that match the album and artist information associated with the song, but it *doesn't* rename the files to match the song names in your iTunes library.

Figure 9.21 From the Advanced menu, choose Consolidate Library when you want to move all your song files into your iTunes Music folder.

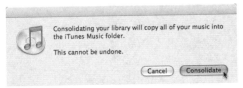

Figure 9.22 Click Consolidate as long as you're sure you want everything moved to your iTunes folder.

Path before consolidation.

Figure 9.23 The Summary tab in the Information window for a song before consolidation.

Path after consolidation.

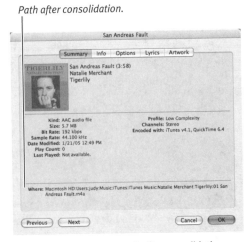

Figure 9.24 The Summary tab after consolidation.

Managing Podcasts

Podcasts are special, complex creatures. Unlike songs, podcasts set you up for an ongoing relationship. And like all relationships, there's a little work involved. iTunes has to do extra work to keep your podcasts coming. You may have to do extra work to manage your podcasts. It's no wonder that iTunes has a special interface for managing podcasts, accessed by clicking Podcasts in the Source list (**Figure 9.25**). iTunes lists any podcasts you've subscribed to or even downloaded a single episode from. There's lots of information available here and a number of tasks you can accomplish.

Blue dots next to podcast names indicate that there are episodes still to be listened to.

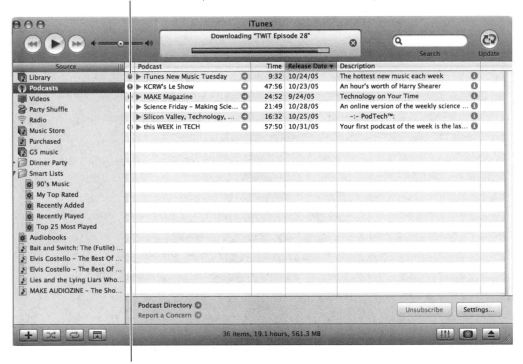

Exclamation points indicate that iTunes automatically unsubscribed you because you haven't listened to any episodes from this podcast in quite a while.

Figure 9.25 Click Podcasts in your source list to be able to manage your podcasts.

To show podcast episodes:

◆ Click the disclosure triangle for the podcast in which you're interested (**Figure 9.26**).

You see the specific episodes you down-loaded (the items that are in your library), as well as (if you subscribed) older epi-sodes that you may want to get (by click-ing the Get button).

To change the frequency with which iTunes checks for new episodes:

◆ Click the Settings button in the lower right corner of the iTunes window (refer to Figure 9.25), which opens the iTunes Preferences window to the Podcasts tab, and choose from the "Check for new episodes" pop-up menu (**Figure 9.27**).

To specify what episodes to keep in your library:

◆ Click the Settings button in the bottom right corner, and choose from the Keep pop-up menu (**Figure 9.28**).

A blue dot next to a podcast episode indicates that the episode has not been listened to at all; the blue dot goes away if you even start to listen to the episode.

Figure 9.26 Click the disclosure triangle for a podcast to show individual episodes.

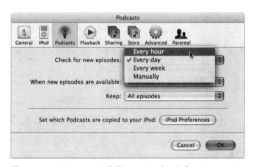

Figure 9.27 You can tell iTunes to check for new episodes more or less frequently than its default of every day.

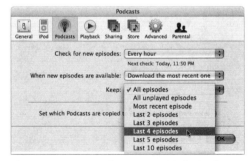

Figure 9.28 You can tell iTunes get rid of episodes after a while.

Figure 9.29 It's easy to tell iTunes to stop downloading episodes. Just select the podcast (or one of its episodes) and click Unsubscribe.

Figure 9.30 It's also easy to subscribe to a podcast.

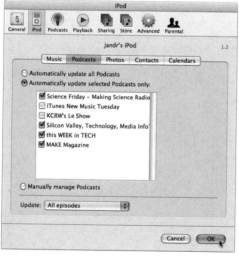

Figure 9.31 You can pick the podcasts that should go on your iPod.

To unsubscribe (so you don't get future episodes):

◆ Select the podcast (or any episode from that podcast), and click the Unsubscribe button down in the bottom right corner (**Figure 9.29**).

To subscribe to a podcast you've unsubscribed from or have only downloaded individual episodes:

◆ Click the Subscribe button next to the podcast name (**Figure 9.30**).

To specify which podcasts should be copied to your iPod:

◆ In the Podcasts tab of the iTunes Preferences window (refer to Figure 9.27), click the iPod Preferences button, and select the podcasts you want routinely copied to your iPod (**Figure 9.31**).

✔ Tip

■ You can cancel the download of a podcast episode by clicking the x button in the status display. If you do so, a listing remains in the Podcast list, and you can later click Get to tell iTunes to download the episode anew.

CUSTOMIZING YOUR iPOD

10

This chapter covers topics that let you personalize your listening experience. When you were getting familiar with your iPod, you probably didn't need to know any of this stuff—you couldn't even guess, for example, that you might want to change what you see in your iPod's main menu—but now you're beginning to figure out what you do and don't like about the operation of the iPod.

We start the chapter showing how to pick specific items to copy to your iPod and then move on to demonstrating how to change what you see in your iPod menus. We also cover settings that impact what you hear—playback order, playback speed, playback volume, and playback tonal quality. In case you haven't already discovered it, we show you how to view artwork and lyrics for songs on your iPod. We also cover the ultimate in making the iPod exclusively yours: locking it with a combination.

We end the chapter with an overview of your options for playing your iPod without headphones—in your home and in your car.

Once again, we need to mention that much of what's in this chapter doesn't apply to the iPod shuffle. Shuffle owners will find a couple of sections at the beginning of the chapter, exclusively for them. The sections at the end, about playing your iPod at home and in your car, also apply. Other than that, everything requires a display on your iPod.

✔ Tip

- We'll show you how to make lots of settings adjustments to your iPod in this chapter. If you make a mess, you can always restore your iPod's default settings. From your iPod's main menu, choose Settings, then choose Reset All Settings, and then choose Reset.

Putting Only Selected Items on Your iPod

Figure 10.1 Click the iPod Options button if you want to change your updating preferences.

Are there specific songs you know you want on your iPod and others you definitely don't want? Are you sick of having iTunes automatically add or delete songs? Do you just want to be in complete control? You can drag individual songs and playlists to your iPod, just as if it was a playlist. First, you'll need to change your updating preferences.

To change iPod updating preferences to manual updating:

1. Connect your iPod to your computer, and in iTunes select the iPod in the Source pane.

2. Click the iPod Options button at the bottom right of the iTunes window (**Figure 10.1**).

   This opens the iTunes Preferences window to the iPod tab.

3. Choose "Manually manage songs and playlists." (**Figure 10.2**).

4. When iTunes warns you that you'll have to manually eject your iPod if you switch to manual updating mode (**Figure 10.3**), click OK.

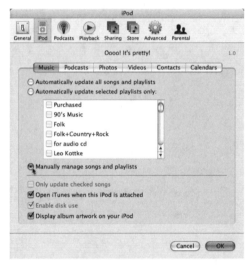

Figure 10.2 If you set your iPod for manual updating, you'll be able to drag individual songs or playlists to your iPod.

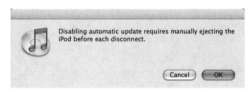

Figure 10.3 When you switch to manual updating, iTunes warns you that you'll have to eject the iPod before disconnecting it.

Figure 10.4
Click the disclosure triangle to hide and show the playlists on the iPod.

Figure 10.5 Once you're in manual updating mode, you can drag songs directly from your iTunes library to your iPod.

5. Click OK to close the Preferences window.

All files and playlists that had previously been on your iPod are now viewable and *manipulable* in the song list. You can see the playlists on your iPod by clicking the disclosure triangle to the left of the iPod entry in your Source pane (**Figure 10.4**).

You'll find you can't use your iPod—the display shows nothing but the "Do not disconnect" warning—until you eject it. (One method for doing this is to click the eject icon next to the iPod icon and name in your Source pane. We cover other methods later in this chapter; see "Ejecting Your iPod.")

The updating choice you make in the iPod Preferences window is applied to the iPod, so until you change your updating preferences again, whenever you connect the iPod to a computer it will be in manual update mode and you can add and delete songs and playlists as we describe next.

To manually add songs to your iPod:

1. Select the source (your library or any playlist, for example) that contains the song(s) you want on the iPod.

2. Select and drag the songs to the iPod icon or to any playlist on the iPod. (**Figure 10.5** shows an example of dragging songs from an iTunes playlist to an iPod playlist.)

After you drag items to the iPod or its playlists, the Status display informs you that iTunes is updating the iPod.

To manually add playlists to your iPod:

◆ Select and drag any playlist or folder of playlists to the iPod icon. (**Figure 10.6**).

If you drag a playlist, iTunes copies it to the iPod and it appears indented directly below the iPod icon.

If you drag a folder of playlists, iTunes adds to your iPod a new playlist that contains the contents of all playlists that were in the folder.

✔ Tips

■ Although you can drag specific podcast episodes to your iPod, you'll probably want to tell your iPod to always copy newly downloaded episodes from certain podcasts. See "Managing Podcasts," in chapter 9.

■ Wondering why, after switching to manual updating, you now have to eject your iPod? You may have noticed that when you switch to manual mode, iTunes automatically checks "Enable disk use" and locks it (so you can't uncheck it). Enabling disk use is what allows you to use the iPod as a hard disk (see next chapter), but it also requires you to eject the iPod before disconnecting it.

Figure 10.6 You can drag entire playlists to your iPod.

Copying Music from Multiple Computers to Your iPod

Do you have more than one iTunes library on different computers—one at home and one at work, for example? If you want to be able to add music from both of your iTunes libraries, we suggest that you start by syncing your iPod with one computer using an automatic update; but *before* you eject the iPod, switch to manual updating. When you plug your iPod into another computer, you won't see the message that your iPod is already linked to another library (as in Figure 4.5 in Chapter 4) and you will be able to drag new songs and playlists to it. (If you forgot to switch to manual updating, just click No when you see that message and go ahead and switch to manual updating on the computer you're on.) As long as you keep your iPod set to manual updating, there should be no problem adding songs from any computer that's running iTunes.

If you're transferring songs from both Windows and Macintosh computers, you'll have to establish the initial connection on the Windows computer. This is because the iPod needs to be formatted for Windows; a Mac can read a Windows-formatted disk but not vice versa. (Note: Apple has said that you *should not* share an iPod between Mac and Windows computers, but we can report that we've been doing it without problems. Your mileage may vary.)

Apologies to iPod shuffle users: iTunes doesn't let you copy music from different libraries to your shuffle. If you click No in response to the question of linking your iPod to a new library, you won't be able to view the shuffle in iTunes.

Why Can't I Transfer Songs from My iPod to iTunes?

You may be in a position where you really want to drag a song from your iPod library to your iTunes playlist. Sorry. You can't do it using iTunes. Apple, to discourage rampant illegal copying from one library to another using the iPod as the transfer mechanism, made it impossible to copy songs from an iPod to an iTunes library.

However, there are some ways around this design limitation. (We trust you've got a good—and legal—reason for copying from your iPod to a computer!)

For one thing, the files are actually stored in an invisible folder on your iPod. If you know how to show invisible (or *hidden*) files and folders, you'll be able to see the song files on the iPod in the Finder (Mac) or in Explorer (Windows).

Some third-party tools let you transfer files from an iPod to a computer. We've found several at www.ilounge.com/index.php/ipod-software/. Choose your platform (Windows, Mac OS X, Mac OS 9, or Linux) in the gray bar, and look through the listings.

Being Picky About What's on Your iPod Shuffle

In Chapter 4, we covered how you get a random assortment of songs from your library onto your iPod shuffle. In Chapter 5, we showed you how to finesse that a bit, autofilling from only selected playlists. On this page, we want to go over a few additional options for gaining more control over what goes on your shuffle.

Methods for controlling what goes on your shuffle:

◆ Select the iPod shuffle in the Source pane, and uncheck "Choose songs randomly" (**Figure 10.7**). This way iTunes will copy the songs in the order they are listed in the song list.

◆ Rate your songs (as described in Chapter 3), and—as long as you have "Choose songs randomly" checked—check "Choose higher rated songs more often" (refer to Figure 10.7).

◆ In your library, uncheck songs you don't want copied to your iPod shuffle, click the iPod Options button in the bottom-right corner of the iTunes window (refer to Figure 10.1), and then check "Only update checked songs" (**Figure 10.8**).

◆ Add and delete songs manually, as described on the next page.

Figure 10.7 If complete randomness isn't for you, uncheck "Choose songs randomly." (Or, leave it checked and check "Choose higher rated songs more often" to tell iTunes to put only the best on your shuffle.)

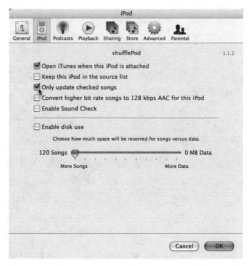

Figure 10.8 You can also uncheck songs and then tell iTunes not to copy unchecked songs to your shuffle.

Conserving Space on a Shuffle

Because you have very limited space on an iPod shuffle, you can have iTunes convert higher bit-rate files (those 160 kbps and higher) to AAC files at 128 kbps before transferring them to your iPod. (See Chapter 8 for more information on different audio formats.)

To set this conversion, click the iPod Options button for the iPod and check "Convert higher bit rate songs to 128 kbps AAC for this iPod."

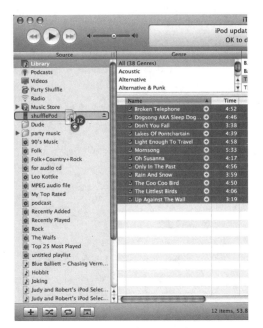

Figure 10.9 You can always drag songs from your iTunes library to the shuffle.

Adding and Deleting Individual Songs on Your iPod Shuffle

Unlike other iPods, you don't need to change your updating mode to copy specific items to your iPod shuffle; you can drag individual songs to it and delete them at any time! What's even cooler is that you can drag songs to your shuffle and delete songs from it even when that little device isn't physically connected; iTunes can keep an icon for your shuffle in the Source pane at all times.

To add specific songs to your shuffle:

◆ Drag songs from your library to your shuffle (**Figure 10.9**).

If there's no room for a new song (as would likely be the case if you previously autofilled it), you'll see a message to that effect; you'll have to do some deleting.

You can also drag playlists from your library to the shuffle; the songs in the playlist get copied to the shuffle.

To delete songs from your shuffle:

◆ Select your shuffle in the Source pane, select the song or songs you want to delete, and press the Delete key on your keyboard (or use any of the options for deleting songs in iTunes that we covered at the end of Chapter 2).

ADDING AND DELETING INDIVIDUAL SONGS

To set your iPod shuffle so you can add and delete songs even when it's not connected:

1. Select the shuffle in your Source pane, and click the iPod Options button (refer to Figure 10.1).

   The iTunes Preferences window appears, opened to the iPod tab.

2. Check "Keep this iPod in the source list" (**Figure 10.10**).

3. Click OK.

When you disconnect your iPod, you'll find that an entry for it still appears in your Source pane. You can add songs to it or delete songs from it. (Added songs that haven't yet made it to the physical device have a dot next to them, as in **Figure 10.11**.) When you next connect the shuffle, it is automatically updated, so what's on it matches what you had put in its song list in iTunes.

✔ Tip

■ Remember the Sound Check option we covered in Chapter 8? It's the feature that helps to even out the volume across multiple songs. If you've turned it on in iTunes, you should check Enable Sound Check on the iPod tab of the Preferences window (refer to Figure 10.10).

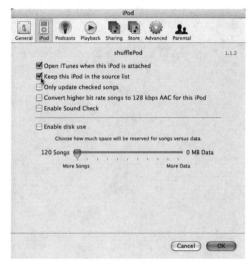

Figure 10.10 If you want to specify the songs you want on your shuffle even when it's not physically connected, you can tell iTunes to keep the shuffle in the Source pane, virtually. When you connect the shuffle, iTunes copies the songs.

Figure 10.11 You can tell which songs haven't yet been copied to the shuffle by the dots that appear to the left of the songs.

Figure 10.12
To eject an iPod, click the eject icon.

Figure 10.13 If the iPod is selected, you click the iPod Eject button.

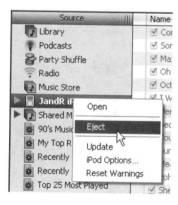

Figure 10.14
Or, control-click (Mac) or right-click (Windows) to show this contextual menu, and choose Eject.

Ejecting Your iPod

You generally don't want to unplug your iPod from your computer if its display reads "Do not disconnect" or if the shuffle's status light is blinking orange. If you're transferring data to your iPod when you unplug it, for example, you could corrupt the iPod's hard drive, which means you'd have to reformat the tiny device. And once you switch to manual updating, you'll always have to eject before disconnecting. Apple gives you a slew of one-step methods for ejecting your iPod. Use your favorite!

Ways to eject your iPod:

◆ Click the eject icon for the iPod in the Source pane (**Figure 10.12**).

◆ Select the iPod in the Source pane, and click the iPod Eject button (in the lower right of the iTunes window, **Figure 10.13**).

◆ Control-click (Mac) or right-click (Windows) the iPod in the Source pane, and choose Eject (**Figure 10.14**).

◆ Select the iPod in the Source pane, and from the Controls menu choose Eject "*iPod name.*"

◆ (Mac only) Drag the iPod icon from the Desktop to the Trash.

◆ (Mac only) Choose Eject "*iPod name*" from the menu that appears when you click and hold the iTunes icon in the Dock.

◆ (Windows only) Use the Safely Remove Hardware icon in the system tray.

◆ (Windows only) Choose the Eject item in the menu that appears when you click the iTunes icon in the system tray.

Once you eject it, the iPod disappears from the Source list. It also no longer appears as an icon on the Desktop (Mac) or in My Computer (Windows). You can safely disconnect it.

✔ Tips

■ To remount your iPod after ejecting (but before disconnecting), you can quit iTunes and then reopen it or disconnect and reconnect the iPod.

■ If the iPod doesn't appear in your Source pane but still reads "Do not disconnect," try to eject it from the Mac Finder or Windows Explorer. If it still reads "Do not disconnect," it's OK to disconnect it.

EJECTING YOUR IPOD

Changing Your iPod's Main Menu

Did you know you have almost complete control over what you see in your iPod's main menu? For example, if you use your iPod primarily to listen to podcasts, you can put podcasts in the main menu so you don't have to navigate to the Music menu to find your favorite podcasts. Or, if you never use the Shuffle Songs feature, you can remove it from the main menu.

To add or remove items in your iPod's main menu:

1. In your iPod's main menu, select Settings (**Figure 10.15**).

2. In the Settings menu, select Main Menu (**Figure 10.16**).

3. In the list that appears, scroll to an item that you do or don't want to appear in your main menu and press the Select button to switch from on to off, or vice-versa (**Figure 10.17**).

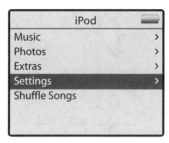

Figure 10.15
Select Settings in the main menu.

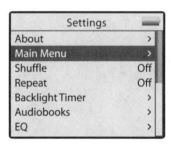

Figure 10.16
In the Settings menu, select Main Menu.

Figure 10.17
Turn displayed items on or off by highlighting them and pressing the Select button.

Renaming Your iPod

When you first set up your iPod (as we covered in Chapter 1), you gave it a name. If you ever want to rename it (for example, if it wasn't *you* that set it up, it was your Uncle Harvey and the iPod is a hand-me-down), you can do it quite simply in iTunes. Just click on its name in the Source pane and type a new name.

CHANGING YOUR IPOD'S MAIN MENU

Figure 10.18 Turn Compilations on in the Settings menu.

Figure 10.19 Compilations appears as a choice in the Music menu.

Grouping Compilations on Your iPod

If you have a color iPod, another change you can make to your menus is to change how songs from compilations appear: you can set it so that you can browse your compilations separately from the rest of your albums. (This is similar to what you can do in iTunes; see "Grouping Compilations for Better Browsing" in Chapter 9.)

To group compilations:

1. In your iPod's main menu, select Settings (refer to Figure 10.15).

2. In the Settings menu, highlight Compilations and press the Select button to set Compilations to On (**Figure 10.18**).

   When you view the Music menu, you'll see a choice of Compilations (**Figure 10.19**). When you select it, you'll see a list of compilation albums. When you check your Artists menu, you'll likely see fewer artists listed, as any artist that's represented only on compilation albums will no longer show up in the Artists menu.

Bragging Rights

The About screen on your iPod (**Figure 10.20**) has some useful information; among other things, it tells how many songs, photos, or videos are on it. To see it, select Settings from the iPod's main menu and then select About from the Settings menu.

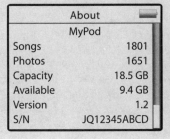

Figure 10.20 Choose About in the Settings menu to get stats on your iPod.

Setting Shuffle and Repeat Options

As in iTunes, you can set specific songs to shuffle or repeat on your iPod. These shuffle and repeat options, once set, apply to any song or song lists you listen to in the future. (This contrasts with the Shuffle Songs choice you can pick in the main menu, which immediately starts playing songs chosen randomly from your entire library; we mentioned this in Chapter 4.)

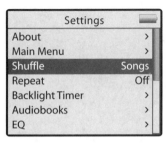

Figure 10.21 In the Settings menu, you can tell your iPod whether to shuffle by songs, by albums, or not at all.

To set shuffle options for your iPod:

Select Settings in the main menu, scroll to highlight Shuffle (**Figure 10.21**), and press the Select button to switch between the following:

Figure 10.22 You can tell you've turned the Shuffle feature on by the icon in the upper right corner of the iPod screen.

◆ Choose **Songs** if you want the songs in whatever song list you select from to play in a random order. If you check the Now Playing screen you'll see the shuffle icon (**Figure 10.22**).

◆ Choose **Albums** if you want your iPod to randomly select an album from the song list you've chosen to play from, play all the songs on that album, and then randomly select another album from which to play all songs, and so on until all the songs in the list are played. The Now Playing screen displays the same shuffle icon as if you selected Songs (refer to Figure 10.22).

◆ Choose **Off** if you want songs played in the order they appear.

Repeat 1 icon

Figure 10.23 Can't stop obsessing over that one song? You can set your iPod so it continually repeats any song you play.

Repeat icon

Figure 10.24 You can also set your iPod to repeat through the list of songs you're listening to.

To set repeat options for your iPod:

Select Settings in the main menu, scroll to highlight Repeat, and press the Select button to switch between the following:

◆ Choose **One** if you want any song you play to repeat indefinitely, until you go to another song. The Now Playing screen, if you check it, shows the "repeat 1" icon (**Figure 10.23**).

◆ Choose **All** if you want your iPod to play all the songs in the list from which you selected, and then start over again at the top of the list. The Now Playing screen shows the standard repeat icon (**Figure 10.24**).

◆ Choose **Off** if you don't want anything to repeat.

Adjusting Playback Speed of Audiobooks

If you're an audiobook listener, you'll be pleased to know that you can change the rate at which audiobooks are read, *without changing the pitch of the narrator*: You can slightly slow down the rate if the rate of speech is too fast for your comprehension, or slightly speed up the rate if you want to do something akin to skimming.

To adjust playback speed of all the audiobooks in your iPod:

1. On the main menu, select Settings.

2. On the Settings menu, select Audiobooks (**Figure 10.25**).

3. On the Audiobooks menu, select Slower, Normal, or Faster (**Figure 10.26**).

To adjust playback speed of the audiobook to which you're listening:

1. When playing an audiobook, press the Select button until your iPod displays a screen with the word *Speed* in the lower left of the display (**Figure 10.27**).

   The current speed, indicated in the lower right, is probably *Normal*.

2. Use your wheel to scroll to change the speed: scroll right to change to *Faster*, scroll left to change to *Slower*.

Figure 10.25 You'll find Audiobooks in your Settings menu.

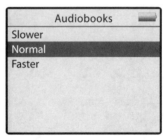

Figure 10.26 When you select Audiobooks in your Settings menu, you'll see speed choices. Highlight the one you want, and press the Select button on your iPod.

This will change to Faster or Slower if you scroll right or left.

Figure 10.27 If you just want to speed up or slow down a specific audiobook, start playing it and then press the Select button until you see the word *Speed* in the lower left. Then use your iPod's wheel to scroll right to speed up or left to slow down.

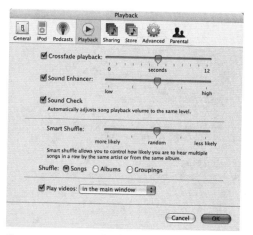

Figure 10.28 You'll first need to turn Sound Check on in iTunes.

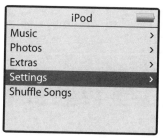

Figure 10.29
On your iPod,
go to Settings...

Figure 10.30
...and turn
Sound Check on.

Adjusting Volume Across Multiple Songs

Do you find yourself constantly adjusting volume on your iPod because some songs are so much louder or softer than others? You can do something about this. Remember the Sound Check checkbox we covered in "Adjusting Sound Settings" in Chapter 8? It adjusted volume across songs so that none was dramatically different than the others. If you want to make sure that the same thing happens on your iPod, follow the steps listed here.

To turn Sound Check on for songs on your iPod:

1. In iTunes, turn Sound Check on as described in "Adjusting Sound Settings" in Chapter 8 (**Figure 10.28**).

2. On your iPod's main menu, select Settings (**Figure 10.29**).

3. In the Settings menu, scroll to highlight Sound Check and press the Select button to set Sound Check to On (**Figure 10.30**).

✔ Tip

■ iPod shuffle owners can turn Sound Check on for their iPod using iTunes (refer to Figure 10.10).

Choosing Equalizer Settings

Yet another task that parallels what you can do in iTunes is to pick equalizer settings. (See "Using the Equalizer" in Chapter 8.) Your iPod also lets you pick an equalizer setting when you need your music to sound just right.

To pick equalizer settings on your iPod:

1. On your iPod's main menu, select Settings (refer to Figure 10.29).

2. On the Settings menu, select EQ (**Figure 10.31**).

3. In the EQ menu, select an appropriate equalizer setting for the music to which you plan to listen (**Figure 10.32**).

    The EQ setting is applied to future songs you play. If you decide you don't like it, you can always return to the EQ menu and choose Off.

✔ Tip

■ If you set EQ settings in iTunes for particular songs, those settings will apply on your iPod as long as the iPod's EQ setting is not set to Off (refer to Figure 10.32). It's a good idea to leave your iPod EQ set to Flat, which has no impact on songs with no iTunes-set EQ settings but allows iTunes-set EQ settings to "shine through."

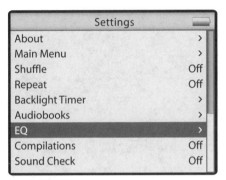

Figure 10.31 Select EQ in the Settings menu.

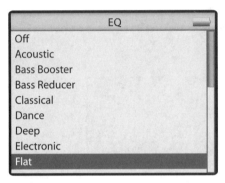

Figure 10.32 Pick an equalizer setting in the EQ menu.

Figure 10.33 Thumbnails of artwork appear on the Now Playing screen.

Figure 10.34 Press the Select button twice to see artwork that fills the iPod's display.

Figure 10.35 Starting from the Now Playing screen, press the Select button two or three times (depending on whether the song also has artwork) to see this Lyrics screen.

Viewing Artwork and Lyrics on Your iPod

Since songs can have artwork (that came with purchased songs or that you added yourself as we describe in Chapter 8), you can view that artwork on any color iPod. Less frequently, songs also have lyrics associated with them (usually added by you, as we describe in Chapter 9); these, too, are viewable on only the newest iPods (the nano and the video iPod).

To view artwork (if any):

◆ When you're playing a song, you'll see a thumbnail of the associated artwork (**Figure 10.33**); press the Select button twice to see a "full screen" view of the artwork (**Figure 10.34**).

To view lyrics (if any):

◆ When you're playing a song, press the Select button two or three times, or until you see a screen with text (**Figure 10.35**).

✔ Tip

■ Not seeing artwork when you think you should? In the iPod Options window (refer to Figure 10.2) there's a "Display album artwork on your iPod" checkbox; if this is not checked, you won't see the artwork on your iPod.

Locking It Down

Do you have top-secret voice memos on your iPod? Or perhaps material that might be inappropriate for an inquisitive child to happen upon? If you've got a nano or video iPod, you can set a combination and then lock your iPod screen. Anybody who wants to use the iPod will need to enter the combination. Talk about high security!

To set a combination and lock your screen:

1. From the main menu, choose Extras, then Screen Lock, and then Set Combination (or Change Combination) (**Figure 10.36**).

2. Use your wheel to change the first digit (**Figure 10.37**).

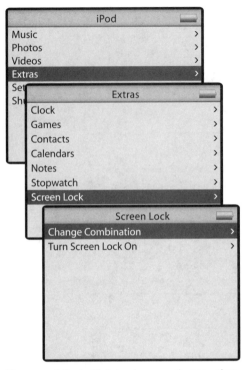

Figure 10.36 Start with Extras in your main menu, then choose Screen Lock, and then Change Combination.

Figure 10.37 Scroll to set a number for each place.

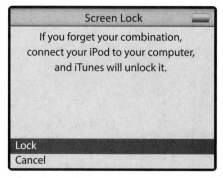

Figure 10.38 When you tell your iPod to turn screen lock on (refer to Figure 10.36), it tells you what to do if you forget (or on a nano, reminds you of your combination) and gives you a chance to cancel.

3. Press the Select button.

4. Use the wheel to change the second digit, and then press the Select button.

5. Repeat for the last two digits.

6. Select Turn Screen Lock On (refer to Figure 10.36).

   Your video iPod tells you how to get your combination back if you forget it (**Figure 10.38**). Your iPod nano reminds you of your combo. Both provide menu choices of Lock and Cancel.

7. Select Lock.

   An Enter Code screen appears (looking much like the Enter New Code screen in Figure 10.37). To use the iPod, you'll need to re-enter your code.

✔ Tip

■ When setting a combo or entering it, you can use your iPod's Forward or Back buttons to move between digits.

Listening at Home Without Headphones

Until you got your iPod, when you wanted to listen to your music at home (presumably without headphones) you probably tapped into your CD collection. Now you can connect your iPod to your stereo and take advantage of the massive library you have (or will soon have). No more CD changing. Not only that, if you create playlists, you can have songs play in the order you want, not the order dictated by your CDs.

Here are your basic options for hooking up your iPod to play in your home.

Figure 10.39 The Dock is a great way to connect your iPod to your home stereo. (Image courtesy of Apple Computer.)

Options for listening to your iPod at home:

◆ Buy an iPod Dock, if you don't have one (**Figure 10.39**), to link your iPod and home stereo system. (This option isn't available for the iPod shuffle.)

The Dock has a *line-level output*, ideal for plugging into your home stereo system to get the best quality sound. Also, when your iPod is in the Dock you can charge it. With this setup, you control volume only from your stereo. (You'll also need to buy a mini-stereo to RCA-stereo cable to go from the Dock to the stereo.)

Figure 10.40 These portable Altec-Lansing speakers designed to be used with an iPod have been useful in our home as well as on the road. (Image courtesy of Altec-Lansing.)

◆ Use a cable to connect your iPod to your home stereo system.

All you need is a mini-stereo to RCA-stereo cable (available in just about any electronics store). It's not as good as using a Dock, because of charging and audio quality issues, but it's certainly cheap and easy. You'll be able to control volume from the iPod or your stereo.

◆ Connect your iPod to powered speakers.

You can use many kinds of powered speakers with the iPod—from those specifically designed to use the Dock connector on the bottom of your iPod (**Figure 10.40**) to those that are not iPod-specific and are designed for use with any mini-headphone jack. (iPod shuffle users will have to go with the latter option.)

Serious Shopping

On these pages, we've tried to give you an overview of your options for connecting your iPod to your home or car stereo.

When it's time to buy, you'll want to know exactly what's out there. You'll find many of these devices at the Apple Store (http://store.apple.com) Two other places to browse (where you'll also find reviews) are www.ilounge.com and http://playlistmag.com.

To learn more about the wide range of available devices for your iPod, pick up a copy of Peachpit's *Your iPod Life: A Guide to the Best iPod Accessories from Playlist.*

Listening in Your Car

Listening to your iPod in your car is a natural extension of listening to your iPod. But please, please, don't use your headphones while driving; it's just not safe and may be illegal in your state.

You have even more choices for listening in your car than you do for listening at home.

Options for listening to your iPod in your car:

- Buy a cassette adapter.

  This is the most common and universal option and will work with all iPods, including the shuffle. As long as your car has a cassette player, you can get an adapter that looks like a cassette with a wire coming off that will plug into the iPods headphone jack. Some iPod cassette adapters will even allow simple control of the iPod from your car stereo.

- Buy an FM transmitter.

  If your car stereo has only a CD player, you may need to go the FM transmitter route. These work by taking the output of the iPod and transmitting over the air like an FM radio station. The transmitter gives you a choice of stations—you need to pick one of those that's not already in use by a "real" radio station; when you tune your radio to that station, you'll hear the output of the iPod.

- Modify your current car stereo.

  You can find kits that will use your car stereo's CD changer connection port to control the iPod.

- Buy a new car stereo.

  Many car stereo makers, such as Alpine and Clarion, support the iPod with their new after-market car stereos. (See www.apple.com/ipod/ipodyourcar/accessories.html for more.)

  Some newer car stereos also have ports that allow you to plug in via a headphone jack; you'll simply need to buy a mini-stereo–to–mini-stereo cable to connect from your iPod to the stereo.

- Buy a new car.

  We admit this is a bit extreme, but if you're in the market for a new car, Apple is working with a handful of carmakers to integrate iPods with new cars. As of this writing, Apple lists a dozen makers that support iPods, including the Mini Cooper and BMW (http://www.apple.com/ipod/ipodyourcar/); in some cases the solutions can even be adapted to your not-so-new car.

Backlighting

The iPod's backlight is something you'll need, particularly in the car or any dark place where you might be using your iPod. The backlight illuminates the iPod screen; it uses lots of battery power too, so use it sparingly. You turn on the backlight by just touching the controls (or pressing and holding the menu button).

If you're getting frustrated with how quickly the backlight turns off, or if you find that it's staying on longer than you need it, you can set the amount of time the backlight stays on. To do this, go to the Settings menu, choose Backlight Timer, and then choose the amount of time you want the backlight to stay on. Ten seconds is the default on newer iPods and works well in many places, although in the car you may want to set it to be longer.

USING THE iPOD AS MORE THAN A MUSIC PLAYER

The world's most popular music-playing device is really much more than a music player. Depending on what model you have, it's also a video player, slide-show projector, voice recorder, address book, calendar, alarm clock, portable hard drive, and photo album. No wonder everyone wants one.

In this chapter, we start by covering what you need to know if you're using your iPod to display photos or videos. Then we move on to showing you how to use it as a portable hard disk and as a pretty sophisticated clock. Voice recording (requiring additional hardware), address-book functions, calendars, and text file display follows. What versatility!

iPod shuffle users, take note: The usual disclaimer applies—most of the material in this chapter applies to iPods with displays, so you'll want to skip to the section "Using Your iPod as a Portable Hard Disk."

Putting Photos on Your iPod

Starting with the aptly named iPod photo (first available in 2004), all iPods have color displays and can show photos. You can use iTunes to specify which photo-cataloguing application or folder on your computer has the photos you want copied to your iPod. From there, iTunes optimizes the photos for iPod viewing and copies them to your iPod.

To copy photos from your computer to your iPod:

1. With your color-display iPod connected, select the iPod in the Source pane and click the iPod Options button in the lower right of your iTunes window (**Figure 11.1**).

   The iTunes Preferences window opens to the iPod tab.

2. Click the Photos tab.

3. Click the "Synchronize photos from" checkbox, and choose a source to get photos from.

   If you're using a Mac, your digital photos may already be stored in iPhoto. But you can also select a folder (**Figure 11.2**).

   Windows users can choose Adobe Photoshop Elements or Adobe Album or a folder (**Figure 11.3**).

Figure 11.1 Select your iPod in the Source pane, and click the iPod Options button.

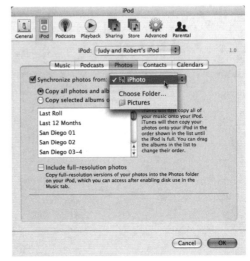

Figure 11.2 This is the iPod Photos tab for a Mac. Indicate the source where you want photos to come from.

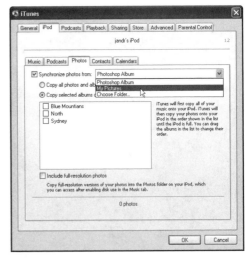

Figure 11.3 This is the iPod Photos tab for a Windows computer. Choose the source for your photos, and then click OK.

Figure 11.4 Choose which specific albums (or folders) you want. (In this example, we chose not to clog up our iPod with all 1645 photos from our trip to Australia.)

Different Ways To Get to iPod Options

In this chapter, you'll frequently be accessing the iPod Options screen (which is really just a tab in your iPod Preferences window). Normally, we'll just direct you to click the iPod Options button, in the lower-right part of the iTunes window, but you may want to substitute these other methods:

◆ Control-click (Mac) or right-click (Windows) the iPod icon in iTunes' Source pane; from the contextual menu that appears, choose iPod Options.

◆ Open your iTunes Preferences window—choose Preferences from the iTunes menu (Mac) or Edit menu (Windows)—and click the iPod tab.

---

4. If you don't want all the photos from the selected application or folder copied, click the radio button for "Copy selected albums only" or "Copy selected folders only" and select which albums or folders you want copied (**Figure 11.4**).

You can shift-click to select contiguous items; Command-click (Mac) or Ctrl-click (Windows) to select items that are not adjacent.

5. Click OK.

All iPod-compatible images—basically all standard formats including JPEG, BMP, TIFF, GIF, PNG, and PSD (Mac only)—from the source you selected in step 3 are copied to your iPod.

✔ Tips

■ If you have a large music library, too large for your iPod, you'll need to be selective about your music—switching to manual updating or at least having only selected playlists automatically updated—if you want to have room for photos. This is because iTunes copies music first to your iPod and then copies photos only if there's room.

■ If you're not sure there's room for all your photos on your iPod, and you've chosen to copy selected photo albums or folders (refer to Figure 11.4), drag to reorder them so the most important albums or photos are at the top of the list—iTunes copies them in the order they're listed.

■ Check "Include full-resolution photos" if you want to be able to copy the photos to another computer. This way you'll see them in the Mac Finder or Windows Explorer in the iPod's Photos folder. (You'll need to enable disk use for your iPod; see "Using Your iPod As a Portable Hard Disk," later in this chapter.)

Copying Photos Directly from a Camera

For all color iPods except the nano, you can purchase an iPod Camera Connector that goes into your iPod's docking connector. You can then just plug in your digital camera and transfer photos directly to your iPod. This is especially useful when you're on the road and need a place to offload images so you can fit more on your camera's flash memory card.

You can browse these imported photos on your iPod but not in the same way as you view photos imported from your computer. To view photos imported directly from your camera, navigate to the Photos menu, select Photo Import, and then pick the roll you want to view.

You're better off, however, transferring these imported photos to your computer in the place you normally store photos; this way the next time you connect your iPod to your computer, iTunes will move these photos into your iPod's photo library, so you can access and view them with the rest of your photos.

How do you get these photos from the iPod to your computer's photo collection? Some applications, such as iPhoto and Adobe Photoshop Album, will recognize that your iPod contains imported-from-camera photos next time you connect it to your computer and will offer you the option of importing them into your normal photo library. In other cases, you'll find the photos in a DCIM folder put on your iPod during the import (as covered later in this chapter in "Using Your iPod As a Portable Hard Disk"); if that's the case, you can manually add those photos to your photo library.

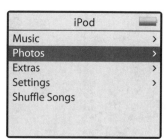

Figure 11.5
When you want to view your photos, select Photos from the iPod's main menu.

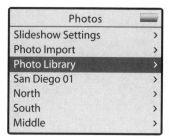

Figure 11.6
Select which group of photos you want to view.

Figure 11.7
Your photos appear as a colorful grid of thumbnails.

Figure 11.8
When you select a photo, it expands to a full-screen size.

Displaying Photos on Your iPod

So you've got those photos on your iPod. Now what? You can view them yourself and entertain (or bore, as the case may be) your friends and family. You can show photos individually (as we cover on this page) or as a slide show (as we cover on the next page).

To view photos on your iPod:

1. From the main menu, choose Photos (**Figure 11.5**).

2. From the Photos menu, choose Photo Library if you want to see your entire collection of folders or choose from one of the subcollections listed below that (**Figure 11.6**).

   Your photos appear as thumbnails (**Figure 11.7**).

3. Use your iPod's wheel to scroll through the thumbnails. You can also jump to the next or previous screenful of thumbnails by pressing the Forward or Backward button.

   You'll notice that as you scroll, one photo is always highlighted with a yellow border.

4. Press the Select button to show the highlighted photo (**Figure 11.8**).

   You can then use your wheel to scroll through the images in this full-screen mode.

✔ Tip

- Scrolling through photos displayed in full-screen mode is actually a very effective way to find an individual photo. You'll be amazed at the speed at which you can scroll and still clearly see each photo. You also have complete control over the speed at which the photos advance.

Presenting a Slide Show with Your iPod

Your color iPod's slide-show features come in handy, whether you want to show off your vacation photos, display a portfolio of scanned artwork, or even show slides from a corporate presentation (PowerPoint and Keynote slides can be exported as individual images and then copied to your iPod).

Slide shows are easy to play and fun to customize. You can watch a slide show on the iPod or (if you have a color iPod other than the nano) you can output the slide show to a TV (with an optional $19 iPod AV cable, available at the Apple Store, http://store.apple.com, as well as at various electronics stores).

To play a slide show on your iPod:

1. In the Photos menu (refer to Figure 11.6), select a Photo Library or an album and press the Play/Pause button.

2. Users of some iPods may see a Start Slideshow screen (**Figure 11.9**). If you see this, select TV Off.

3. Watch your slide show!

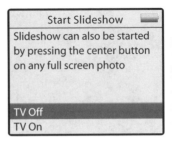

Figure 11.9
If you see this screen, tell your iPod whether you want to show the slide show on TV or not.

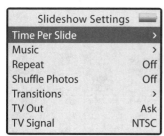

Figure 11.10
You can customize your slide show—for example, you can choose specific music, transitions, and where you want to view your slide show.

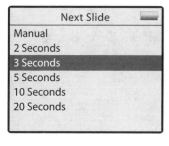

Figure 11.11
You can choose how long you want each slide to be displayed.

Figure 11.12
You can also choose the music you want to play during your slide show.

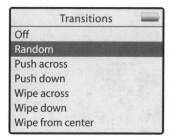

Figure 11.13
Your iPod provides a decent selection of slide-show transitions to choose from.

To customize your slide show:

1. Select Photos from the main iPod menu.

2. Select Slideshow Settings (refer to Figure 11.6).

3. In the Slideshow Settings menu (**Figure 11.10**) choose from the following:

   ▲ **Time Per Slide** is the amount of time each slide is displayed (**Figure 11.11**). The default is 3 seconds, and that works pretty well.

   ▲ **Music** lets you tell your iPod to use the music you currently have playing as slide-show accompaniment or to pick a playlist from your iPod (**Figure 11.12**).

   ▲ **Repeat** allows you to set the slide show so it starts again each time it reaches the end. Press the Select button to toggle between On and Off.

   ▲ **Shuffle Photos** can also be On or Off. If On, your iPod shows your photos in a random order.

   ▲ **Transitions** allows you to choose from a list of transitions to use between each pair of slides in the show (**Figure 11.13**). Pick Random, and the iPod will randomly choose different transitions between slides.

   ▲ **TV Out** toggles between On, Off, and Ask. If you always play your slide shows on your iPod, leave it as Off. If you always play slide shows while your iPod is connected to a television, change this to On. If you choose Ask, the iPod will ask if you'd like to display the output on a TV before each slide show (refer to Figure 11.9). TV Out is not available on the nano.

   ▲ **TV Signal** tells the iPod how to format the signal for the particular country standard, NTSC or PAL.

To play a slide show on a TV:

1. In the Slideshow Settings menu (refer to Figure 11.10), make sure TV Out is set to Ask or On. (Use Ask if you also sometimes like to view slide shows on your iPod; use On if you always like to view them on TV.)

2. Make sure your iPod is connected to your TV with the iPod AV cable.

3. In the Photos menu (refer to Figure 11.6), select a Photo Library or an album and press the Play/Pause button.

4. If you had set TV Out to Ask, you will see a Start Slideshow screen (refer to Figure 11.9); select TV On.

5. Watch the slide show on your TV.

   While the slide show appears on your TV, your iPod displays the previous, current, and next slides (**Figure 11.14**).

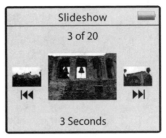

Figure 11.14 When you view a slide show on your TV, your iPod displays the current, previous, and next slide.

Controlling a Slide Show

You can use the controls on your iPod, whether you're displaying your slide show on the iPod or on TV:

◆ Press the Forward button to immediately show the next slide or the Backward button to jump back if you need to see a previously viewed slide.

◆ Press the Play/Pause button to pause and then resume the slide show; a pause or play icon shows on the screen where your slide show is playing (**Figure 11.15**).

◆ If you have customized your slide show to play music (refer to Figure 11.12) spin your iPod's wheel to raise or lower the volume.

◆ Press Menu to exit the show.

Figure 11.15 When you pause a slide show, a pause icon appears on your screen for a few seconds.

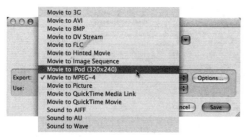

Figure 11.16 QuickTime Player Pro 7 provides an export-to-iPod option.

Tech Specs for iPod Video

If you prefer to use a tool other than QuickTime Player, you'll need to set that tool to create files that will play on the iPod. Here's what Apple has to say about what's required:

H.264 video: up to 768 Kbps, 320 x 240, 30 frames per sec., Baseline Profile up to Level 1.3 with AAC-LC up to 160 Kbps, 48 Khz, stereo audio in .m4v, .mp4 and .mov file formats

MPEG-4 video: up to 2.5 mbps, 480 x 480, 30 frames per sec., Simple Profile with AAC-LC up to 160 Kbps, 48 Khz, stereo audio in .m4v, .mp4 and .mov file formats

About Producing Videos for the iPod

Although you're guaranteed that the videos you purchase at the iTunes Music Store will be copied to your video iPod and play just fine, you may have other video files on your computer that you'd like to put on your video-compatible iPod. (It's just *so* last-century to pull out a wallet with baby photos; now, you can pull out an iPod with baby videos!)

The iPod isn't quite as evolved when it comes to video as it is with audio, however. The video formats the iPod supports are quite limited (unlike the large variety of audio formats the iPod can handle). And, iTunes can't convert video files into an iPod-compatible format as it does with audio. (Not yet, anyway.)

For a video file to play on an iPod, it needs to be an MPEG-4 or QuickTime file, compressed with either the H.264 compressor or the MPEG-4 compressor. The file needs to meet various other requirements, too; see the sidebar "Tech Specs for iPod Video." Fortunately, you can convert most videos you may have—whether they're from your digital camera or camcorder, as well as those downloaded from the Web—to one of these formats.

Perhaps the easiest way to ensure that your video will work on the iPod is to convert it using Apple's own QuickTime Player Pro (version 7.0.3 or later). You'll have to pay Apple thirty dollars to upgrade to the Pro version from the standard version you have on your computer (it was installed when you installed iTunes if you didn't have it already). To upgrade, open QuickTime Player and choose Buy QuickTime Pro from the QuickTime Player menu (Mac) or the Help menu (Windows). Once you've got QuickTime Player Pro running, open your movie in that application, choose Export from the File menu, and then choose Movie to iPod (**Figure 11.16**).

Copying Videos to Your iPod

To get videos onto your iPod, you'll need to add them to your iTunes library first.

iTunes will download any videos you buy from its Music Store automatically to your iTunes library.

You can add other properly formatted video files (see previous page) to your iTunes library just as you add audio files; dragging the files right into the iTunes window is the simplest method, but we cover other methods of adding files to your iTunes library in Chapter 2.

If your iPod is still set for automatic syncing, you'll need to also set your iPod preferences to automatically copy videos. To do this, open the iPod Options window and click the Videos tab; here, select "Automatically update all videos" or select "Automatically update selected playlists only" and pick some playlists (**Figure 11.17**).

If you've set your iPod for manual updating (as we described in the previous chapter), you can drag video files and playlists containing video to the iPod, just as you do songs.

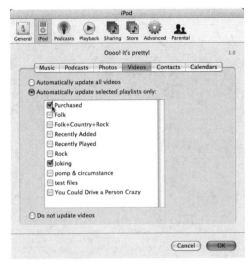

Figure 11.17 If you want your videos copied to your iPod automatically, select one of the "Automatically update" options in the iPod Options window.

An Odd Workaround: Make Your Movies Music Videos

If you have lots of your own videos to copy to your iPod, you may find it useful to set their video kind as "Music Video." Why? Because on your iPod, all ordinary movies are lumped together with no submenu; you'll find them all under Movies. Music Videos, on the other hand, are subdivided by Artist, so you could select Music Videos and then, for example, "Hawaii" to see all your clips from your Hawaiian vacation.

To do this, open the Information window for each movie and on the Options tab, set the video to "Music Video" rather than "Movie." You'll also need to provide an "Artist" name (on the Info tab) that's actually a useful category name ("Hawaii" in the above example).

COPYING VIDEOS TO YOUR IPOD

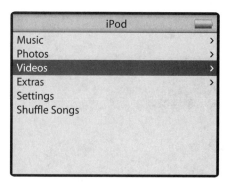

Figure 11.18 To watch videos on your iPod, start by choosing Videos in the main menu.

Figure 11.19 Videos are divided into subcategories.

Figure 11.20 When you get to a screen with a list of videos, select the one you want to view.

Playing Videos with Your iPod

Almost universally, people are impressed with how good video (especially video from the iTunes Music Store) looks on the video iPod. They're equally wowed when they see the video from their iPod playing on a TV.

You'll find that viewing videos is remarkably similar to listening to music—the methods for browsing and playing are largely the same. And as with showing photos, the optional iPod AV cable allows you to show your videos on a TV.

To browse to a video and begin playing:

1. From the main menu, choose Videos (**Figure 11.18**).

2. Choose from the categories of Videos (Video Playlists, Movies, Music Videos, TV Shows, or Video Podcasts; **Figure 11.19**).

3. Continue to make selections until you reach a list of videos (**Figure 11.20**).

4. Scroll to highlight the video you want to view, and click the Select button.

continues on next page

PLAYING VIDEOS WITH YOUR IPOD

5. If you see a screen that lists TV Off and TV On, choose TV Off if you want the video to play on your iPod or choose TV On if you want the video to play on your TV. (You may not see this screen at all.)

The video begins to play, on your iPod or your TV (assuming the cable is connecting the TV to the iPod). If it is playing on your TV, your iPod shows a screen much like you see for audio-only files (**Figure 11.21**).

✔ Tips

- If you don't see the screen that lists TV Off and TV On and you want to view the video on a TV, choose Video Settings in your Videos menu (refer to Figure 11.19) and set TV Out to Ask. (You can also set it to On if you will always play your video out to TV; see **Figure 11.22**.)

- It may take several seconds after you press the Select button before the video actually starts to play.

- Music videos and video podcasts, although you'll find them listed under Videos in the iPod's main menu, also appear under your iPod's Music menu. When you access them under Music, however, you'll only be able to hear the audio track. This is useful when you only want to *hear* a video (and save your batteries in the process).

Figure 11.21 If you play the video out to TV, your iPod screen looks like this.

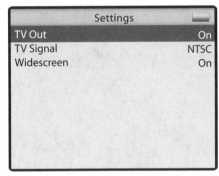

Figure 11.22 Set TV Out to On or Ask if you plan to view on TV.

Figure 11.23 When you pause a video, a pause icon shows on your display screen (whether the iPod or TV) for a few seconds.

Figure 11.24 When you begin playing again, a play icon shows for a few seconds.

Figure 11.25 When you spin the wheel on your iPod, you change volume; a volume indicator appears.

To pause or play a video that you've browsed to:

◆ Press the Play/Pause button on your iPod's wheel.

If the video is playing, the screen freezes and displays a pause icon in the upper left of the display for several seconds (**Figure 11.23**). If the video is paused, it begins to play again, first showing a play icon in the upper left of the display for several seconds (**Figure 11.24**). If you are playing out to TV, the play and pause icons appear on your TV as well.

To control volume:

◆ Once you've started playing a video (even if it's currently paused), simply spin the wheel: clockwise raises the volume and counterclockwise lowers it.

As soon as you start spinning, the iPod knows you're trying to control volume and shows a graphic representation of the volume (**Figure 11.25**).

PLAYING VIDEOS WITH YOUR IPOD

To fast-forward or fast-reverse using the wheel when watching video:

1. When the video is playing, press the Select button once.

   A scrubber bar appears, filled in to show the current location in the video (**Figure 11.26**).

   If you're showing the video on TV, you'll see a standard scrubber bar (with a diamond showing current location) on your iPod, as well.

2. Immediately (in less than 5 seconds), spin the wheel clockwise to move to a later point in the video or counterclockwise to move to an earlier point in the video.

   If you wait 5 seconds or more, the bar disappears and scrolling the wheel changes volume. You'll need to press the Select button again to see it.

Figure 11.26 Here's the scrubber bar used to fast-forward video. Scroll right to fast-forward, left to rewind.

✔ Tips

■ You can also press and hold down the Forward button or Backward button to fast-forward or fast-reverse the video.

■ TV shows that you purchase from the iTunes Music Store are set to remember your playback position (like audiobooks and podcasts), so if you have to stop watching (because your morning commute is over, for example), you'll find yourself at the right place when you play again. The same is not true by default for music videos or any of your own movies you put on the iPod, although you can use iTunes to set your movie to remember playback. (See the sidebar "Setting a Song to Remember Playback Position" in Chapter 8.)

Check this

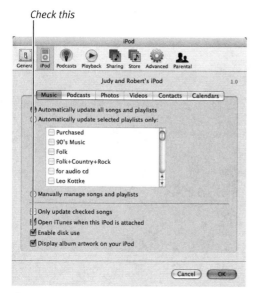

Figure 11.27 Having "Enable disk use" checked is the key to using your iPod as a hard disk.

Figure 11.28 The iPod looks and acts like any disk.

Using Your iPod as a Portable Hard Disk

If your iPod can hold all those songs (and maybe even photos and videos), you know it has some decent storage capabilities. As a matter of fact, it can hold any files that a hard drive can hold and can mount on your desktop just as any other hard disk would. You can even use the relatively tiny iPod shuffle for storing files.

To use your iPod (other than a shuffle) as a hard disk:

1. In iTunes, select your iPod, click the iPod Options button in the lower right of the window, and check "Enable disk use" (**Figure 11.27**).

2. If this was not checked previously, iTunes may warn you that this choice means that you will need to manually eject your iPod before disconnecting. Click OK to dismiss this dialog.

3. Click OK to close the Preferences window. In the Mac Finder or Windows Explorer, you'll see your iPod as you would any other hard drive (**Figure 11.28**). Copy and delete files as you would with any other hard drive.

To use your iPod shuffle as a hard disk:

1. In iTunes, select your iPod, click the Options button, and check "Enable disk use" (**Figure 11.29**).

2. Click OK to dismiss the dialog in which iTunes warns you that you will need to manually eject your iPod in the future.

3. Use the slider to indicate how much space on your shuffle you want reserved for files (refer to Figure 11.29).

4. Click OK to close the Preferences window.

5. If your shuffle asks if you'd like iTunes to remove songs to make room for data, click Yes (**Figure 11.30**).

   You'll be able to use the shuffle as you would any other hard drive.

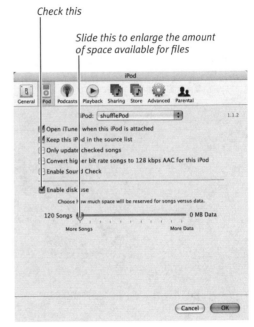

Figure 11.29 "Enable disk use" is available for the shuffle, too.

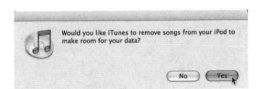

Figure 11.30 You probably need to let iTunes delete some songs on the shuffle if you want to use it as a hard disk.

Figure 11.31 This new and improved Clock screen appears on a nano and a video iPod when you first select Clock from the main menu.

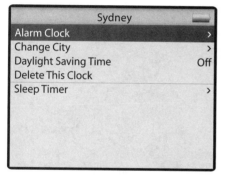

Figure 11.32 When you select a clock from the Clock menu, nanos and video iPods display additional alarm and clock-setting options.

Figure 11.33 iPods other than the nano and video iPod go straight to this screen when you first select Clock.

Using Your iPod's Clock Features

Did you know that your iPod keeps time? Given this, wouldn't it be lovely to wake up to an upbeat selection of your tunes? How about falling asleep to that really relaxing playlist? You can, of course, do both using any iPod, although you'll need to have a way to hear the iPod (see "Listening At Home Without Headphones" in Chapter 10), unless you're willing to sleep with your headphones on. Alternatively, you can set the alarm to beep: A simple, somewhat melodic sound will play through the iPod's external speaker (this is a pathetic little speaker, not good for anything more than this simple alarm sound).

The newest iPods (nano and video) have an impressive world clock built right in—so you can keep track of the time in multiple cities across the globe.

To set an alarm:

1. In the iPod's Main menu, select Extras.

2. In the Extras menu, select Clock.

3. If you have a nano or video iPod, you'll see a screen with multiple clocks listed (**Figure 11.31**); press the select button. (Older iPods won't show this screen.)

4. On the screen that appears next (**Figures 11.32** and **11.33**), select Alarm Clock.

continues on next page

5. Highlight Alarm and press the Select button to set the Alarm to On (**Figure 11.34**).

6. Select Time, and use the wheel to set the time you want the alarm to go off (**Figure 11.35**). Press the Menu or Select button to return to the Alarm Clock menu.

7. Select Sound and then select the playlist you want to play when the alarm goes off (**Figure 11.36**). Or select Beep, if you don't expect to have your headphones on or your iPod connected to external speakers when the alarm goes off.

Your alarm is set. Happy dreams!

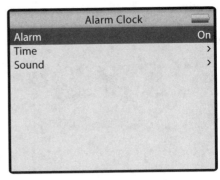

Figure 11.34 If you select Alarm Clock on any iPod, you'll see this screen. Toggle Alarm to On, and then select Time.

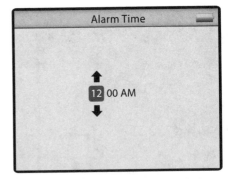

Figure 11.35 Set the time you want the alarm to sound.

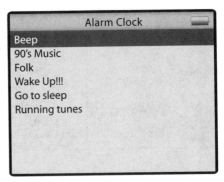

Figure 11.36 You can pick what you want to hear when your alarm goes off.

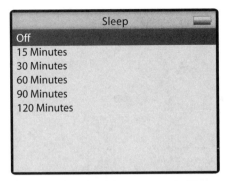

Figure 11.37 You can pick a set amount of time until you want the iPod to go to sleep.

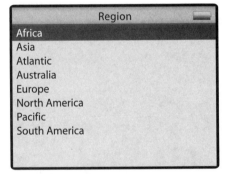

Figure 11.38 (Nano and video iPod only) When creating a new clock or editing an old one, you'll have to select a region....

Region	
Adak	12:42 PM
Anchorage	1:42 PM
Atlanta	5:42 PM
Austin	4:42 PM
Boston	5:42 PM
Calgary	3:42 PM
California	2:42 PM
Chicago	4:42 PM
Columbus	5:42 PM

Figure 11.39 ...and then a city.

To set the sleep timer:

1. Follow steps 1 and 2 of the previous task.

2. Select Sleep Timer (refer to Figure 11.32).

3. Select a time (**Figure 11.37**).

   Any audio playing after the number of minutes you designated will automatically stop.

To add a clock to use in a different time zone (nano and video iPod only):

1. From the main menu, select Extras and then Clock.

   You'll see at least one analog clock and a digital representation of the time, plus a city name. Below that you'll see New Clock (refer to Figure 11.31).

2. Select New Clock; you'll be asked to choose a region (**Figure 11.38**) and then a city (**Figure 11.39**).

   You'll be returned to the Clock menu, with your new clock listed.

   You can switch to your new clock when you travel.

Using Your iPod as a Voice Recorder

If you normally carry a separate device around as a recording device—perhaps to record interviews or dictate memos— you'll be glad to know you can use your iPod as a voice recorder. To do so, you'll need to purchase either a Belkin Voice Recorder for iPod or Griffin Technology iTalk iPod Voice Recorder. (At the time of this writing, these aren't available for the video iPods, but Apple lists "voice recording" in the spec for this iPod, so we hope that by the time you read this at least one voice recorder will be available for the newest iPod models.)

To record a voice memo:

1. Connect your voice recorder to your iPod (**Figure 11.40**).

    The iPod immediately switches to the Voice Memo screen (**Figure 11.41**) when it detects that the voice recorder is plugged in.

    If your voice recorder was already connected, go to Extras, then Voice Memos, and then Record Now.

Figure 11.40
Voice recorders connect directly to your iPod. (Image courtesy of Griffin Technology)

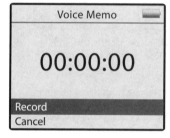

Figure 11.41
When you connect a voice recorder you'll see this screen. When you're ready to speak, select Record.

Figure 11.42
As you record, the iPod keeps track of how long you've been recording.

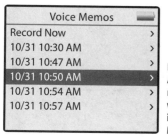

Figure 11.43
Anything you record and save will appear in the Voice Memos menu.

2. Prepare to speak, and select Record.

   You'll see a screen with a timer (**Figure 11.42**) already starting to keep time; the word *Recording* also appears.

3. Start speaking.

4. If you need to pause, press your iPod's Play/Pause button or Select button. Press either of these to resume recording, as well.

5. When you're done, press the Menu button. (You can also scroll to "Stop and Save" and press Select, but that takes more work.)

   The word *Saving* appears on the screen, and then you are returned to the Voice Memos menu, where you'll find all voice memos listed.

To listen to a voice memo:

1. In the Extras menu, choose Voice Memos.

2. In the Voice Memos menu, select the listing for the time that you made the recording you want to listen to (**Figure 11.43**).

3. Select Play.

Using Your iPod as an Address Book

Having your contacts with you on your iPod can be helpful when you need that phone number or address. You can transfer contacts from your Address Book (Mac) or Microsoft Outlook or Outlook Express (Windows). iTunes will make sure to keep the contacts on your iPod synchronized with those on your computer.

Copying your contacts to your iPod using iTunes:

1. In iTunes, with your iPod connected, access the iPod options in the Preferences window, and click the Contacts tab.

2. On Windows, check the "Synchronize contacts from" checkbox and choose, from the drop-down menu, either Outlook Express or Microsoft Outlook (**Figure 11.44**).

   On the Macintosh, check "Synchronize Address Book contacts" (**Figure 11.45**).

3. Choose "Synchronize all contacts," or choose "Synchronize selected groups only" and check the groups of contacts you want included.

4. Click OK to close the Preferences window.

   Your contacts are automatically added to the iPod. Contacts that you update or add to your computer will automatically be added to your iPod every time you connect it.

Figure 11.44 (Windows) In iTunes, you'll need to specify whether to synchronize contacts from Outlook or Outlook Express.

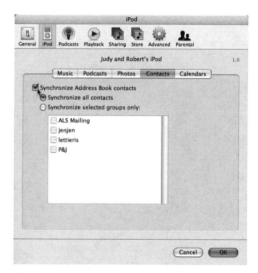

Figure 11.45 (Mac) You can sync contacts from Mac OS X's Address Book.

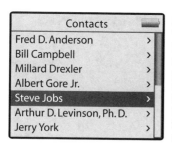

Figure 11.46
Your address book entries are listed on your iPod in the Contacts menu (which you'll find if you go to Extras from the iPod's main menu).

Viewing contacts on your iPod:

1. In the main menu, select Extras, and then Contacts.

2. In the Contacts menu, select the contact you want to view (**Figure 11.46**).

   You may need to use your wheel to scroll to see all the information.

Putting Your Contacts on Your iPod Without iTunes

If you're using a tool other than the Mac OS X Address Book or Microsoft Outlook or Outlook Express on Windows, there may still be a way to get your contacts on your iPod. You'll need to export your contacts as *vCards*—consult your tool's documentation to see if and how it does this—and then drag those vCards into the Contacts folder on your iPod in the Mac OS X Finder or Windows Explorer. (This assumes you have enabled disk use on your iPod.)

Games, Games, Games

This book doesn't cover the games on your iPod (and if you've got a video iPod, chances are you won't miss this coverage anyway). But if you're stuck at the airport and want to kill an hour, choose Extras from the main menu and then choose Games to explore the handful of games Apple has provided for your gaming pleasure.

Keeping Your Calendars on Your iPod

If you use the calendar in Outlook (Windows) or iCal (Mac), make sure to keep a copy of your calendars on your iPod.

To copy calendars to your iPod:

1. Connect your iPod, and access the iPod options in the Preferences window.

2. Choose Calendars from the row of tabs.

3. On Windows, check "Synchronize calendars from Microsoft Outlook" (**Figure 11.47**).

   On the Macintosh, check "Synchronize iCal calendars" and then either select the "Synchronize all calendars" radio button or select "Synchronize selected calendars only" and select the calendars you want on your iPod (**Figure 11.48**).

4. Click OK.

   iTunes copies your calendars to your iPod. (Outlook will ask about another program accessing its data; you'll need to agree to this every time you sync.)

   Any time you connect your iPod in the future, its calendars will be updated to match the calendars on your computer.

Figure 11.47 (Windows) iTunes can automatically sync your calendars from Outlook.

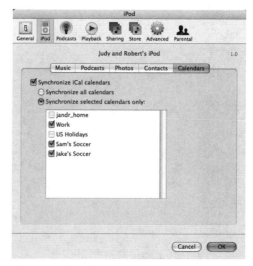

Figure 11.48 (Mac) iTunes can sync your iCal calendars—all of them or a subset.

Figure 11.49
The calendar for the current month shows. Use your wheel to highlight a day and then press the Select button to view...

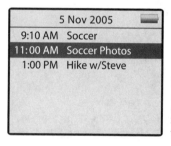

Figure 11.50
...the events for a particular day. Select an event to view...

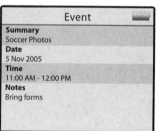

Figure 11.51
...the details for that event.

To view calendars on your iPod:

1. From the main menu, select Extras, then Calendars, and then select the calendar you want to view.

2. The calendar for the current month appears; days that have events display a tiny flag (**Figure 11.49**).

   ▲ Press the Forward or Back buttons to show the next or previous month.

   ▲ Use the wheel to move forward or backward day by day. If you continue scrolling, the next or previous month displays.

   ▲ Press the select button to view the highlighted days events (**Figure 11.50**), and then select any particular event to see its details (**Figure 11.51**).

✔ Tip

■ If events in your calendar have alarms associated with them, your iPod will alert you on-screen and will beep. If this isn't happening for you, choose Extras, then Calendars, and make sure Alarms is set to Silent (if you only want a visual reminder) or Beep (if you also want to hear a sound through the iPod's minuscule external speaker).

Storing and Accessing Notes

Using an iPod as a text reader seems, well, kind of weird. We've found it useful, however, to keep such documents as travel itineraries and directions on our iPod, especially when we're on the road for extended periods of time.

Also, you'll find certain types of information already available out there, in a format that you can easily put on your iPod in the form of notes. In the San Francisco Bay Area, for example, BART (Bay Area Rapid Transit) has made its transit schedule available for just this purpose.

To copy notes to your iPod:

1. Set your iPod up for use as a hard drive, as covered earlier in this chapter.

2. Using the Finder (Mac) or Explorer (Windows), copy text files into the Notes directory on the iPod.

   You can also include folders with files inside of them.

To view notes:

1. From the main iPod menu, choose Extras, and then Notes.

   You'll see files and folders listed (**Figure 11.52**).

2. Select files to view them. Select folders to view their contents (**Figure 11.53**).

✔ Tips

- Files need to be saved as text files. Most word processing programs let you save files as text. Microsoft Word, for example, has an option to save as "Text Only."

- Files you can put on your iPod are limited to 4 kilobytes; if you put a file that's larger than 4 kilobytes on your iPod, part of the text won't appear on screen.

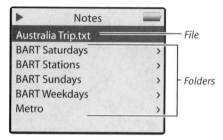

Figure 11.52 The Notes menu lists files and folders that you've dragged to the Notes folder on your iPod.

Figure 11.53 Here's how a note appears on your iPod.

- The iPod can actually read some very basic html tags in a text file. More information can be found here: http://developer.apple.com/hardware/ipod/ipodnotereader.pdf

- If you want those BART schedules we mentioned, go to www.bart.gov. (They also have color system maps for viewing on an iPod; these you'll access through the Photos area of your iPod.)

INDEX

INDEX

INDEX

INDEX

X–Y–Z

INDEX